Oil on the Wounds

A CONTEMPORARY EXAMINATION OF
THE EFFECTS OF DIVORCE AND ABORTION
ON CHILDREN AND THEIR FAMILIES

EDITED BY

Livio Melina
Carl A. Anderson

Cover Designer: Jeannie Tudor
Typesetter: Gary A. Rosenberg

Square One Publishers
115 Herricks Road
Garden City Park, NY 11040
(516) 535-2010 • (877) 900-BOOK
www.squareonepublishers.com

Library of Congress Cataloging-in-Publication Data

Oil on the wounds : a response to the aftermath of divorce and abortion / Livio Melina, Carl Anderson (eds.).
   p. cm.
   Includes bibliographical references and index.
   "International Congress ... organized in collaboration between the Pontifical John Paul II Institute and the Knights of Columbus"--Pref.
   ISBN-13: 978-0-7570-0360-8
   ISBN-10: 0-7570-0360-5
   1. Divorce—Religious aspects—Catholic Church—Congresses. 2. Abortion—Religious aspects—Catholic Church—Congresses. I. Melina, Livio. II. Anderson, Carl A. III. John Paul II Institute for Studies on Marriage and Family. IV. Knights of Columbus.
   BX2254.O35 2011
   261.8'3589—dc22
                            2010017329

Copyright © 2011 by Knights of Columbus

All rights reserved. No part of this publication may be reproduced, stored in a retrieval system, or transmitted, in any form or by any means, electronic, mechanical, photocopying, recording, or otherwise, without the prior written permission of the copyright owner.

10   9   8   7   6   5   4   3   2   1

Contents

Preface, vii

Address to the Participants at the International Congress, xi
His Holiness Benedict XVI

Introduction, 1
LIVIO MELINA AND CARL A. ANDERSON

PART ONE   The Children of Divorce

I   THE DRAMA OF A BROKEN TIE

Impact of Separation and Divorce on Children: Research Insights on What Children Need, 7
JOAN B. KELLY, PH.D.

Broken Ties and the Next Generation: Effects of Marital Separation on Adolescent and Young Adult Children, 25
RAFFAELLA IAFRATE

The Spiritual Lives of Children of Divorce, 37
ELIZABETH MARQUARDT

Parents in the Wake of Divorce: Some Points of Reference on Theological Ethics, 49
OLIVIER BONNEWIJN

II A Pastoral Approach

A Pastoral Care Plan for Children of Divorce, 83
JOSÉ NORIEGA

Building a Ministry With Children of Divorce:
Obstacles & How to Overcome Them, 87
LYNN CASSELLA-KAPUSINSKI

An Educational Initiative Addressing Children
of Divorce in the Church, 107
ANA MARIA ANASTASIADES, MD

"Voice Groups" for Children of Divided Families, 151
COSTANZA MARZOTTO

PART TWO The Aftermath of Abortion

I The Hidden Sufferings of Abortion

Being the "Good Samaritan": Between Works of Healing
and the Responsibility to Educate, 169
MARIA LUISA DI PIETRO

The Dark Side of Maternity, 173
EUGENIA ROCCELLA

The Psychological Consequences of Abortive Mentality
in the Family, 179
PHILIPPE DE CATHELINEAU

The Psychological Aftermath of Abortion for Children
and Families: A Clinical Perspective, 193
E. JOANNE ANGELO, MD

Abortion of the Sick Child, 205
AGNETTA SUTTON

II Towards a Pastoral Outreach of Mercy

To Act According to the Merciful Example of God, 213
  Jean Laffitte

Project Rachel: A Sacramental Response
to the Grief of Abortion, 219
  Vicki Thorn

A Sacramental Journey to an Inheritance of Mercy, 231
  Mother Agnes Mary Donovan

AGAPA: Following Christ, Welcoming and
Accompanying Those Who Experience Suffering
as a Result of Abortion, 237
  Dominique Vandier

The Gift of Support, 247
  Serena Taccari

Preface

The International Congress *Oil on the Wounds: A Contemporary Examination of the Effects of Divorce and Abortion on Children and Their Families*, organized in collaboration between the Pontifical John Paul II Institute and the Knights of Columbus, was intended to promote reflection on the suffering of those who have experienced the pain of their own parents' divorce or the trauma of abortion. Our goal has been to find concrete ways in which we can develop a more effective pastoral response to those who suffer—a response which will alleviate their pain and bring about true healing through the ministry of the Church and of all men and women of good will.

Those who participated in the Congress saw a great event, crowned by the meeting with the Holy Father, an audience which took place on April 5, 2008. The words and the welcoming attitude of the Pope manifested the paternity of the Church, which makes her own the drama, the pain, the hope, but also the initiatives undertaken to alleviate the sufferings provoked by divorce and abortion. The Holy Father expressed all of this, showing a great understanding of our work and our intentions. Very often, public opinion focuses only on the negative aspect of the Church's judgment concerning these themes, denouncing a rigid and detrimental attitude towards personal liberty. In reality, the Church feels called to make her own the attitude of Jesus and the Good Samaritan. She feels, along with many men and women of good will, the call to approach the individuals who are suffering, to descend from her horse, and to stoop to cure their wounds.

In preparation for the Congress, we had at heart from the beginning the words of Benedict XVI in his encyclical, *Deus caritas est:* "The Christian's program—the program of the Good Samaritan, the program of Jesus—is 'a heart which sees.' This heart sees where love is needed and acts accordingly" (n.31). Being aware of these dramas, how could we, the Institute of Marriage and Family and the Knights of Columbus, pass by without attending to those who have been their victims, both the innocent, such as the children, sons and daughters of divorce, or those who are not yet born and extinguished in their mother's womb, and also the other persons, who in different measures are both guilty and victims of the wounds which they have provoked?

Behold here the program of the recent Congress and of the present volume, which, inspired in its movements by the icon of the Good Samaritan, articulates two distinct moments. The first moment is "a heart which sees," which draws near, feeling compassion and searching to know the situation from a sociological and psychological, but overall human, and therefore, ethical, point of view. The second moment involves "acting accordingly," taking care of and bearing the weight of the other, bringing him to the inn, entrusting him to the care of others, and finally returning. In this second moment, one resolves to search for a pastoral response of solidarity, listening to the experience of many centers and initiatives for help which are already present in various parts of the world.

At the beginning of this volume, it is necessary to thank all of the people who, with their generosity and intelligence, have made possible this moment of reflection.

A thank you above all to Prof. Carl Anderson, the Supreme Knight of the Knights of Columbus and Vice-President of the United States Session of the Pontifical John Paul II Institute. During a cycle of lessons on familial politics, he offered to the students a vivid image of the unjust violence of divorce and abortion and of the hidden sufferings of so many persons, while indicating, however, the existence of many initiatives which have arisen above all in the United States to address these wounds.

Thank you to those students, who allowed themselves to be surprised and struck by their professor's words, and who reacted by proposing to organize this event at our Institute.

Thank you to Mr. Victor Soldevila who looked after, together with other colleagues and students of the Institute, the organization of the event, contributing in a definite way to its success, and thank you to Mr. Patrick Kelly and all the staff of the Knights of Columbus, who supported them in this difficult task.

Thank you to the presenters, who brought a profound richness, both at the levels of academic and professional experience, and of humanity. Each one testified to a "heart which sees," which is capable of listening, of identifying, of finding the words and gestures, the forms of contact and help, which can alleviate the sufferings of our brothers who are victims of abortion and divorce. They have had, in this occasion, the possibility of meeting and coming to know others who share the same commitment and of nourishing their mission with the experiences of colleagues.

And finally, a thank you to the Holy Father, who with his words illuminated our walk and will continue to guide us in our work in service of the vineyard of the Lord, so that it may produce good wine, which, with the oil, may heal the wounds of the smallest among us and brighten the faces of men and women for the glory of God.

Father Livio Melina
Rome, April 19th 2009
2nd Sunday of Easter, Divine Mercy Sunday
4th anniversary of the election of Pope Benedict XVI

Address to the Participants at the International Congress

His Holiness Benedict XVI

Clementine Hall
Saturday, April 5, 2008

Your Eminences,
Venerable Brothers in the Episcopate and in the Priesthood,
Dear Brothers and Sisters,

I meet you with great joy on the occasion of the International Congress on *"Oil on the wounds: A contemporary examination of the effects of divorce and abortion on children and their families,"* promoted by the John Paul II Pontifical Institute for Studies on Marriage and Family in collaboration with the *Knights of Columbus.* I congratulate you on the topical and complex theme that has been the subject of your reflections in these days and in particular for the reference to the Good Samaritan (*Lk* 10: 25–37), which you chose as a key to approach the evils of abortion and divorce that bring so much suffering to the lives of individuals, families and society. Yes, the men and women of our day sometimes truly find themselves stripped and wounded on the wayside of the routes we take, often without anyone listening to their cry for help or attending to them to alleviate and heal their suffering. In the often purely ideological debate a sort of conspiracy of silence is created in their regard. Only by assuming an attitude of merciful love is it possible to approach in order to bring help and enable victims to pick themselves up and resume their journey through life.

In a cultural context marked by increasing individualism, hedonism and all too often also by a lack of solidarity and adequate social support, human freedom, as it faces life's difficulties, is prompted in its weakness to make decisions that conflict with the indissolubility of the matrimonial bond or with the respect due to human life from the moment of conception, while it is still protected in its mother's womb. Of course, divorce and abortion are decisions of a different kind, which are sometimes made in difficult and dramatic circumstances that are often traumatic and a source of deep suffering for those who make them. They also affect innocent victims: the infant just conceived and not yet born, children involved in the break-up of family ties. These decisions indelibly mark the lives of all those involved. The Church's ethical opinion with regard to divorce and procured abortion is unambivalent and known to all: these are grave sins which, to a different extent and taking into account the evaluation of subjective responsibility, harm the dignity of the human person, involve a profound injustice in human and social relations and offend God himself, Guarantor of the conjugal covenant and the Author of life. Yet the Church, after the example of her Divine Teacher, always has the people themselves before her, especially the weakest and most innocent who are victims of injustice and sin, and also those other men and women who, having perpetrated these acts, stained by sin and wounded within, are seeking peace and the chance to begin anew.

The Church's first duty is to approach these people with love and consideration, with caring and motherly attention, to proclaim the merciful closeness of God in Jesus Christ. Indeed, as the Fathers teach, it is he who is the true Good Samaritan, who has made himself close to us, who pours oil and wine on our wounds and takes us into the inn, the Church, where he has us treated, entrusting us to her ministers and personally paying in advance for our recovery. Yes, the Gospel of love and life is also always the *Gospel of mercy*, which is addressed to the actual person and sinner that we are, to help us up after any fall and to recover from any injury. My beloved Predecessor, the Servant of God John Paul II, the third anniversary of whose death we celebrated recently, said in inaugurating the new Shrine of Divine Mercy in Krakow: "Apart from the mercy of God there is no other source of hope for mankind" (August 17, 2002). On the basis of this mercy the Church cultivates an indomitable trust in human beings and in their capacity for recovery. She knows that with the help of grace human freedom is capable of the definitive and faithful gift of self which makes possible the marriage of a man and woman as an indissoluble bond; she knows that even in the most difficult circumstances human freedom is capable of extraordinary acts of sacrifice and solidarity to welcome the life of a new human being. Thus, one can see that the "No" which the Church pronounces in her moral directives, on which public opinion sometimes unilaterally focuses, is in fact a great "Yes" to the dignity of the human person, to human life and to the person's capacity to love. It is an expression of the constant trust with which, despite their frailty, people are able to respond to the loftiest vocation for which they are created: the vocation to love.

On that same occasion, John Paul II continued: "This fire of mercy needs to be passed on to the world. In the mercy of God the world will find peace" (*ibid.*, p. 8). The great task of disciples of the Lord Jesus who find themselves the travelling companions of so many brothers, men and women of good will, is hinged on this. Their program, the program of the Good Samaritan, is a " 'heart which sees'. This heart sees where love is needed and acts accordingly" (*Deus Caritas Est,* n. 31). In these days of reflection and dialogue you have stooped down to victims suffering from the wounds of divorce and abortion. You have noted first of all the sometimes traumatic suffering that afflicts the so-called "children of divorce," marking their lives to the point of making their way far more difficult. It is in fact inevitable that when the conjugal covenant is broken, those who suffer most are the children who are the living sign of its indissolubility. Supportive pastoral attention must therefore aim to ensure that the children are not the innocent victims of conflicts between parents who divorce. It must also endeavor to ensure that the continuity of the link with their parents is guaranteed as far as possible, as well as the links with their own family and social origins, which are indispensable for a balanced psychological and human growth.

You also focused on the tragedy of procured abortion that leaves profound and sometimes indelible marks in the women who undergo it and in the people around them, as well as devastating consequences on the family and society, partly because of the materialistic mentality of contempt for life that it encourages. What selfish complicity often lies at the root of an agonizing decision which so many women have had to face on their own, who still carry in their heart an open wound! Although what has been done remains a grave injustice and is not in itself remediable, I make my own the exhortation in *Evangelium Vitae* addressed to women who have had an abortion: "Do not give in to discouragement and do not lose hope. Try rather to understand what happened and face it honestly. If you have not already done so, give yourselves over with humility and trust to repentance. The Father of mercies is ready to give you his forgiveness and his peace in the Sacrament of Reconciliation. To the same Father and his mercy you can with sure hope entrust your child" (n. 99).

I express deep appreciation for all those social and pastoral initiatives being taken for the reconciliation and treatment of people injured by the drama of abortion and divorce. Together with numerous other forms of commitment, they constitute essential elements for building that civilization of love that humanity needs today more than ever.

As I implore the Merciful Lord God that he will increasingly liken you to Jesus the Good Samaritan, that his spirit will teach you to look with new eyes at the reality of the suffering brethren, that he will help you to think with new criteria and spur you to act with generous dynamism with a view to an authentic civilization of love and life, I impart a special Apostolic Blessing to you all.

Introduction

LIVIO MELINA AND
CARL A. ANDERSON

"Not only oil, but also wine over his wounds"

This introduction does not have the intention of offering a preliminary synthesis of the work undertaken during the two days of presentation and debate of the Congress *Oil on the Wounds: A Contemporary Examination of the Effects of Divorce and Abortion on Children and Their Families.* It expresses, instead, a desire for the beginning, or continuation, of a conversion of the heart, which unfolds into a compassion motivating the search for methods and language more appropriate for helping those who have experienced in their own lives the pain and the profound wound of a divorce or an abortion.

Millions of people each year are affected by the trauma resulting from both abortion and divorce. And as each year passes, the cumulative effect becomes more staggering. Rather than being a quick solution, abortion unwittingly leads many—both men and women—into a harrowing and complex psychological journey of depression, anxiety, and other emotional disturbances that often lead to a series of broken relationships. And for the many children of divorce, their parents' separation is frequently linked to loss of faith, higher rates of depression, behavioral and relational difficulties, and even suicide. A culture that readily embraced the "right to choose" and the

---

Livio Melina is the President of the Pontifical John Paul II Institute for Studies on Marriage and Family.

Carl A. Anderson is the Supreme Knight of the Knights of Columbus and Vice-President of the United States Session of the Pontifical John Paul II Institute, Washington, D.C.

"no-fault divorce" is beginning to learn that these quick fixes have exacted a heavy price.

This Congress is a response to the growing awareness that the personal, relational, and societal effects of abortion and divorce have brought us to a point where something must be done.

On the fundamental question of the dignity of every human life, the Church has always and everywhere raised her prophetic voice. Now more than ever, on the question of the deep emotional trauma brought about by abortion and divorce, we see that her prophetic voice is being matched by her concern for those who carry this sorrow.

Indeed, the Church is not a newcomer to these issues. The young Father Karol Wojtyla's experience as a pastor led him to a deep understanding of the trauma that takes place after abortion. In 1960 in *Love and Responsibility*, he discussed a woman's complex emotional response:

> "Apart from its physical effects, artificial abortion causes an anxiety neurosis with guilt feelings at its core, and sometimes even a profound psychotic reaction. In this context we may note the significance of statements by women suffering from depression . . . who sometimes a decade or so after the event remember the terminated pregnancy with regret and feel a belated sense of guilt on this account."[1]

Pope John Paul II's understanding of post-abortion trauma would later find voice in *Evangelium Vitae*. Speaking directly to post-abortive women, he said:

> "Do not give in to discouragement and do not lose hope . . . If you have not already done so, give yourselves over with humility and trust to repentance. The Father of Mercies is ready to give you his forgiveness and his peace in the Sacrament of Reconciliation. You will come to understand that nothing is definitively lost and you will also be able to ask forgiveness from your child, who is now living with the Lord. With the friendly and expert help and advice of other people, and as a result of your own painful experience, you can be among the most eloquent defenders of everyone's right to life."[2]

It is fitting that we have discussed these topics during the second week of Easter, a time when the Church calls us to reflect on the meaning of our salvation in and through Jesus Christ. Jesus is known as the "Salvator," which literally means "one who brings good health." A great writer of the Patristic time, Origen, interpreted the parable of the Good Samaritan using Christ as the key: Christ is the true Good Samaritan, who makes himself man, descending from heaven in order to help all of humanity which lies at the edge of the road, stripped and wounded by sin, incapable of reaching the goal. It is he who cures humanity, paying in person and, loading humanity upon himself, brings it to the inn which is the Church. It is he who promises to return at the end of time. Origen explains that "Samaritan" is not an improper title for Jesus, who, in effect, does not refuse it when it is directed towards him as an accusation by the Pharisees. Etymologically, "Samaritan" means "keeper." This calls to mind, in antithesis, Cain's response to God after the first murder. To the question, "Where is your brother?" he responds, "Am I my brother's keeper (Samaritan)?" Jesus is the true keeper of his brothers, and we also, in Him and in the Church, are called to become keepers of our brothers, stripped and wounded at the edges of the roads which we travel.

In our present day—indeed, perhaps now more than ever, the Church is called to be the "inn" we hear about in the parable of the Good Samaritan, a place where the wounded can be brought back to health. It is Christ himself who calls us to have "a heart which sees" and to act accordingly. Those who have suffered the pain of their parents' divorce or the trauma of abortion should experience the healing mercy of God in the embrace of the Church.

This must be our mission: to bring the healing power of Christ to those who have suffered, and to show them that their suffering can have a purpose. We are now seeing that those who have lived through the experience of abortion and divorce are able to help others experience the healing mercy of God. And in doing so they witness to the legacy and memory of John Paul II, who showed us so many years ago—both through his teaching and example—that "suffering is present in the world in order to release love, in order to give birth to works of love toward neighbor, in order to transform the whole of human civilization into a civilization of love."[3]

"Oil on the Wounds": At this point, we will allow ourselves a small "correction" by finishing the title of this volume, which could have been more faithfully rendered "Wine and Oil on the Wounds," since the Good Samaritan, along with the oil, also poured wine on the wounds of the traveler.

Why? Any doctor would be able to explain that before alleviating the pain, it is necessary to disinfect the wound, eliminating all that could infect it and expose the patient to further danger. This is a good reply; however, it is not enough by itself to explain the intention of this book. In fact, wine in the Sacred Scriptures is connected with the feasting banquet. Wine helps to celebrate and allows the banqueters to be cheerful; it brings joy. One cannot cure a person without bringing joy, without having it oneself. To truly cure, one must have great hope, but as Charles Péguy says, "One does not have hope if one has not first received great joy," and the joy that one can and one must communicate is that which comes from God. Here is the importance for Christians of having present not only the oil, but also the wine. Christians are called to be a joyful people, capable of announcing this joy even in the midst of these dramas and of alleviating the wounds not only with the oil of consolation, but also with the joy of a hope, which begins today while still awaiting its final completion: that of the new wine which we will drink in the Kingdom of Heaven, where all wounds and tears will be dried.

REFERENCES

1. Karol Wojtyla (Pope John Paul II), *Love and Responsibility*, trans. H.T. (Willetts, Farrar, Straus and Giroux: New York), 1981, 284–485.

2. Pope John Paul II, *Evangelium Vitae* (1997), no. 99.

3. Pope John Paul II, *On the Christian Meaning of Human Suffering* (February 11, 1984), no. 30.

PART ONE

THE CHILDREN OF DIVORCE

I The Drama of a Broken Tie

Impact of Separation and Divorce on Children: Research Insights on What Children Need

JOAN B. KELLY, PH.D.

Parental divorce has been viewed for many decades as the cause of a wide range of enduring behavioral, emotional and social problems in children and adolescents. Divorced families have been viewed as flawed structures in which to raise children whereas all married families were assumed to offer healthy and nurturing environments. Such simplistic views regarding these family structures have been abandoned in the past 20 years as evolving social science research has contributed an increasingly complex understanding of both marriage and divorce. Although children and adolescents generally fare better in well-functioning two-parent families than in divorced families, not all married families provide appropriate parenting and environments for their children and many divorced families offer the nurturance and support necessary for positive child and adolescent outcomes (see Clarke-Stewart & Brentano, 2006; Cummings & Davies, 1994; Kelly, 2000; Kelly & Emery, 2003).

This paper summarizes social science research which helps to identify the range of needs of children and adolescents whose parents have separated and divorced. The differences between divorced and married family children and adolescents are first described. Then, identified factors that increase the divorce-related risk of enduring psychosocial, emotional, and academic problems, and protective factors that reduce or ameliorate the potential negative impacts of divorce are described. More recent research focusing on young adults' views of their parents' divorce and their post-divorce living (custody and access) arrangements provides more insight into what aspects of divorce were difficult, manageable, painful, and potentially avoidable. Finally, services to families in the midst of separation and divorce which address the needs

---

Joan B. Kelly is with the Northern California Mediation Center, California

of children and their parents and have been demonstrated to be effective in promoting more positive adaptations to divorce are discussed.

Child Adjustment in Divorced and Married Families

Divorce is not a single event but rather an extended process unfolding over one or more years' time that involves multiple and potentially difficult changes and challenges for most children and adolescents. A large body of empirical research confirms that divorce essentially doubles the risk for adjustment problems in children and adolescents (for reviews, see Amato, 2000; Clarke-Stewart & Brentano, 2006; Emery, 1999, 2004; Hetherington & Kelly, 2002; Kelly, 2000; Kelly & Emery, 2003). This research compared the psychosocial and emotional adjustment of school-aged children (primarily Caucasian) living in both married and divorced families, using widely accepted methodologies, standardized and objective measures and appropriate statistical analyses. The vast majority of the divorced family children and adolescents lived primarily in the custody of their mothers and had varying amounts of contact with their nonresidential fathers.

Children of divorce are more likely to have behavioral, psychological, social, and academic problems when compared to children from married families. In continuously married families 10–12% of children have serious psychological, social and academic problems whereas 20–25% of children from divorced families have similar symptoms (Hetherington & Kelly, 2002). Some of these youngsters from divorced families are already at considerable risk when their parents separate, the result of spousal violence (Kelly & Johnson, 2008); high conflict (Cummings & Davies, 1994: Johnston & Campbell, 1988; Kline, Johnston & Tschann, 1991), impaired mental health of one or both parents (Dickstein, Seifer, Hayden, et al, 1998; Emery, 1999; Kelly, 2000; Kline et al, 1991; Pruett, Williams, Insabella, & Little, 2003), poor parenting practices (Cummings & Davies, 1994), and/or parental substance abuse (McMahon & Giannini, 2003). Longitudinal studies (following families over a period of time) indicate that nearly half of the adjustment problems in children and adolescents attributed to divorce were evident prior to parental separation (see Cherlin, Furstenberg, Lindsay, Chase-Lansdale, et al, 1991; Kelly, 2000; Sun, 2001).

Groups of divorced and never divorced children are not two distinct groups, however, and they overlap considerably in their functioning. The magnitude of the differences between them, while statistically significant, is quite small (Amato, 2000; Emery, 1999; Clarke-Stewart & Brentano, 2006). Just as there are married family children with major psychological, social and emotional adjustment problems, so too do we find children and adolescents from divorced families who are functioning quite well on psychological, social, emotional, and academic dimensions. Indeed, between 75–80% of children and adolescents from divorced families fall within the average range of various indices of adjustment and achievement (Hetherington & Kelly, 2002). It is also apparent that while the majority of youngsters are functioning at an average or better level in the years following divorce, there is considerable ongoing stress and pain associated with parental divorce for some, particularly where there is continuing co-parental high conflict (Carlson, 2006; Fabricius & Hall, 2000; Fabricius & Leucken, 2007; Laumann-Billings & Emery, 2000; Marquardt, 2005).

The most consistent adverse effects associated with divorce are conduct disorders, aggression, impulsive and antisocial behaviors, and problems with authority figures, peers and parents (Amato, 2000; Emery, 1999; Hetherington & Kelly, 2002). Children from divorced families, compared to those in married families, are also more likely to have symptoms of depression, anxiety, and lower self-esteem, although these findings are less consistent. Divorced adolescents use more alcohol, cigarettes, and marijuana than their peers in married families, in part due to impaired parenting practices including inadequate monitoring and entrusting them to friends and peer groups that use substances.

Divorce has been associated with modestly lower academic performance and achievement test scores, although the differences between divorced and never divorced children are reduced when comparing the socioeconomic differences between married and divorced families. The school dropout rate of divorced children, particularly for White as compared to Black and Hispanic youngsters, is more than twice as high as that of never-divorced children (McLanahan, 1999). Some of these academic problems existed prior to separation, with parents who later divorced providing less help with homework, talking less about educational achievement, and less involved in school, compared to still married parents (Sun & Li, 2001).

Risk Factors for Children and Adolescents Following Divorce

The identification of factors associated with increased risk for children and adolescents following divorce is one of the more important outcomes of recent empirical research (see Amato, 2000; Clarke-Stewart & Brentano, 2006; Emery, 1999; Hetherington & Kelly, 2002; Kelly, 2000; 2007; Kelly & Emery, 2003). These findings provide valuable guidance to parents, divorce educators, family courts, and other institutions committed to reducing the negative impacts of divorce on children and adolescents.

Highly Stressful Separation

For the majority of children and adolescents, the parental separation is a very stressful experience, although the severity, duration, and number of stressors vary from family to family, and within families, and may affect siblings differently. For those youngsters whose parents engaged in violence and explosive conflict in the marriage, the separation is often experienced as a relief (Wallerstein & Kelly, 1980). The strength of the child's psychological and social resources will in part determine their responses to separation and their longer-term outcomes. Contributing greatly to the stress of the separation is the failure of parents to talk with their children about the separation and how it will affect their lives. Most striking are findings that in 23% of families, neither parent talked to their children at all at the point of separation and another 45% gave one line explanations (Dunn, Davies, O'Connor, & Sturgess, 2001). Thus, children were left with high anxiety about the many changes and challenges they would face, including where they would live, what school they would attend, when if ever they would see the parent who moved out of the residence, and in high conflict separations, whether they would be permitted to love and be loved by both parents.

Adjustment of Parents

Children and adolescents who live in the custody of mothers with depression, high anxiety, personality disorders, and mental illness are significantly more likely to experience more symptoms of all kinds, compared to divorced children living with better adjusted parents (Carlson & Corcoran, 2001; Dickstein, et al, 1998; Kline, et al, 1991; Pruett et al, 2003). Angry, erratic, and dysfunctional behaviors are more likely to increase in response to the stress of parental separation and dominate the children's household (Johnston & Roseby, 1997; Wallerstein & Kelly, 1980). Adjustment problems and substance abuse in either mothers or fathers not only provide poor role models but are associated with more negative parenting practices and parent-child relationships, which in turn are linked to more symptoms in their children.

Quality of Parenting

Quality of parenting has emerged as a critical factor in child and adolescent adjustment following separation and divorce. Parenting is negatively impacted by many parental experiences associated with divorce: sustained anger and high conflict, violence, strong separation reactions, absorption in dating and new partners, and financial instability (Kelly, 2000). Separated parents are often preoccupied with their own emotional reactions to separation, stressed by financial and litigation pressures, emotionally unavailable, and rarely focused on being by their child or adolescent's side (Johnston & Roseby, 1997). Divorced parents use more coercive, harsh forms of discipline, are more angry, have less positive involvement, and express less affection with their children, when compared to married family parents (Hetherington & Kelly, 2002).

Loss of Paternal Involvement

Children report the erosion or loss of the relationship with their father as the most negative aspect of divorce, and loss of important relationships is a major theme in children's divorce experiences. Up to 25% of children do not see their fathers by two to three years post-divorce, and this absence of the father has powerful and longer-term emotional and economic consequences for children and adolescents. Traditional "visiting" guidelines or engrained societal attitudes limiting fathers to every other weekend "visits" with their children significantly limit fathers' opportunities to parent with a resulting diminution in the important interactions of discipline, homework, projects, and opportunities to provide emotional support. Many children express their intense dissatisfaction with the 12-day separation from their father typical of the every other weekend parenting plan. Such arrangements fail to consider children's ages, gender, developmental needs and achievements, the history and quality of the child's relationship with each parent, and family situations requiring special attention (Kelly, 2005, 2007). Father-child relationships often weaken and deteriorate over time as a result, and financial support for the children decreases.

A number of studies indicate that the majority of children and adolescents want more and longer periods of time with fathers, and many favor substantially equal time. The painful memories and feelings among young adults described as a residue of the divorce experience are in part associated with long-term sadness and longing for more father involvement (Fabricius &

Hall, 2000; Finley & Schwartz, 2007; Laumann-Billings and Emery, 2000; Smith & Gallop, 2001). As many as two-thirds of university students reported that they missed not having their fathers around and many questioned whether their fathers loved them. They also viewed their mothers as opposing more contact with their fathers. In contrast are those children and adolescents, a minority, who resist or refuse contacts with their fathers after separation, either in response to the trauma of spousal violence, abusive child rearing practices, or strong alignments with some angry mothers who discourage the father-child relationship. In bitter divorces, relationships with grandparents or other loved relatives may also be severed, resulting in even more pervasive loss of love and support.

High Conflict

Although conflict after divorce decreases or stops for the majority of parents, an estimated 8–20% of parents remain angry and highly conflictual in their co-parental relationship two to three years after divorce (Hetherington & Kelly, 2002; King & Heard, 1999). Continued high conflict is a risk factor for children and adolescents, whether perpetrated by one or both parents. The intensity and the focus of the parental conflict are more predictive of adjustment problems in children than is frequency. Explosive, intense conflict, and conflict focused on the child are most problematic. The most damaging conflict is when one or both parents use their children to express their anger, by making demeaning comments about the other parent, asking children to carry hostile messages, asking intrusive questions about the other parent, and demands for loyalty and alignments (Booth & Afifi, 2006; Buchanan, Maccoby, & Dornbusch, 1991).

In a substantial number of families after divorce, one parent has emotionally disengaged from their former partner, while the other parent remains full of rage and vindictive motivation, and continues to create problems which often require further court assistance. In such cases, the label of "high conflict parents" is not only inaccurate but a disservice to the parent who has been able to work through their emotional responses to the divorce and resume appropriate functioning.

There are longer-term negative impacts of parent anger and conflict after divorce. Maternal hostility at separation is associated with fewer father-child contacts and overnights several years later (Maccoby & Mnookin, 1992). High levels of parent conflict after divorce is linked to deterioration in the father-child relationship (Ahrons & Tanner, 2003). And when a parent demeans the other parent or interferes with the child or adolescent's contacts with the nonresident parent, one of the longer-term effects is more anger and a more distant relationship with that parent in young adulthood (Fabricius & Hall, 2000).

Relocation

The relocation of one parent, with or without children, to a new, more distant location reorganizes the nature and frequency of contacts between parents and their children. Between 25% to 45% of children move with their custodial parent within two years following separation, some many times (Booth & Amato, 2001; Braver, Ellman, & Fabricius, 2003; Hetherington & Kelly, 2002). Relocations of more than 75–100 miles appear to create substantial barriers to continuity in nonresident parent-child relationships, and studies indicate that distances of 400–500 miles are typical (Ahrons & Tanner, 2003; Hetherington & Kelly, 2002). When parents have limited economic resources, inflexible work schedules, and distances which cannot be managed by car, a pattern of diminishing contacts, drifting apart, and deterioration in attachments and closeness in nonresident parent-child relationships is a common outcome, particularly for very young children (Kelly & Lamb, 2003). The hostility of one or both parents exacerbates logistic and communication problems leading to breakdowns in planning and managing trips (Hetherington & Kelly, 2002; Kelly & Lamb, 2003). Relocation may be problematic regardless of whether mothers move with children or fathers move away from their children, with college students reporting a less favorable view of parents as role models and source of emotional support, and more internal turmoil and distress, compared to students where neither parent moved after divorce (Braver et al, 2003). It is important to note that relocation can benefit children when they are distanced from abusive, self-centered, or coercive and controlling nonresident parents, although no empirical research exists on this issue (Hetherington & Kelly, 2002; Kelly & Lamb, 2003).

Repartnering and Remarriage

The risk for behavioral and emotional problems for children and adolescents is not diminished by a parent's remarriage. Estimates are that one-third of children of divorce live in a cohabitating or remarried family during their minor years and many challenges arise as parents date, form partnerships, cohabit and remarry. The remarriages of either parent lead to decreased contact between fathers and their children over time. Fathers' remarriages, particularly when a child is born within the new union, diminish paternal commitment to the children of the former marriage, seemingly as a result of inability to maintain or deal with multiple commitments, conflicting loyalties and time demands (Bray, 1999; Hetherington & Kelly, 2002). Many parents have numerous sequential relationships following separation and divorce to which the children and adolescents are expected to respond with positive affect and approval. These transitional relationships are often accompanied by family conflict, problems with discipline, angry relationships with new partners and the partners' children, and a risk of child physical abuse and partner violence and conflict.

Economic Decline

Persistent economic instability and reduced access to important resources such as better schools, neighborhoods and extracurricular activities are additional risk factors for the children of divorce. The economic problems of divorced households have been estimated to account for half of the adjustment problems seen in children of divorce (McLanahan, 1999).

Protective Factors for Children and Adolescents Following Divorce

The known risks of divorce described above for the future psycho-social well-being of children and adolescents have been well-established and continue to be refined and differentiated by ongoing social science research. With approximately three-quarters of those from divorced families settling into positive outcomes several years after divorce, researchers sought to identify specific factors which appeared to ameliorate or lessen risk. These protective factors include the positive adjustment of residential and nonresidential parents, specific aspects of competent parenting for mothers and fathers, reduced conflict, expanded contacts with adequate nonresident parents, cooperative or parallel co-parenting arrangements, a limited number of family transitions, and stable economic circumstances.

Good Adjustment of Custodial Parent

When the psychological and social adjustment of residential (custodial) parents is adequate or better, their children are significantly more likely to be well-adjusted after divorce compared to children whose primary parents have significant psychiatric problems or personality disorders (Kline, et al; Simons et al, 1999). Better adjusted parents are more likely to deal with their own divorce-related stress in a timely and effective manner, and can help their children cope with divorce-related emotional, social and academic difficulties that may arise.

Competent Parenting

The quality and type of parenting have emerged as one of the most important post-divorce predictors of child and adolescent adjustment. Effective parenting may prevent the longer-term negative impacts of divorce on children and adolescents. Research has demonstrated that there are critical components of mothers' effective parenting after divorce including warmth, authoritative discipline (setting limits, noncoercive discipline and control, appropriate expectations), academic skill encouragement, and monitoring of their children's activities. These dimensions of parenting are strongly associated with positive emotional, social and psychological functioning in their children and adolescents (Amato & Fowler, 2002). Parental warmth is often not available to children if one or both parents are extremely angry and absorbed with their own feelings. And appropriate discipline of children and adolescents is frequently missing following separation as many mothers fear that disciplining children will result in the child's choosing to live with fathers or feel sorry for their children and do not hold appropriate expectations.

Critical dimensions of fathers' parenting after divorce associated with positive outcomes include active involvement in their children's lives, authoritative parenting, and monitoring of child/adolescent activities. Active involvement encompasses help with homework and projects, emotional support and warmth, talking about problems, and involvement in school (Amato & Fowler, 2002; Hetherington & Kelly, Simons, et al, 1999). In order for fathers to be actively involved, they must have negotiated agreements or court orders that permit sufficient time with their children and adolescents not just on alternate weekends but also during the school week. When fathers show an interest in their child or adolescent's school and homework, such as attending parent-teacher conferences, or visiting the classroom to see their children's work at "Back to School" nights, their children are significantly more likely to succeed at school, and less likely to drop out, compared to fathers who are less involved in school (Nord & Zill,

1996). Many nonresident fathers falter in providing effective discipline because they want their children to enjoy their time with them. Fathers also are less likely than mothers to monitor their child or adolescent when in their care, in part because mothers in the married family more often take responsibility for such parental oversight.

Reduced Conflict

When parents cease or diminish their conflict after divorce, children and adolescents are more likely to have positive adjustment, when compared to those whose parents continue in chronic high conflict. Fortunately, the majority of parents do reduce conflict, particularly when they use alternative divorce processes such as mediation which have been demonstrated to reduce conflict during the separation, when compared to those parents using more traditional adversarial divorce processes (Kelly, 2004). Parents who instigate and sustain conflict at high levels, who remain vengeful, often litigating their disputes repetitively in court, are more likely to have severe personality disorders or mental illness (Johnston & Roseby, 1997; Kelly, 2003). College students whose parents divorced a decade earlier reported more painful experiences when their parents had high levels of conflict, compared to those experiencing lower parental conflict.

Buffers have been identified which appear to shield children from the negative impacts of high continued parent conflict. These include a good relationship with at least one parent, caregiver or mentor, parental warmth, and the shared support of siblings. Thus, for example, we see children who sustain good adjustment and academic performance in the face of continued parent conflict because they have the love and support of one if not two good parents, each functioning well in their own home environments. Another protective buffer identified is when parents are able to encapsulate their conflict, i.e., take their children out of the middle of their disputes, not use their children to express their anger and hostile messages, and refrain from disputing in front of the children. In such situations, adolescents were as well adjusted as adolescents of low conflict parents after divorce (Buchanan et al, 1991; Hetherington & Kelly, 2002; Kelly & Emery, 2003). In contrast, children of angry parents who did not encapsulate their conflict were more depressed and anxious (Buchanan et al, 1991).

Contact with Nonresidential Parents

Frequency of contact (visits) by itself is not a good predictor of child outcomes, in part because fathers vary considerably in the quality of parenting they provide. When children have close relationships with their fathers and the fathers are actively involved in their lives following separation, then frequent contact is significantly linked to more positive adjustment and better academic achievement in school age children and adolescents, compared to those with less involved fathers (Amato, 2000; Amato & Fowler, 2002; Hetherington & Kelly, 2002; Menning, 2006). In comparing the effects of father involvement in six different family structures (e.g., married, never married, married-divorced-single, married-divorced-remarried), greater amounts of father involvement reduced the effects of family structure differences, and those adolescents with more involved fathers had fewer behavioral problems on all measured outcomes (behavioral and delinquency problems, less depression, less anxiety (Carlson, 2006). Boys and girls benefitted equally from this paternal investment of time and emotional support. Academic functioning of adolescents was found to be linked to the amount and type of activities that the adolescent and father shared. When fathers and their adolescents engaged in a variety of activities (church and school related activities, cultural and sporting events, and discussion about adolescent issues), the probability of school failure was lowered, compared to those fathers who had limited contacts and discussions. Ongoing school-related discussions between fathers and adolescents about grades and homework were the most important factor in lowering the probability of school failure (Menning, 2006).

Among university students whose parents divorced 8–10 years earlier, the majority stated that they desired (but did not have) shared physical custody arrangements. Indeed, those students who had substantial time-sharing between parents reported greater closeness to their fathers, even when there was conflict between parents (Fabricius & Hall, 2000; Fabricius & Leucken, 2007; Laumann-Billings & Emery, 2000). A meta-analysis of 33 studies found that children in shared physical custody (typically in the range of 35% to 50% of time with the nonresident parent) had better adjustment on multiple measures of psychological and behavioral adjustment and academic achievement when compared to children in the sole custody of one parent (Bausermann, 2002). More painful experiences associated with the divorce were reported by students who lived primarily with their mothers with limited time with their fathers, compared to students with shared physical custody arrangements (Laumann-Billings & Emery, 2000).

Young adults from divorced families, compared to those in continuously married families, were reported to be less trusting of their fathers and less affectionate, with fewer intergenerational exchanges of financial and emotional assistance and support (Amato & Booth, 1996; King, 2002). However, when there is a strong adolescent-father relationship and frequent contact with the father following separation and divorce, distrust is diminished and these youngsters are no different from married family adolescents.

More father involvement is also important for the adjustment and development of very young children as well. For infants and children under the age of 6, higher levels of father involvement were associated with better adaptive, communication and social skills, compared to those young children with less father involvement. Further, a consistent pattern of overnight visits with fathers in children from birth to age 6 was associated with positive psychological and developmental benefits compared to families where the children had no overnight visits with their fathers (families with a history of domestic violence and substance abuse were excluded from this study). Mothers and fathers have important and unique contributions to make to their young children's attachment formation and developmental achievements, and post-divorce living arrangements should enable both mothers and fathers to have substantial and meaningful time with their children (Kelly & Lamb, 2000; Pruett, Ebling, & Insabella, 2004).

CONCLUSIONS

An extensive social science literature investigating multiple dimensions of outcomes of children and adolescents following separation and divorce confirm that on average divorced children have twice the risk of behavioral, psychological, and academic problems when compared to children in still-married families. The majority of divorced children and adolescents function within the average range or better on measures of adjustment in the years after divorce, although many do so following a prolonged period of stress, pain, and anxiety. Identified risk and protective factors provide the opportunity to assist children and adolescents from separating and divorced families by implementing and encouraging involvement in effective divorce programs and offering pastoral outreach to parents that will focus on what parents can do to diminish the pain of those affected by parental divorce whenever possible and facilitate positive outcomes for their children.

Social science research indicates that children and adolescents from separated and divorced families have multiple needs related to their post-divorce adjustment and well-being, some of which diverge significantly from the compelling and often chaotic emotional needs of their parents. Unlike parents who want to sever their former marital ties completely, children and adolescents express strong desires to continue meaningful involvement with both of their parents (assuming they are adequate parents) and do not want parent-child ties severed. Children and adolescents need and benefit from appropriate parenting (nurturance, support, appropriate discipline, expectations) during separation and after divorce, and parents are often unable to provide this structure and support without parent education or counseling. Children and adolescents need re-stabilized, mentally healthy parents, and new family environments free of violence and intense parent and parent-child conflict.

These identified needs can be addressed in a variety of services and programs. Well-designed divorce education programs for parents that focus on those factors known to increase risk of maladjustment and continued pain in children have shown measureable success. These group programs openly discuss how children's needs are often different from parents interests and needs, what parental behaviors and attitudes are likely to be destructive to children's well-being, encourage parents to seek further help for their own emotional reactions to the divorce, and offer strategies for parents to help their children cope with the family disruption. Divorce education programs are best when parallel child and adolescent groups are provided to enable these youngsters to discuss their own situations, including their anger, fears, and distress, in a supportive and healing environment. Beyond education, parents (and indirectly their children) will benefit considerably from effective and empathic pastoral outreach and counseling provided by those knowledgeable about divorce and its effects on children and adolescents. The message should be one of empathy, understanding and inclusion, rather than one of condemnation and exclusion. Helping the most troubled parents deal with their grief, depression, anger and distress so that they can re-stabilize or improve their adult and parental functioning is critical for children of these parents. Custody and divorce mediation have demonstrated effectiveness in reducing parent conflict, increasing parental support and cooperation, and retaining father involvement at higher levels over time (Emery, 20004; Kelly, 2004).

We should not delegate children of divorce to the permanent category of "victims," with no hope for a productive, meaningful and loving life. Instead, institutions and individuals can express the will and intent to focus on those attitudes, behaviors, programs and services that will sustain children's positive adjustment and diminish the wounds and pain of divorce for children and adolescents as they move toward young adulthood.

REFERENCES

Ahrons, C. & Tanner, J. L. (2003). Adult children and their fathers: Relationship changes 20 years after parental divorce. *Family Relations, 52,* 340–351.

Amato, P. (2000). The consequences of divorce for adults and children. *Journal of Marriage and Family, 62,* 1269–1287.

Amato, P. R. & Afifi, T. D. (2006). Feeling caught between parents: Adult children's relations with parents and subjective well-being. *Journal of Marriage and Family, 68,* 222–235.

Amato, P. R. & Booth, A. (1996). A prospective study of divorce and parent-child relationships. *Journal of Marriage and the Family, 58,* 356–365.

Amato, P. R. & Fowler, F. (2002). Parenting practices, child adjustment, and family diversity. *Journal of Marriage and Family 64,* 703–716.

Amato, P. R. & Gilbreth, J. (1999). Nonresident fathers and children's well-being: A meta-analysis. *Journal of Marriage and the Family, 61,* 557–573.

Bauserman, R. (2002). Child adjustment in joint-custody versus sole-custody arrangements: A meta-analytic review. *Journal of Family Psychology, 16,* 91–102.

Booth, A. & Amato, P.R. (2001). Parental predivorce relations and offspring postdivorce well-being. *Journal of Marriage & Family, 63,* (1), 197–212.

Braver, S.L., Ellman, I.M. & Fabricius, W.V. (2003). Relocation of children after divorce and children's best interests: New evidence and legal considerations. *Journal of Family Psychology, 17,* 206–219.

Buchanan, C., Maccoby, E., & Dornbusch, S. (1991). Caught between parents: Adolescents' experience in divorced homes. *Child Development, 62,* 1008–1029.

Carlson, M. J. (2006). Family structure, father involvement, and adolescent behavioral outcomes. *Journal of Marriage and Family, 68,* 137–154.

Carlson, M. J. & Corcoran, M. E. (2001). Family structure and children's behavioral and cognitive outcomes. *Journal of Marriage and Family, 63,* 779–792.

Cherlin, A., Furstenberg, F., Jr., Lindsay, P., Chase-Lansdale, P., Kiernan, K., Robins, P.,

Morrison, D., Teitler, J. (1991). Longitudinal studies of the effects of divorce on children in Great Britain and the United States. *Science, 252,* 1386–1389.

Clarke-Stewart, A. & Brentano, C. (2006). *Divorce: Causes and consequences.* New Haven, CT: Yale University Press.

Cummings, E. & Davies, P. (1994). *Children and Marital Conflict.* New York: Guilford Press.

Dickstein, S., Seifer, R., Hayden, L., et al (1998). Levels of Family Assessment: II. Impact of maternal psychopathology on family functioning. *Journal of Family Psychology, 12,* (1), 23–40.

Dunn, J., Davies, L., O'Connor, T., & Sturgess, W. (2001). Family lives and friendships: The perspectives of children in step-, single-parent, and nonstop families. *Journal of Family Psychology, 15,* 272–287.

Emery, R. (1999). *Marriage, divorce, and children's adjustment.* (2nd Edition). Thousand Oaks: Sage.

Emery, R. (2004). *The truth about children and divorce: Dealing with emotions so you and your children can thrive.* New York: Viking/Penguin.

Fabricius, W. V. & Hall, J. (2000). Young adults' perspectives on divorce: Living arrangements. *Family & Conciliation Courts Review, 38*(4), 446–461.

Fabricius, W. V., & Luecken, L. J. (2007). Post-divorce living arrangements, parent conflict, and long-term physical health correlates for children of divorce. *Journal of Family Psychology. 21* (2), 195–205.

Finley, G. E., & Schwartz, S. J. (2007). Father involvement and young adult outcomes: The differential contributions of divorce and gender. *Family Court Review, 45*(4), 573–587.

Hetherington, E. M., & Kelly, J. (2002). *For better or for worse.* New York: Norton.

Johnston, J.R. & Campbell, L. (1993). A clinical typology of interparental violence in disputed-custody divorces. *American Journal of Orthopsychiatry, 63,* (2), 190–199.

Johnston, J. R. & Roseby, V. (1997). *In the Name of the Child. A Developmental Approach to Understanding and Helping Children of Conflict and Violent Divorce.* NY: Free Press.

Kelly, J. B. (2000). Children's adjustment in conflicted marriage and divorce: A

decade review of research. *Journal of Child and Adolescent Psychiatry, 39,* 963–973.

Kelly, J. (2003). Parents with enduring child disputes: Multiple pathways to enduring disputes. *Journal of Family Studies, 9(1),* 37–50 (Australia).

Kelly, J. B. (2004). Family mediation research: Is there support for the field? *Conflict Resolution Quarterly, 22,* 3–35.

Kelly, J. B. (2005). Developing beneficial parenting plan models for children following separation and divorce. *Journal of American Academy of Matrimonial Lawyers, 19,* 237–254.

Kelly, J. B. (2007). Children's living arrangements following separation and divorce: Insights from empirical and clinical research. *Family Process, 46,* 35–52.

Kelly, J.B. & Emery, R.E. (2003). Children's adjustment following divorce: Risk and resilience perspectives. *Family Relations, 52,* 352–362.

Kelly, J.B. & Lamb, M.E. (2003). Developmental issues in relocation cases involving young children: When, whether, and how? *Journal of Family Psychology, 17,* 193–205.

King, V. & Heard, H. E. (1999). Nonresident fathers' visitation, parental conflict, and mother's satisfaction: What's best for child well-being? *Journal of Marriage and Family, 61,* 385–396.

King, V. & Sobolewski, J. M. (2006). Nonresident fathers' contributions to adolescent well-being. *Journal of Marriage and Family, 68,* 537–557.

Kline, M, Johnston, J. & Tschann, J. (1991). The long shadow of marital conflict: A model of children's postdivorce adjustment. *Journal of Marriage and the Family, 53,* 297–309.

Laumann-Billings, L & Emery, RE. (2000). Distress among young adults in divorced families. *Journal Family Psychology, 14* (4), 671–687.

Maccoby, E. & Mnookin, R. (1992). *Dividing The Child.* Cambridge, MA: Harvard University Press.

Marquardt, E. (2005). *Between two worlds: The inner lives of children of divorce.* New York: Crown.

McLanahan, S. S. (1999). Father absence and children's welfare. In E. M. Hetherington (Ed). *Coping with divorce, single parenting, and remarriage: A risk and resiliency perspective* (pp. 117–146). Mahway, NJ: Lawrence Erlbaum Associates.

McMahon, T.J. & Giannini, F. D. (2003). Substance-abusing fathers in family court: Moving from popular stereotypes to therapeutic jurisprudence. *Family Court Review, 41,* 337–353.

Menning, C. L. (2006). Nonresident fathering and school failure. *Journal of Family Issues, 27,* 1356–1382.

Nord, C., Brimhall, D., & West, J. (1997). Fathers' involvement in their children's schools. National Center for Education Statistics, U.S. Department of Education, Washington, D.C. 20208-5574.

Pruett, M. K., Ebling, R., & Insabella, G. (2004). Critical aspects of parenting plans for young children. *Family Court Review, 42,* 39–59.

Pruett, M. K., Williams, T. Y, Insabella,, G., & Little, T. D. (2003). Family and legal indicators of child adjustment to divorce among families with young children. *Journal of Family Psychology, 17* (2), 169–180.

Simons, R.L., Lin, K-H., Gordon, L.C. et al. (1999). Explaining the higher incidence of adjustment problems among children of divorce compared with those in two-parent families. *Journal of Marriage and the Family, 61,* 1020–1033.

Smith, A.B., & Gallop, M. M. (2001). What children think separating parents should know. *New Zealand Journal of Psychology, 30,* 23–31.

Sun, Y. (2001). Family environment and adolescents' well-being before and after parents' marital disruption: A longitudinal analysis. *Journal of Marriage and Family, 63,* 697–713.

Sun, Y. & Li, Y. (2001). Marital disruption, parental investment, and children's academic achievement. *Journal of Family Issues, 22* (1), 27–62.

Wallerstein, J. & Kelly, J. (1980). *Surviving the Breakup: How children and parents cope with divorce.* NY: Basic Books.

Broken Ties and the Next Generation: Effects of Marital Separation on Adolescent and Young Adult Children

RAFFAELLA IAFRATE

The abundant quantity of international research on family psychology agrees in emphasizing the quality of family relationships for children's well-being and psychosocial adjustment (Scabini and Cigoli, 2000; Scabini and Iafrate, 2003; and Cigoli Scabin, 2006).

In view of the crisis that the family is facing today, both as an institution and as a privileged place of bonding between genders, generations and ethnic groups, the study of the implications of family instability for the new generations and for their future becomes particularly interesting.

Because of the progressive weakening of the marital bond, resulting in the increasing number of separated and divorced couples, more researchers and scholars choose to investigate the short-term, mid-term, and in most recent studies, long-term consequences of this phenomenon for "children of divorce." This definition includes children, adolescents and young people who experienced their parents' separation (Amato, 2000; Kelly, 2000; Wallerstein, 2005; Emery, 2008).

In general, the majority of the studies, especially in the international area, show that the event of separation, even if unpredictable and traumatic for children (and psychologically unexpected and disruptive for family members), always causes a significant amount of suffering. In the best case scenario, this event is not pathological in itself; however, it is undeniable that it requires a dramatic change, both from the point of view of family organization and as far as individuals' emotions are concerned.

Raffaella Iafrate is Associate Professor of Social Psychology, School of Psychology, Università Cattolica del Sacro Cuore, Milan (Italy).

Current research highlights the role of resilience, that is, the ability to cope with traumatic events, as well as to come through them with increased emotional strength. However, it is impossible to overestimate the distress that parental separation causes in the family. The studies that emphasize the resilience of children of divorced parents do not mention the associations with the experience they lived through. They also neglect to explore how resilience is influenced by the long process needed to come to terms with the pain for the loss experienced by these children (Amato, 2001; Emery, 2008). It is only through a painful journey that trust in emotional bonds may be re-established.

Research and clinical practice show that if the event of separation overlaps with other critical events, including predictable ones, such as the transition to adolescence or to adulthood, the impact on young generations may be even more problematic. For this reason, it is important to pay special attention to the consequences that separation has on adolescent and young adult children who live through these changes. (Iafrate, 1996a, 1996b; Lanz, Iafrate, Rosnati, Scabin, 1999; Darlington, 2001; Cigoli, Giuliani, Iafrate, 2002; Kirk 2002)

Data on this issue is largely available, considering the rich production of international as well as Italian studies (see the studies carried out in the Ateneo Center for Studies and Research on the Family of the Catholic University of Milan). This richness of data allows us to identify some key trends, especially with regard to separated families with teenage and young adult children, focusing on a number of aspects.

We will try to illustrate these trends in four distinct points, deeply connected to each other.

THE CENTRALITY OF RELATIONSHIPS

Research has shown that the quality of the relationship between ex-partners, and between parents and children, has a significant influence on the good functioning of the family as a whole and on children's adjustment.

Family relational processes, such as conflict management between ex-partners, parental cooperation, and parent-child communication, seem to cause more negative consequences for children than structural factors (according to research findings of the last few decades), such as children's gender and age, or the time of the event (for a review, see Iafrate and Cigoli, 1997; Cigoli, 1998; Emery, 2008).

Many studies also show that the structural dimension of being a separated or non-separated family in itself does not necessarily cause major consequences for children; however, research also indicates that the conflict level between spouses, which can also be very high before the separation, is responsible for many negative effects on children (Hetherington and Kelly, 2002).

A critical point in this respect concerns the function of boundaries: marital separation entails a renegotiation of relationships by family members, and requires them to redefine the boundaries in those relationships. The ability of parents and children to face this complex work of renegotiation is crucial for their future well-being (Emery, 1998; Iafrate, 1996b; Cigoli, Giuliani and Iafrate, 2002).

The difficulties concerning the redefinition of boundaries, as well as (as we will see later) children's perception of these boundaries, can be observed on different levels:

1. boundaries within the familiar subsystem (the subsystem consisting of the children of the parental couple);

2. boundaries between generations;

3. family boundaries (Greek, 2006).

1. Regarding the familiar subsystem, difficulties can arise when the boundary between the couple and the children subsystem becomes confused and ambiguous; this may lead children to be inappropriately involved in their parents' relationship.

According to the literature, it seems that parents' ability to manage their ex-spousal relationship can reduce the negative effects of divorce, so as not to let the child feel "caught in the middle" of an intolerable loyalty conflict. In literature, scholars define children "caught between parents" when they are used instrumentally by each of the two ex-spouses as an allied partner against the other parent.

The extent to which children perceive such a loyalty conflict may explain the quality of their relationship with their parents after divorce. This is particularly true when we consider children's (teenagers or young adults) satisfaction with the relationship with their parents and their tendency to avoid emotional closeness with them (Afifi and Schrodt, 2003).

Females seem to be most affected by the consequences of marital conflict, and therefore show signs of distress, such as anxiety and depression, more frequently than males (Buchanan, Maccoby and Dornbusch, 1991).

2. Regarding the boundary between the two generations, research has shown that in nuclear families after divorce, parent-child relationships tend to become structured on a horizontal level, rather than a hierarchical one. This means that the parent who was left alone (in many cases, the mother), frequently asks the child for support, in a way which often is not respectful of the child's developmental needs.

Children may therefore become their parent's confidants, and, for example, take upon themselves the responsibility (which is very often experienced as a burden) of emotionally supporting the parent, in a role reversal (or "parentification" of the child).

The research that studied these phenomena, which paid particular attention to the ethical aspects of the parent-child relationship, i.e. issues of justice/ injustice in the intergenerational exchange, showed very interesting results. It seems that children with separated parents experience parentification more often and more intensely than peers from intact families (Jurkovic, Thirkield & Morrell, 2001).

Parentified children carry out the instrumental and emotional caretaking roles they are given in the family. If parents fail to acknowledge children's efforts, and if their duration in time is not limited, children's development may be negatively affected. (Earley and Cushway 2002; Johnston, 1990; Jurkovic, 1997).

3. As far as the family boundary is concerned, research has indicated that children's perception is often ambiguous: namely, children seem unable to understand "who's in and who's out of the family" (Carroll, Olson, Buckmiller, 2007).

Above all, it is the father figure, at times very present in the children's psychological world, but distant from their everyday life, that seems to be affected by such an ambiguous arrangement. From a psychological point of view, this difficulty in defining the familial boundary indicates a potential risk factor, particularly for adolescents. This is because adolescents are already, as individuals, in a position of "ambiguity" of "boundaries": they are moving between the safety of childhood and the uncertainties of adult life (Iafrate, 1996).

OUTSTANDING IMPORTANCE OF COGNITIVE-AFFECTIVE ASPECTS

Research shows with increasing clarity that socio-behavioral aspects are insufficient in describing the experience of children with divorced parents. It is therefore essential that the observations of the "effects" of parental separation are not limited to children's "behavior" or signs of "social adjustment." A shift of focus is needed which includes the child's feelings, emotions and perceptions, as these reveal in a more significant way the suffering caused by parental divorce or separation.

In particular, research confirms the importance of the study of individual perceptions of the family experience, because these perceptions are predictive of the effects observed on the quality of family relations (Grych, Fincham, Jouriles and McDonald, 1990).

It is therefore important to remember that external behavior may not be able to reveal a type of distress which, very often, is deeply internalized. Instead, this must be detected with appropriate methods, in order to be recognized, monitored and possibly "treated."

Research which uses only children's observable behavior as an indicator of discomfort may leave such difficulties unnoticed. These, more easily noticed in females (as shown above), are expressed in a subtle, "internalized" way, as in the case of anxiety, low self-esteem and tendency to depression (Laumann-Billings & Emery, 2000).

Some recent studies investigate the cognitive-affective aspects of the effects of divorce on children, such as the experience of "being caught in the middle" (or of feeling caught between parents) mentioned above, the perception of family boundaries ambiguity and the "feeling of injustice" (or unfairness) resulting from parentification and early "adult-ization." We could say, as Cigoli (2008) noticed, that children's perception of divorce always oscillates between "being in mid air," as in a "limbo," and "being desolate."

In particular, for young adults, as it is clear from the recent results of our relevant quantitative research (Iafrate, Parmiani, Giuliani, forthcoming), feelings of injustice seem to be much more intense in children with separated/divorced parents than in their counterparts coming from intact families.

These subjects express the perception of being unfairly deprived of their parents' support, and are often constrained in the already mentioned "role reversal," experienced as a deep injustice and a heavy burden.

The effects of these feelings of injustice, even if they relate to the subjects' childhood or adolescence, seem to continue through time, affecting significant relationships, and therefore creating difficulties in the process of psychological separation from the parents during the transition to adulthood.

THE CENTRALITY OF TIME

A third point concerns the attention to the dimension of time, which has become increasingly relevant in recent research.

The most recent literature reports that the "long term" effects of parental separation on children are not to be underestimated: many problems that seem to be moderate, or completely absent, in preschool and school age, can literally "explode" in adolescence or young adulthood, when children need to plan their future life. In this period, they may frequently feel both emotionally and professionally "stuck."

The attention given to the consequences of divorce for adolescent and young adult children suggested the presence of a "sleeper effect" (Wallerstein, 2005), that is, a delayed effect of divorce on children's life. Such sudden resurgence of problems after childhood and preadolescence reveals a latent stress, which could not be observed before. That is why a growing number of studies focuses on adult children of divorce and uses longitudinal methods, with the aim of detecting the consequences of divorce many years after it occurred.

The results of these studies are heterogeneous; still, empirical evidence shows that overall, in children with separated/divorced families (compared with peers of intact families) there is a decrease in the ability to commit to long term emotional relationships, and a tendency to experiment in emotional and sexual relationships at an earlier age. Moreover, children with divorced parents will experience more difficulties in career planning and in achieving a stable financial situation (Hetherington, Law and O'Connor, 1993; Cigoli and Iafrate, 1997; Wallerstein, Lewis and Blakeslee, 2000).

In the research we conducted on adolescent children of divorce, we observed the tendency to express distrust and fear in emotional relationships, combined with a certain difficulty in planning their future adult life (Giuliani, Iafrate and Rosnati, 1998).

For children, on one hand, the experience of parents' marital separation seems to cause the fear of repeating their parents' "failure." Children of separated/divorced parents, when compared with their peers from intact families, express more worries and uncertainties toward marriage. On the other hand, the need to redeem the image of the lost family unity, pushing young adult children to invest—sometimes in an idealized way—in their own future family, can also emerge.

PROBLEMS RELATED TO FATHER'S ABSENCE/DISENGAGEMENT

Scholars agree that distance from the father, associated with feelings of disappointment and loss, is a major source of disturbance for children with separated parents (Laumann-Billings & Emery, 2000).

In this regard, two recurring phenomena in studies of separated families are discussed: "parental alienation syndrome" and "malicious mother syndrome." Without addressing the specific characteristics of these phenomena, we can say that they both indicate a tendency, in one-parent separated families, (especially maternal-led) to distance the non-resident parent (usually the father), and to undermine his relationship with the children at its very roots (Gardner, 1998; Hodges, 1991). This does not imply a "brainwashing" of the child by the custodial parent against the non-custodial one, but rather a genuine "alienation" of the other, a cancellation of the recognition of that bond. This way, children are brought to depreciate the non-resident parent as well as their paternal family roots.

An Italian research study conducted ten years ago (Giuliani, Iafrate, 1995) had already shown that over 80% of the interviewed children with divorced parents claimed to have restricted accessibility to their father, meaning not only the possibility of contacting him, but also the actual chance of relying on him during important moments of their lives.

Even in the ongoing research on young adult children with separated families, one of the most important findings is, once more, the lack of paternal involvement in children's (in particular daughters') lives and the substantial lack of material support from their fathers. The emotional climate of the father-child bond is often described as formal and stiff. Even the places where fathers and children meet seem to be alien and formal: cafés, restaurant, workplaces, as opposed to the comfortable environment of the child's family home (Cigoli, Giuliani and Iafrate, 2002).

One of the areas most affected by the deterioration of the father-child relationship, especially for females, is their insecurity in intimate relationships (Frank, 2006; Mullett, & Stolberg, 2002).

This data, showing specific effects of children's gender, is illustrated by our qualitative research on young adult children of separated couples (Cigoli, Giuliani, Iafrate, 2002). This study showed different kinds of suffering for males and females in the period of young adulthood, associated with different ways of dealing with the issue of paternal absence.

For sons, fathers' absence seems to be experienced as the lack of the parent who sets the rules and transmits useful life lessons—in other terms, the lack of the head of the house, of a teacher and a guide.

For daughters, who easily identify with their mothers' suffering, this paternal lack is mainly perceived as the absence of a partner for the mother, responsible for the mother's loneliness. They feel the lack of her husband/partner as the one who could limit her excessive and invading presence in their lives.

What are the defense mechanisms that children adopt in these situations? Looking at the male sample, there appeared to be a significant devaluation of the father, both as a person and as a parent. Children emphasized only the negative aspects of the relationship with the father, resulting either from the effects of the divorce, and/or his personality.

In contrast, the recurring pattern among females is the idealization of the father. He is attributed with heroic and mythical characteristics and typified as a charismatic figure.

The outcomes of these defense mechanisms are, for females, fears of intimacy and abandonment in the couple relationship; males, on the other hand, are concerned about the risk of repeating their fathers' mistakes, as well as doubt their own ability to perform a parental role in the future.

It should also be noted that paternal absence seems to have a negative impact on parent-child relationships in single-parent families. In particular, in single-parent homes, where the access to the father is more difficult, the mother-son/daughter relationship appears to be much more problematic than in intact families. We could say that paternal absence and relational difficulties with the non-custodial parent have a "pervasive" effect, and influence even the seemingly "privileged" relationship with the custodial parent (Iafrate, 1996a). In other words, children, especially daughters, express a "call for the father;" he is needed as "other" in the relationship with the mother.

This presence becomes particularly relevant during the developmental stage of "detachment" from the family of origin, as well as for the process of psychological separation from the mother.

Finally, the lack of access to "the other," that is, the other parent, often implies also the lack of access to another lineage, which actually represents a crucial indicator of many at-risk situations.

In this regard, the little research that has addressed this issue (Cooney and Smith, 1996), indicates that "children of divorce," while still considering grandparents as important points of reference for their growth, find it more difficult to access both family histories.

They tend to openly declare their belonging to one family lineage only (either on the maternal or the paternal side), excluding the other, this way reproducing the rift caused by parental divorce.

In particular, we witness the grandchildren's alignment to the grandparents who raised them (usually the maternal grandparents) and the subsequent detachment from the other grandparents (Giuliani, Iafrate, 1995; Cigoli, Giuliani, Iafrate, 2002).

The importance of these results should encourage the development of research addressing the issues of "children of divorce" from a social and intergenerational point of view, going beyond a merely individual or—in the best cases—dyadic approach to the problem.

CONCLUDING REMARKS

In view of these results, we may wonder which paths can be taken today as "carrying the family ties to safety" even in these situations of crisis and fracture. This is not to deny the suffering and hardships of this experience, but to find a way to give it a purpose, and find a meaning that the generations involved could recognize.

The adult generation's responsibility towards the children has a central role here.

Separated parents, in particular those who have custody of the children, are first of all requested to allow the child access to the "missing half": the actual chance to access both the other parent, and his/her symbolic history. The "single parent" has a duty to respect the child's roots, as children are always the result of two histories, as well as of a variety of social and family ties.

"Creating a space for the absent" and ensuring access to the other parent may open the door to pain or conflict but, at the same time, may allow the child access to her or his own history. This process would be able to relieve pain by bringing hope and giving a sense of transformation of the turmoil experienced in family ties.

It is true that the access to the other in a divorce situation implies taking the risk of facing the conflict between the ex-spouses. This is a serious problem because children will be able to deal with their history and lineage only if they have the chance to access them. If they do not, either because fathers are detached, uninvolved, or because of mothers' choice, a risk may arise and children themselves—not to mention the future generations—will pay the consequences for this.

As we observed, hope in familial ties and trust in the perceived ability to create lasting bonds are at risk for children of divorced parents. This means that the very concept of the person as potentially able to generate beneficial ties is put to the test.

It is therefore of paramount importance to guarantee and to foster, beyond the marital break-down, the continuity of the parental relationship, ensuring children's access to both parental lineages, respecting their right to confront their own origins, which are—as we said before—both familial and social.

The denial of this right is one of the greatest acts of injustice that only a parent can do against his/her own children, burdening them with the failure of the conjugal relationship. This way, parents fail to respect children's right to enjoy the symbolic dimension of the parental bond, of which they remain the indissoluble sign.

REFERENCES

Afifi, T. D, Schrodt, P. (2003). "Feeling caught" as a mediator of adolescents' and young adults' avoidance and satisfaction with their parents in divorced and non-divorced households. *Communication Monographs*, 70(2), 142–173.

Amato, P. R. (2000). The consequences of divorce for adults and children. *Journal of Marriage and the Family*, 62, 1269–1287.

Amato, P. R. (2001). Children of divorce in the 1990s; an update of the Amato and Keith (1991) meta-analysis. *Journal of Family Psychology*, 152, 355–369.

Buchanan, C. M., Maccoby, E. E., & Dornbusch, S. M. (1991). Caught between parents: Adolescents' experience in divorced homes. Child Development, 62, 1008–1029.

Carroll J. S., Olson C. D., & Buckmiller N., (2007). Family Boundary Ambiguity: A 30-Year Review of Theory, Research, and Measurement. *Family Relations*, 56, 210–230.

Cigoli V. (1998). Psicologia del divorzio. Il Mulino, Bologna.

Cigoli V., Scabini E. (2006). *Family Identity: Ties, Symbols and Transitions.* Lawrence Erlbaum Associates Publishers, London.

Cigoli V. (2008). Prefazione all'edizione italiana. Divorziare e rigenerare il legame familiare, in R. Emery La verità sui figli e il divorzio. Gestire le emozioni per crescere insieme. Franco Angeli, Milano, pp. 7–13.

Cigoli, V., Giuliani, C., & Iafrate, R. (2002). Il dolore del divorzio: adolescenti e giovani adulti tra riavvicinamento e distacco alla storia familiare. Psicologia clinica dello sviluppo, IV, 3,423–442.

Cooney, T.M., &Smith, L.A., (1996).Young adults' relations with grandparents following recent parental divorce. *Journal of Gerontology Series B Psychological Sciences and Social Sciences,* 51(2), pp. 91–95.

Darlington, Y. (2001). "When all is said and done": The impact of parental divorce and contested custody in childhood on young adults' relationships with their parents and their attitudes to relationships and marriage. *Journal of Divorce & Remarriage,* 35(3–4), 23–42.

Earley, L., & Cushway, D. (2002). The parentified child. *Clinical Child Psychology & Psychiatry,* 7(2), 163–178.

Emery R. (1998). Il divorzio. Rinegoziare le relazioni familiari. Raffaello Cortina, Milano.

Emery R. (2008). La verità sui figli e il divorzio. Gestire le emozioni per crescere insieme. Franco Angeli, Milano.

Frank, H. (2006). Young adults' relationship with parents and siblings: The role of marital status, conflict and post-divorce predictors. *Journal of Divorce and Remarriage,* 46, 105–124.

Gardner R.A. (1998). The parental alienation syndrome: What is it and what data support it? *Child Maltreatment,* Vol 3(4), pp. 309–312.

Giuliani, C., & Iafrate, R. (1995). Nuclei monogenitoriali: genitori e figli a confronto. Bambino Incompiuto, 6,19–43.

Giuliani, C., Iafrate, R., & Rosnati, R. (1998). Peer-group and romantic relationships in adolescents from intact and separated families. *Contemporary Family Therapy,* 20,1,93–105.

Greco, O. (2006) Il lavoro clinico con le famiglie complesse: il test "la doppia luna" nella ricerca e nella terapia, Franco Angeli, Milano.

Grych, J. H., Fincham, F. D., Jouriles, E. N., & McDonald, R. (1990). Interparental conflict and child adjustment: Testing the mediational role of appraisals in the cognitive-contextual framework. *Child Development,* 71, 1648–1661.

Hetherington, E.M., Law, T.C. & O'Connor, T.G., (1993). Divorce, challenges, changes and new chances, in normal family processes, in Walsh F. (ed.), *The Guilford Press,* New York, pp.208–234.

Hetherington, E. M., & Kelly, J. (2002). *For better or for worse: Divorce reconsidered.* New York: Norton.

Hodges, W.F. (1991). *Interventions for Children of Divorce,* (second edition), Wiley, New York.

Iafrate, R. (1996a). Comunicazione, soddisfazione ed influenza parentale in famiglie intatte e separate con figli adolescenti. Archivio di Psicologia, Neurologia e Psichiatria, 2–3,175–193.

Iafrate, R. (1996b). Conflitto, cooperazione e percezione dei confini familiari in famiglie separate con adolescenti. Ricerche di Psicologia, 2, 79–113.

Iafrate, R., & Cigoli, V. (1997). Dallo sviluppo della ricerca empirica sul divorzio all'uso clinico della C.T.U. In V. Cigoli, G. Gulotta, G. Santi e coll., Separazione, divorzio e affidamento dei figli, (pp. 403–476). Giuffrè, Milano.

Iafrate, R., Parmiani, L., & Giuliani, C. (in preparazione). Intergenerational relationships and developmental tasks in young adults: the role of parental divorce and gender in an Italian sample.

Johnston, J. R. (1990). Role diffusion and role reversal: Structural variations in divorced families and children's functioning. *Family Relations,* 39, 405–413.

Jurkovic, G. J. (1997). Lost childhoods: The plight of the parentified child. Brunner/Mazel, Philadelphia.

Jurkovic, G. J., Thirkield, A., Morrell, R. (2001). Parentification of adult children of divorce: a multidimensional analysis. *Journal of Youth and Adolescence,* 30, 2, 245–257.

Kelly, J. B. (2000). Children's adjustment in conflicted marriage and divorce: A decade review of research. *Journal of the American Academy of Child & Adolescent Psychiatry,* 39(8), 963–973.

Kirk, A. (2002). The effects of divorce on young adults' relationship competence: The influence of intimate friendships. *Journal of Divorce & Remarriage,* 38(1–2), 61–90.

Lanz, M., Iafrate, R., Rosnati, R., & Scabini, E. (1999). Parent-child communication and adolescents' self-esteem in "normal," separated, and inter-country adoptive families. *Journal of Adolescence,* 22,785–794.

Laumann-Billings, L., & Emery, R. E. (2000). Distress among young adults from divorced families. *Journal of Family Psychology,* 14, 4, 671–687.

Mullett, E., Stolberg, A.L. (2002). Divorce and its impact on the intimate relationships of young adults. *Journal of Divorce and Remarriage,* 38 (1–2), 39–60.

Scabini E., & Cigoli V. (2000). Il Famigliare.Cortina, Milano.

Scabini, E., & Iafrate, R. (2003). Psicologia dei legami familiari.Il Mulino, Bologna.

Wallerstein, J. S., Lewis, J. M., & Blakeslee, S. (2000). The unexpected legacy of divorce: A 25-year landmark study. Hyperion, New York.

Wallerstein, J. S. (2005). Growing up in the divorced family. *Clinical Social Work Journal,* 33, 4, 401–418.

The Spiritual Lives of Children of Divorce

Elizabeth Marquardt

Abstract: In a first-ever national study in the United States, the author finds that even amicable divorces profoundly shape the inner lives of children of divorce. The grown children of divorce overall are less religious and less likely to be a member of a house of worship. Of those who were active in a church at the time of their parents' divorce, *two-thirds* say that no one from the clergy or congregation reached out to them at that time. The paper shares stories and data about the inner lives of these young people and offers practical suggestions to faith communities of how to minister to today's generation of young adults who are so profoundly affected by divorce. More information about the study can be found in Elizabeth Marquardt's book, *Between Two Worlds: The Inner Lives of Children of Divorce* (Crown, 2005) or at www.betweentwoworlds.org.

INTRODUCTION

Despite the widespread occurrence of divorce in many of our nations, there has been very little investigation of the moral and spiritual lives of children and young people from divorced families. Too often, churches miss opportunities to minister to these young people because they do not understand their lives. Even worse, their lack of understanding can evoke the losses these young people have already experienced in their families and cause further suffering.

Elizabeth Marquardt is vice president for family studies, Institute for American Values, New York City.

The church must learn about the experience of children of divorce because it is called to minister to the most vulnerable, especially children. Importantly, too, the life of the church will be dramatically enriched and strengthened if it can effectively minister to young adults from divorced families who now make up so much of the young adult population.

In a first-ever national study in the United States, reported in my book *Between Two Worlds* (Crown, 2005), the grown children of divorce say there is no such thing as a "good" divorce. Even amicable or "good" divorces require children to grow up *between two worlds,* forced alone to make sense of their parents' often dramatically different beliefs, values, and ways of living. When parents divorce, the tough job of dealing with the conflict between their worlds does not go away. Instead, divorce hands the job of making sense of two worlds to the child alone. The result is that divorce sows lasting inner conflict in children's lives.

THE MYTH OF THE GOOD DIVORCE

Many experts say that a so-called "good" or amicable divorce will prevent children's suffering. If divorced parents stay on good terms with each other and stay involved in their children's lives, they say, then the children will be fine. This study shows quite the contrary; that while a good divorce is better than a bad divorce, it isn't good. Even "good" divorces hand children the lonely job of making sense of their parents' different worlds, a job that formerly belonged first to their parents. In this study, the children of "good" divorces often fare worse than children of *unhappy* marriages, so long as those marriages are low-conflict (as most are that end in divorce)—and they fare *far* worse than children of happy marriages.

Most people think that conflict between divorced parents is the main problem with divorce. In truth, we found that the majority of grown children of divorce say their parents did *not* have a lot of conflict after the divorce. Yet they nevertheless experienced serious and lasting conflicts between their parents' two different worlds. For example, though only a few of the grown children of divorce had parents who conflicted "a lot," the majority of them, two-thirds, view their parents as polar opposites. Many say they had to be a different person in each parent's world. They often felt the need to keep secrets, even when their parents did not ask them to. They consistently speak of feeling divided inside.

Quite strikingly, when their parents did have conflicts, nearly all those from intact, married families felt very confident that their parents would "get over it" (74 percent strongly agreed), while only a quarter (27 percent) of grown children of divorce felt the same way. The divorce itself made the child view the parents' worlds as forever locked in conflict, *even when* the parents themselves did not have a lot of conflict.

This inner conflict burdens children, making them grow up too soon. They feel like divided selves, torn between their parents' worlds. They feel much more alone. They become guarded and often secretive. They don't know where they belong. They feel like they have to figure out the big questions in life alone. They struggle with huge losses that impact their spiritual lives. And they do all this in isolation and silence, because no one ever talks about this job they've been given, to make sense *alone* of their parents' two different worlds.

Selected findings from *Between Two Worlds: The Inner Lives of Children of Divorce* (Crown, 2005). (For information about study methodology, visit www.betweentwoworlds.org):

STUDY FINDINGS ABOUT THE GROWN CHILDREN'S INNER LIVES AND THEIR RELATIONSHIPS WITH THEIR MOTHERS AND FATHERS

Only a fifth (20 percent) recall their parents having "a lot" of conflict after the divorce, but two-thirds say that after the divorce their parents seemed like *polar opposites,* compared to just one-third of young adults from intact families (66 percent vs. 34 percent).

Twice as many—close to half—say that after the divorce they felt like a *different person* with each of their parents (43 percent vs. 21 percent).

Half said their divorced parents' *versions of truth were different,* compared to just a fifth of those from intact families.

Fewer than half of the children of divorce say their *parents' household rules were the same,* while the vast majority of those from intact families said their parents' rules were the same (44 percent vs. 85 percent).

Over twice as many said that after the divorce they were asked to *keep secrets* (27 percent vs. 10 percent)—and many more felt the need to keep secrets, even when their parents did not ask.

Almost twice as many said that after the divorce it would *upset them if one parent said they looked like the other parent* (28 percent vs. 15 percent).

Over three times as many said that after the divorce, *"I was alone a lot as a child"* (44 percent vs. 14 percent), and they were seven times more likely to strongly agree with that statement (21 percent vs. 3 percent).

Just one third said they *went to one or both parents for comfort* after their parents' divorce, compared to two-thirds from intact families who said the same thing (33 percent vs. 69 percent). The children of divorce were more likely to go to peers—either siblings or friends—or to deal with it alone.

Three times as many say there are *things their mother has done that they find hard to forgive* (37 percent vs. 13 percent) and three times as many say the same thing about their *father* (51 percent vs. 17 percent).

Three times as many agree, *"I love my mother but I don't respect her,"* (19 percent vs. 6 percent) and four times as many agree, *"I love my father but I don't respect him"* (26 percent vs. 7 percent).

The majority (64 percent) say that after the divorce it was *stressful in their family,* compared to just 25 percent of intacts, with *holidays* being a particularly stressful time for some. Over twice as many say holidays were stressful (36 percent vs. 15 percent).

STUDY FINDINGS SPECIFICALLY ABOUT RELIGION AND SPIRITUALITY

Children of divorce are much less likely to have had consistent involvement in a religious faith when growing up.

Only 56 percent of children of divorce say they attended religious services every week or almost every week when they were growing up, compared to 74 percent of young people from intact families. A smaller number said their mother encouraged them to practice a religious faith (57 percent, compared to 78 percent from intact families) and an even smaller number said their father encouraged them to do so (31 percent vs. 64 percent).

Even children of divorce who were active in a faith during childhood rarely recall being reached out to at church at the time of their parents' divorce.

Of those children of divorce who were regular attendees at a place of worship, *two-thirds* said no one from the clergy or congregation reached out to them when their parents split up, while only one-quarter said that someone at church did reach out.

When they grow up, children of divorce as a group are much less religious than their peers from intact families.

As young adults, 68 percent from intact families say they are "very" or "fairly" religious, compared to 55 percent of young people from divorced families. Further, 63 percent of young people from intact families, compared to 49 percent of children of divorce, say they are currently a member at a house of worship.

More than a third (37 percent) of children of divorce agree with the statement, "Religion doesn't seem to address the important issues in my life," compared to 29 percent of people from intact families. Almost half of children of divorce (46 percent) agree "I believe I can find ultimate truth without help from a religion," compared to 36 percent of their peers from intact families.

However, generalizations can mask differences. The qualitative interviews made it clear that some children of divorce become more religious as a result of their parents' divorce, and some become less. If children of divorce *are* religious they are more likely to be evangelical. In the survey, 41 percent of young people from divorced families describe themselves as born again or evangelical, compared to 37 percent of their peers from intact families.

Young adults from divorced families feel just as spiritual as their peers, but their spiritual journeys are more often characterized by loss and suffering.

As young adults, 70 percent of children of divorce compared to 73 percent of young adults from intact families say they are "very" or "fairly" spiritual. But their route to spirituality is more often a painful one.

Children of divorce are more likely to say that their relationship with God is an outgrowth of lacking a loving father or parent when they were growing up, with 38 percent of them agreeing (compared to 22 percent from intact families), "I think of God as the loving father or parent I never had in real life."

One fifth of children of divorce (20 percent) but 13 percent from intact families agree, "When I think about bad things that have happened in my life I find it hard to believe in a God who cares." Children of divorce are more likely to agree that, today, "I don't feel that anyone really understands me"—more than one-fifth of them (22 percent), compared to 14 percent from intact families. They are also more likely to feel that the hardships in their life come from God (22 percent vs. 17 percent).

STORIES THAT HELP TO ILLUSTRATE THE DATA

Some of these young people have experienced so much loss, they struggle to find meaning in a faith that does not recognize it. Too often the faith itself *evokes* the losses they felt in their families so many years ago. One example is how they react to the parable of the Prodigal Son.

When people from intact families hear the story of the Prodigal Son they tend to focus on the end of the story, when the son finds himself loved in spite of his mistakes. But children of divorce often think about the beginning of the story instead. The idea of someone leaving home resonates for them, though not necessarily the idea of a *child* who leaves home. Rather, some are reminded of being home alone while their divorced parents were working or socializing, or of the departure that caused the divorce in the first place. In the children of divorce's understanding of the story, the roles are reversed: the story is not about the Prodigal Son but their Prodigal Parents.

Joanna said that, growing up, when she heard the story of the Prodigal Son in church it always made her think, "Well, maybe my father will decide to come back one of these days." After her parents' divorce when she was 5 years old, her father lived in the same town but saw Joanna and her brothers only once a year. During the Christmas holidays he would pick the children up and take them out to breakfast for a couple of hours. When he dropped them off afterwards he would say, "that went really well," Joanna recalled, and "yeah, I'll come around and see you one of these Saturdays." But he never did. Joanna would run to her room crying after these visits. She always wondered why her father would spend far more time being a dad to the five children his second wife brought to their marriage than to his own three children.

Joanna says she has given her father many chances to come back. She is wary and cautious with him, but she wants him to know her and, especially, her baby. She even said to him, "I'll make the effort, but I have to see you making the effort. And I don't mean like you come once and disappear for another year." In the story of the Prodigal Son it is the father who is willing to give his son a second chance, despite his mistakes. Yet this story reminds Joanna of her own willingness to continue hoping—despite the constant rejections as a child—that her father will start showing interest in her life.

Other children of divorce also think of their parents leaving when they hear the story. Alicia's parents divorced when she was seven years old. Each remarried within a year after that, and both later divorced again. When I asked her if the story had any relevance to her life she said, "Well, I don't really see anybody going away and coming back and being welcomed, you know?" She laughed bitterly, "In my life people have either gone away and done something else or gone away and stayed away."

Other children of divorce interpret the story slightly differently. They think about the son coming home, but say that even if they had rebelled and left home there would not have been a stable home for them to come back to. Instead, they see *themselves* as the one who stayed put while their *parents* came and went, or themselves as the ones who traveled back and forth to keep their families connected.

Melissa thought about the story and said, "I thought it was a nice idea if it would ever really work . . . To actually believe that you could just leave and the fact that love would always be constant. For me it was, like, if they love me then why do they live so far away? Or why are they always going out with boyfriends?" As a child of divorce, she said, "You're always staying put in one place and trying your hardest to make something stable."

Melissa concluded, "I figured if I left and went away, when I came back my house would be gone."

Another young woman from a divorced family who I interviewed for an earlier project said she had friends for whom the story of the Prodigal Son meant a great deal. "They feel like they've gone away and rejected their families and came back," she said. But, in her family, "I was always kind of the dutiful one—the one traveling distances to be sure I saw my mother, traveling distances to be sure I saw my father. My family didn't even give me anything to reject! There wasn't a stable enough thing to go away from or come back to."

I also asked young adults from divorced and intact families to reflect on the idea of God as a parent more generally. The responses of the children of divorce revealed a great deal about what they thought of their parents as well as what they thought of God. Many of them find thinking about God painful.

Will had been angry at his father for years because he had cheated on Will's mother. When I asked Will if God is like a father or parent he paused, looking puzzled. "Yeah, I think a father is somebody who is your last string of hope," he said. "He'll watch over you, make sure everything is going to be okay." Then he stopped and looked down at his hands in his lap. "I'm drawing a blank," he repeated, "I'm just drawing a blank."

Kimberly said that God is like a parent because God "is trying to test you . . . in life you're going to have many challenges. And the challenges come from somewhere."

"Do they come from God?" I asked.

"Yeah, I think they do," she said. In Kimberly's unusual perspective, the role of her parents and of God was to confront her with challenges. In the national survey, 22 percent of children of divorce agreed with the statement, "The hardships in my life come from God," compared to 17 percent of people from intact families.

Rochelle said that God is like a parent because God "supplies things I need." She emphasized, "Like you're *supposed* to be able to ask your parents for things and they're *supposed* to take care of you." As we talked she told me many stories of how her father rarely supplied her needs when she was growing up, even when she specifically asked.

Others said that God did *not* seem like a parent. Allison said that thinking of God as a parent "would be a negative relationship for me." Alicia said God is "like a mentor, an older, wiser person . . . not like a parent," revealing a lot about how she saw her parents and God. One young woman said that God is not like a parent because God is "something smarter" than us. Another said that parents are supposed to be nurturing and comforting but, to her, God seems "like a manager, keeping tabs on things."

Daniel referred to the book *The Color of Water* by James McBride. In that book the author, who grew up the child of a black father and a white mother, took comfort in his mother's assurance that God was neither black nor white but was "the color of water." Daniel speculated that, similarly, God is neither father nor mother but the color of water, which felt liberating to him. Melissa said she didn't think of God as a parent, she thought of God as "authority, control, and safety." She told me that she didn't experience "full, untainted love" in her family so she didn't think of God as being "part of the family."

To be sure, some children of divorce *do* find spiritual healing and joy in the church. At a young age Michael embraced the church. Yet like so many children of divorce, he came to God and the church alone, without the company of his parents. "I wasn't raised in a religious home," Michael recalls. His mother and stepfather would go to church "on Christmas and Easter and that was about the extent of it." When he was 14 years old, though, Michael's best friend invited him to go to church. "It was a Baptist church and they had a separate youth worship service and it was really, really neat. The more I went, the more it became somewhere that I really felt safe and like I belonged." After a while, he told me, "I gave my life to Christ and started going to church regularly."

Michael sat back and smiled as he recalled, "I remember being very excited when I got my first Bible. I can remember the smell of it. And I just would spend hours in my room reading it and thinking, this is the most exciting stuff in the world, you know, that God cares for me, that all this is possible for me. There had been this huge void in my life," he told me. "But once I accepted Christ, from that point on, I really looked at life differently." As a child, he said, "I had always believed in God, but now it was like God could be with you . . . God wasn't out there anymore. God was walking with you and living in you." Michael's newfound faith changed every part of his life, including at school. "I had been doing mediocre in school at that point. But it just really gave meaning to life for me, to excel in life. I got more involved in school and my grades got really good."

Michael's growing relationship with God in part filled a huge void created by the tense relationship he had with his own father. Michael's father had left his mother for another woman. At their house the children of his father's first and second marriages vied with each other and Michael's older brother would often turn on him, teasing him mercilessly when they visited their dad. Meanwhile, Michael's father was often out at work or playing golf. "God really became my father," Michael said. "He was that father who never leaves and is always there. Who you can always talk to and who will listen to you."

For some children of divorce, faith and a relationship with God fill a void. They turn to God for love and guidance in place of an absent father or parent, or a lonely home life.

Yet it is clear, whether they become more or less religious, the spiritual journeys of children of divorce consistently reflect stories of loss, pain, and loneliness.

WHAT CAN CHURCHES DO?
PRACTICAL SUGGESTIONS FOR FAITH COMMUNITIES

Teaching and Preaching: Many churches avoid discussing family issues, especially divorce, because they fear alienating or hurting single and divorced adults. Prophetic messages may flow from their pulpit every week that touch on all kinds of social justice issues—health care, public education, the environment, and more—but rarely will there be mention of family structure and its effects on children. Such a message might hit too close to home and actually make some adults uncomfortable. Yet this kind of challenge is exactly what faith communities are called to.

It is fully possible to be compassionate to children of divorce and emphasize the importance of marriage while, at the same time, affirming and supporting single and divorced parents. Yet most church leaders, in all denominations, could be more informed, more prophetic, and more compassionate on the topic of family than they currently are.

Tackling the topic of family might ruffle a few feathers among some, but faith communities are also likely to discover that many young adults respond favorably to honest examinations of marriage and divorce. Today's generation of young adults has grown up in a divorce culture. Even those whose parents did not divorce have seen its effects among their friends. Faith communities often wonder how to involve young adults more fully in their community. I predict that responding honestly to the effects of family change today will make more young adults feel welcome.

Liturgy: Some faith communities are trying to develop rituals and prayers that can be used at the time of divorce. While these efforts are well-intended they often end up being a religious version of "happy talk." The United Methodist denomination in the United States has a prayer to be used at the time of divorce that ends with the words "in the name of the One who sets us free from slavery to the past and makes all things new." This sentiment may reflect the experience of some divorcing adults but children do not experience the breakup of their families as being "set free from slavery to the past," nor do they long to have their families "made new."

More appropriate might be rituals in which parents vow to be kind to one another and remain loving, involved parents to their children, but even this could feel intimidating rather than comforting to young children. Rituals of healing for adult children of divorce, however, might be welcomed by some.

Counseling: While some marriages are so destructive that they must be ended, many low-conflict marriages might be saved. Clergy who marry couples have a distinct responsibility to be aware of quality marriage education and counseling resources in their community and to make sure members of their congregation know where to find them. Marriage education, in particular, should be encouraged for all kinds of couples, not just those in crisis.

When faith communities want to help children of divorce often their first idea is to start a support group. Some children might be helped by support groups around the time of their parents' divorce, especially if leaders use a well-written curriculum that is sensitive to the children's needs. But churches should see support groups only as a beginning. Such groups can isolate the people they help, and no one else in the community has to learn much about the problem or change their behavior in any way.

More important is for faith communities to take a comprehensive approach to marriage and divorce as a whole. For children of divorce, the effects of divorce are not limited to the time around the divorce "but continue to shape us throughout our lives." Churches should respond to the needs of young children of divorce but also adolescents, young adults and older people whose parents may have divorced many years before. They should also make supporting and strengthening marriages in the congregation and community a priority so that, in the future, there will be far fewer children suffering the lifelong pain of their parents' divorce.

* * *

Contact information: Elizabeth Marquardt is an author and vice president for family studies at the Institute for American Values in New York City. The Institute's contact information is available at www.americanvalues.org.

Parents in the Wake of Divorce: Some Points of Reference on Theological Ethics

OLIVIER BONNEWIJN

"I relieved your shoulder of the burden; your hands were freed from the basket." (Ps 81:5).

INTRODUCTION

> They were bringing children to him, that he might touch them; and the disciples rebuked them. But when Jesus saw it, he was indignant, and said to them: Let the children come to me, do not hinder them; for to such belongs the kingdom of God . . . . And he took them in his arms and blessed them, laying his hands upon them. (*Mk* 10:13–16)

This scene takes place after a harsh discussion with the Pharisees on the indissolubility of marriage. Christ now welcomes all the children presented to him. He embraces and blesses them all, without exception. He lays his hands upon them. Perhaps there are some among them whose mothers have been repudiated, whose father has left, whose parents may have married again after divorce. Whatever their family situation, to each one of them "belongs the kingdom of God."

This life dynamism and blessing is the very frame for our research as a theologian and moralist. The point of view in this search is not the time "before" a divorce, but its "after," the situation after the grave decision of one or both spouses, whatever the complex reasons that led to this choice.

Olivier Bonnewijn is Professor of Ethics and Moral Theology, Institut d'Etudes Théologiques, Brussels (Belgium).

This choice is always fraught with consequences for the children. Certainly, a separation of the spouses, with or without a civil divorce, may be beneficial and even necessary in certain situations. It offers in certain cases "a last resort" to the terrible marital conflicts that threaten family life.[1] Everyone can find relief, including the children who seek to escape from being witnesses and hostages to endless fighting. But the decision must be made prudently[2], even if it meets the approval of the children.[3]

Nevertheless, divorce takes into account grave marital failures that have proved to be irresolvable. Unsolved conflicts between adults are carved as a definite failure in the heart and story of the children. It causes a deep upheaval to be compared with an earthquake of great magnitude, despite the parents' good intentions. "It's as if the child had his feet on two tectonic plates separating from each other. He wonders if he will fall into the abyss that grows beneath him."[4] "I felt the ground collapse, and I had the impression that I no longer existed."

Nevertheless, divorce has an aftermath in which parents will continue their educational mission in this new situation marked by grief. How can they still be everyday sources and mediators of life? In which ways can they lead their sons and daughters "to grow, become strong, and be filled with wisdom" (*Lk* 2:40)? How can they contribute practically to a hopeful future for their children? How are they called to raise their children in conditions where some points of reference are objectively blurred?

We are conscious of the difficulty of such a question. There is a great diversity of situations, all of which we seek to respect, hoping both to be able to find out some helping points and to keep in mind the attitude of Moses in front of the burning bush.

We will proceed in two stages. We will disclose an ethical point of reference founded in *Gen* 2:24: *"Therefore a man leaves his father and his mother and clings to his wife, and they become one flesh."* This verse crowns both creation accounts and is referenced by Christ in *Mt* 19:4–6 and *Eph* 5:31. It offers concrete criteria for evaluation, its advice is at the same time human and humanizing, shrewd and practical, and will guide us through the elaboration of the second part, which will be devoted to the discernment of seven practical reflections to help separated parents in the exercise of their educational responsibility.

AN ETHICAL POINT OF REFERENCE

Marriage and Parenthood According to Gen 2:24 and Eph 5:31

The Conjugal Bond According to Gen 2:24

"Therefore a man leaves his father and his mother and clings to his wife, and they become one flesh" (*Gen* 2:24). The two creation accounts develop beautifully into the covenant between man and woman, in their mutual "attachment." In the Scriptures, to attach oneself is to construct a strong affective bond between two beings, a bond of fidelity that spans all the trials of life. This verb is used in the Deuteronomic texts to explain the kind of relationship that must unite Israel to her God[5], in relationship with other expressions such as "to love, to walk in his ways, to keep his commandments." This attachment does not belong only to the order of affection and passion, but also and especially to the commitment of the heart in the biblical meaning of the term. It concerns the essential level of the person and presents itself in the form of a contract. It demands "to leave one's father and mother" to found a new community of life and love.

The attachment in marriage is such that both partners make up "one flesh." The term "flesh" refers to the carnal part of the body common to both humans and animals: bones, skin and nerves. It also indicates the person in his or her totality, considered according to his or her earthly dimension: contingent, bodily, and fragile. More broadly, it refers to the community of life established between the spouses, to the conjugal link that is established between them through the many tasks of the daily life, the material worries, the joys and sorrows. In a more personalistic language, you could translate the phrase in the following manner: "From now on, there is something of myself in you, and of yourself in me (. . .) To divorce, would be to divorce from a part of oneself."[6]

Conjugality and Parenthood

According to the original design of the creator, this "attachment" of the two forming a "single flesh" is the place of conception, of pregnancy, and of the birth and growth of every human being. Conjugality is the origin and the matrix of parenthood. The child is called to be born of and nourish from the relationship between his parents. This anthropological reality is from a profoundly natural order. It is perceptible through philosophical reason[7] as well as through life and social sciences.[8]

"According to the plan of God," writes John Paul II, "marriage is the foundation of the wider community of the family since the very institution of marriage and conjugal love are ordained to the procreation and education of children, in whom they find their crowning. In its most profound reality, love is essentially a gift, and conjugal love, while leading the spouses to the reciprocal 'knowledge' which makes them 'one flesh' (cf. *Gen* 2, 24), does not end with the couple, because it makes them capable of the greatest possible gift, the gift by which they become co-operators with God for giving life to a new human person."[9]

According to certain rabbis—Rachi in particular—"one" ultimately designates the child born from the attachment of the spouses.[10] The child, culmination of their conjugal love, is the place where they preeminently are one flesh.

In the text of John Paul II, the description of love as gift intimately articulates conjugality and parenthood. The mutual donation of the spouses, the profound gift of their being, is neither limited in itself, or its own absolute purpose. From this donation comes a new gift, a "gift-being"—the child— and a strong impetus for education.[11] The anthropological cradle prepared by the Creator for each new person is the loving relationship of the parents. Such is his "house," the "roof" which shelters his free development as a person and as "gift-being."

Conjugality and Parenthood According to Eph 5:31

When the spouses are Christians, their fruitful "attachment" is sacramental. Marital love is the same as the love of Christ towards his Church. "For this reason a man will leave his father and mother and be joined to his wife, and the two will become one flesh. This is a great mystery, and I am applying it to Christ and the Church" (*Eph* 5:31–32). The conjugal covenant thus bears the same characteristics as the new covenant sealed by Christ in the paschal mystery.[12] It is not only a sign, but also an efficient means. Procreation and education are deeply affected by this.

Thus, "the couple, while giving themselves to one another, give not just themselves but also the reality of children, who are a living reflection of their love, a permanent sign of conjugal unity and a living and inseparable synthesis of their being a father and a mother."[13] In Christian spouses, this articulation between conjugality ("giving oneself to one another") and parenthood ("give not just themselves but also the reality of children") is of a sacramental order. Their parental love receives the same quality as their married love, being its extension, free overflow and "coronation"[14]. John Paul II continues: "The sacrament of marriage gives to the educational role the dignity and vocation of being really and truly a ministry of the Church."[15] The spouses are here in some way "consecrated," "in a new and specific way."[16]

Cardinal Marc Ouellet has magnificently developed reflections on this field, considering education in relationship with the mystery of the Holy Trinity. "In the daily loving relationships within the family," he writes, "the Trinitarian relations show through, interlaced as they are by this paternity, filiation and fruitful unity that constitute the Trinitarian sanctity."[17] The fruitful "we" of the spouses refers to the divine "We" himself.[18] Conjugality and parenthood (procreative and educative) are thus always both already united and to unite.

They are united "in Christ"[19], Spouse of the Church and only Son of the Father. By him and in him, the spouses receive the gifts of the Holy Spirit that "immerse their conjugal, parental, and familial relations in the same relations of the Holy Trinity."[20] Here is why and how "the daily relations between parents and children contain a great mystery."[21]

> "Through the parents who love their children and have life in Christ," writes Paul VI, "is the love of the Father, pouring himself out into his beloved son (cf. 1 *Jn* 4:7–11)." Through exercising their authority, they exercise His authority. Through their dedication, his providence as "Father from whom every family in heaven and on earth takes its name." (*Ep* 3:15)[22]

In short, contemplating the link that unites Christ to his Church in the heart of the Holy Trinity, Christian spouses will discern not only the reciprocal nature of their link of "attachment," but also the nature of their educational mission. From this they receive the grace to live, through the course of days, months, and years.

A Reversal of Conjugality and Filiation

On both natural and supernatural levels, filiation finds itself rooted in parenthood, which itself is rooted in conjugality. A divorce necessarily breaks this chain. Its initial link, conjugality, is suddenly gone, placing parenthood and filiation in a trying face-to-face. Certainly, most of all, the child remains infinitely loved by both parents, but this love no longer comes from the couple, which is now either broken or deeply hurt. The system of "custody" illustrates this: "Some days with mom, some days with dad, but never with mom and dad at the same time." As a result, "the child, instead of the parent, becomes the guarantor of the link."[23] They become the principal link between those who have "brought them into the world"—to recall a beautiful French expression—and who, in a certain way, continue to bring them into the world each day.

This situation reinforces a spontaneous tendency among children to consider themselves as responsible for what happens to their parents. The child now feels entrusted with the impossible mission of ensuring and even reconstructing by himself the matrimonial bond which his parents—or at least one of them—no longer want. "I don't like not to see my mother when I am at my dad's house, so I need to call her" confesses one of them.[24] He spends in this exhausting task an unimaginable wealth of conscious and unconscious energy, resorting in certain cases to self-destructive means. It isn't rare, for example, for him to resort to grave folly—running away, bad marks at school, thefts, drugs—for which his parents are obliged to get together, to speak with each other, to come up with solutions for his deeds. By this mostly unconscious behavior, he addresses them in reality with an indirect message which violence awkwardly and sometimes in a dramatic way translates the desperate desire to revive the marriage of his parents, the source of his existence. In short, filiation spontaneously has to deal with a responsibility which is not its own.

He tries in vain to—so to say—breed his parents into marriage again; this role in some way "adultises"[25], "parentifies"[26] him, depriving him of his childhood. In a way, he acts like an adult, responsible for his parents, not like a child. "I must go and live with my father, poor one, he is alone." He unconsciously feels like a guarantor for the safety of those thanks to whom he was born. Paradoxically, this "mission" might give the impression that he has reached maturity at an early age. But at what cost?

> He will have to take it upon his own resources, leave his childhood and pass by what he needs to live to be able to grow. He will pay for it later, at the moment when he himself must become autonomous, for he will lack the resources that every child takes upon, based on trust with adults . . . The loss of basic security creates a vulnerability that resurfaces several years after parental separation.[27]

This exhausting work which handicaps his authentic maturation can only be frustrated and opposed. The child is comparable to the Greek hero Sisyphus who continually tries to push a boulder up a hill in an endless cycle. Overloaded, tirelessly failing in his pseudo-"duty," feeling guilty, the discovery and elaboration of his own identity is profoundly perturbed and affected. His relationship with life, generation and love is to a certain extent reversed.

Couples who divorce cannot ignore this spontaneous tendency of those who were born of their love. By separating, not only will they leave one another, but they also in a way leave their child, even if they also continue to surround him with a real and very attentive love. The natural order, as described in *Genesis* 2:24, is shattered.

> Historically, observes Olivier Abel, it was assumed that children would one day leave their parents. But, with the general trends towards separation, the parents themselves are those leaving, and the children those assuming continuity. Today, the full weight of the social need for sustainability rests on the frail shoulders of the small.[28]

"There was a man who had two sons," says Jesus, recounting the parable. "The younger of them said to his father, 'Father, give me the share of the property that will belong to me.' . . . A few days later the younger son gathered all he had and traveled to a distant country" (*Lk* 15:11–13). In the event of divorce, there is somehow a reversal of roles; the father grasps his children's inheritance and goes to a distant country, while his sons, the ones left home alone, watch intensely for his unlikely return. The parable becomes that of the "prodigal parent."

This reversal between conjugality and filiation finds a powerful echo in contemporary culture marked by deconstruction[29], disassociation, atomization[30], individualization, and disconnectedness. According to this line of thinking, parenthood and conjugality are isolated from one another. They follow independent trajectories and are reinvented through the whims and trends of adults and society. In this movement, fatherhood and motherhood are considered individually and as interchangeable roles. A new term is forged to this effect: the adjective "parental" is substantified in "parenting." More radically still, "parenting" itself is broken into several autonomous elements and is reinvented to suit its circumstances: the biological parents, the birth mother, legal guardians, educators of the moment.[31] One henceforth talks in certain environments about "pluriparentality"[32], a way to replace parenthood with parental functions. Filiation is thus "tinkered with"[33] stemming from the artificial association between different people exercising specific roles. The spiritual and cultural challenge is therefore important. It is a question today of justifying and making clear anew a natural truth, evident to preceding generations: the roots of filiation in marriage.

Harmonizing Conjugality and Parenthood

These anthropological considerations can also be approached from a moral point of view. The reality that they describe not only appears as a truth perceptible by theoretical reasoning, but also as good, apprehensible by practical reason and its specific cognitive dynamic: "God saw everything that he had made, and indeed, it was very good!" (*Gen* 1:31)

This truth of good is expressed in a basic ethical norm, at the same time simple and powerful, able to guide the discernment of acts to perform and acts to avoid, by a loving and responsible adult: "Respect your children absolutely, inasmuch as they are children, give them time to grow at their own pace, help them just play their part as children, fight at their side against this tendency towards an inversion of responsibility which drains and alienates them."

Any action along these lines is good from a moral standpoint, which is to say, humanizing, promoting life, hope and future. A morally good act will be that which permits the child to cry out joyfully with the psalmist: "I hear a voice I had not known: 'I relieved your shoulder of the burden; your hands were freed from the basket'" (*Ps* 80:6–7). The evil, on the contrary, consists in condemning the child—be it by negligence or by any more or less conscious reason—to try to construct the conjugal link, to ensure the work of his own filiation, to "adultisize" himself. No, filiation is not to take precedence over marriage. It is not the foundation of the family.[34] It is not firstly it which is indissoluble, but marriage itself.

Let us note that this point of reference is relevant and applicable not only for families affected by divorce, but more broadly for all families. It indicates a duty and an ethical task that all parents should carry out again and again with the passing days, in a thousand and one ways. "Act in such a way that you treat your child like a child, not as an adult! It is a matter of strict justice. Respect and promote the childhood of our child, it is only this which allows a child what is due to him." We find again, under a form suited to our research, the "personalistic norm" dear to John Paul II. "The person must never be only a means, but always also the end of our action."[35] "Parents," the pope would write many years later, "must want the new creature in the same way the Creator wants it: for itself."[36]

This principle—not always easy to implement in daily life—resolutely opposes any utilitarian attitudes. It is the foundation of a personalistic axiology. The criterion of evaluation reached offers an expression that integrates the historic dimension of the human being in its growth. "You shall respect your child—within his history—as a person. You shall honor his identity within its construction. You will never leave his filiation to his own hands. You will never utilize him as a means or as an instrument at the service of your own development or interests." In short, to speak the language of the first chapters of Genesis: "So as to live and help life, you may joyfully eat of every tree of the garden; but of the tree that reverses the relationship with life and generation, you shall not eat, for in the day that you eat of it you shall die."

This imperative ethic is of the natural order. It acquires a force and a supernatural quality for the Christian spouses. It pours out from the fruitful love of Christ and the Church to which the covenant of marriage, also fruitful, participates. It constitutes an intrinsic demand of this love. It helps to guide and to save its own deployment, profusion, flourishing and fulfilment. The harsh reality of divorce must not question this principle. Like all parents on earth, those who are affected by separation must jealously care to act in the light of this personalistic norm, with all the intelligence of heart they can muster, and beyond.

The sacrament of marriage has truly "consecrated"[37] them to this effect. It "enriches them with wisdom, counsel, fortitude and all the other gifts of the Holy Spirit in order to help the children in their growth as human beings and as Christians."[38] Thus, even if divorced, it works to reveal to the world the reality of the fruitful love of Christ and the Church. Even more, the spouses participate in its extension, its growth and its intensification. The personalistic norm about the respect of the identity and construction of the child is endowed with incomparable nobility when it is grasped, inscribed and elevated in a sacramental dynamic. It mysteriously refers to the life of the Holy Trinity itself, its internal law and its economy.

Indispensable Parents, Very Precious Educational Assistants

Indispensable Parents

This basic norm dispenses reason in the general perspective adopted in our research, that of the parents. Education before all comes under their responsibility, not to that of their offspring. The eminent task of endowing their child with his very humanity is primarily entrusted to them, not to him. Little ones cannot be in charge of the impossible task of bringing themselves up from their own resources, or purely and simply by themselves, even less to bring up their own parents. "No one to this day has managed to be born alone."[39]

Opting for the good of the child urges adults not to resign from their paternity or maternity, whatever the hardships of the divorce.

> The right and duty of parents to give education is essential, since it is connected with the transmission of human life; it is original and primary with regard to the educational role of others, on account of the uniqueness of the loving relationship between parents and children; and it is irreplaceable and inalienable, and therefore incapable of being entirely delegated to others or usurped by others.[40]

This right and duty emanating from their conjugal love gains a particular title when it is elevated to the dignity of sacrament.

> The mission to educate, a mission rooted . . . in their participation in God's creating activity, has a new specific source in the sacrament of marriage, which consecrates them for the strictly Christian education of their children: that is to say, it calls upon them to share in the very authority and love of God the Father and Christ the Shepherd, and in the motherly love of the Church.[41]

"For the gifts and the calling of God are irrevocable!" (*Rom* 11:29). Despite the separation of the spouses, divine grace cuts a path to the child through their hurt conjugality. The source is not dried up. The Holy Spirit is always given. Christ is always united to his Church. The spouses can still be the sign and the instrument of this unity, especially by letting themselves live the mystery of Holy Saturday, i.e. the days of "hope against hope" (*Rom* 4:18).[42] Through the education of their children, they continue to be associated in a privileged manner to the very fecundity of the love of Christ and his Church. "As spouses, parents and ministers of the sacramental grace of marriage, parents are supported day after day, with special spiritual energies, through Jesus Christ who nourishes the Church, his Spouse."[43] This remains true in the most painful moments.

Alongside the parents, the discrete and efficient presence of relatives in the general sense is a precious commodity: grandparents, uncles, aunts, godfathers, and godmothers.

> A particular and difficult, but necessary, task is allocated to the other family members, in a more or less close way. Through a proximity that must not be confused with condescendence, they must aid their relatives and in particular the children. Because of their youth, they are more affected by the consequences of the choices of their parents.[44]

This active presence will continue to demonstrate to the child the frontiers of his family, which divorce can obscure: who is from the family, and who is outside of it.

In case of a remarriage, the new partner will have to accept the child with his own past, a past that he himself will always be excluded from. He will love the child of his partner, as the fruit of another love, another education, which sometimes requires great selflessness and infinite patience. He will need to respect, therefore, the relationship between the child and the absent parent, recognizing existence of this parent within the blended family.

> Even if he is no longer present there, and if a remarriage takes place, he [the absent parent] is still part of the family. The new spouse has the difficult task leaving space for he who may appear to be, sometimes, a rival. This is one of the conditions, important but sometimes ignored, if one hopes to be adopted by the children of the first marriage and therefore, to be able to help them to grow and to be happy.[45]

This observation is a hidden expression of the ethical principle highlighted above, according to which one should honor filiation within conjugality. Remarriage does not deny this law of life, but confirms it in a roundabout way. "I need Dad's place to remain void," confided one child, despite his deep unease at his father's attitude, and his relief in seeing his mother "rebuild her life" with someone else.[46] The parent and his or her new companion cannot ignore this legitimate cry. Even with the best possible intentions, even if the child himself calls for it, they have no right to ask him to substitute their new union for that which was the basis of his existence, to demand that he should "divorce" himself from either parent.

Very Precious Educative Assistants

The educational role of the parents is consequently "something irrevocable and inalienable."[47] All others must see their role as subsidiary and not as a substitution: friends, Church, youth groups, sporting clubs, school, academies, social workers, and therapists. Their help is necessary and infinitely precious.

This call to the educational subsidiarity resonates powerfully in the heart of the Church, particularly when it itself experiences the suffering of the children. The Christian recognizes here the Son of God himself, who "for by His incarnation . . . has united Himself in some fashion with every man"[48], especially with the little ones. "Truly I tell you, just as you did it to one of the least of these who are members of my family, you did it to me (. . .) truly I tell you, just as you did not do it to one of the least of these, you did not do it to me" (*Mt* 25:40,45). By caring for the child, the educator cares for Christ himself. He accomplishes an "almost sacramental" task. "It is in the same movement," as Xavier Thévenot observes,

> that we welcome the child in His name and receive Him, Jesus son of God. For this reason, it is legitimate to say that the educational task of a Christian is a "sacrament," which is to say an "efficacious sign" of the encounter with God.[49]

"Whoever welcomes this child in my name welcomes me" (*Lk* 9:48).

The Church, through the diversity and charisms of its members, cannot afford not to work towards this end.[50] To begin with, it prepares couples for marriage, accompanies them during difficult times and receives them for any occasional or lasting crisis. It also engages in listening to and counseling those who have experienced divorce. In addition, it takes collective actions at the social, legal, and political level.[51] We believe that all the initiatives in this field should be more widely recognized, promoted and propagated. There is a true urgency for such programs. Others remain to imagine and invent, under the action of the Holy Spirit, in the eternal novelty of the two-thousand-year-old Church.

SEVEN SECONDARY ETHICAL POINTS OF REFERENCE

"Act in such a way that you treat your child as a child, not as a parent or as an adult!" This basic ethical principal can more practically be presented in seven secondary ethical points of reference. Although the fundamental statute of this second part is directly taken from the Christian revelation, its theological development will be kept to a minimum. Our approach will be more practical than theoretical, more inductive than deductive.

Becoming Receptive to the Child

Profoundly Distressed Children

During one rainy morning, a 5-year-old child watches a violent dispute between his parents for the first time. Stricken with panic, he flees to find refuge under the kitchen table. His elder sister comes and consoles him. Disoriented, he gets out from his shelter and tremblingly asks: "What is my name? I forgot my name." His origin—the love of his parents—being suddenly damaged before his eyes, this young boy loses his sense of identity and his place in existence. He becomes "a being incomprehensible to himself."[52]

In a way, this event shows the destructive power of severe marital conflict, which, when it becomes habitual and is stigmatized by separation, marks the children forever and profoundly influences their psychological[53] and spiritual development. The impact varies greatly, depending on the child's age and stage of development: the Oedepian phase with the integration and prohibition of incest, the age of reason with its request for clear rules, the adolescence with its need for parental stability so that the child may be allowed to "find himself" and leave the nest.

Whether 2, 5, 7, 12, 15, or 20 years old, young people always feel personally threatened and impaired when their parents break their commitment. They live in widespread fear of being themselves abandoned: "If the love of Mom and Dad can one day disappear, indeed change into indifference or hate, their love for me might follow the same path!"[54] If, as Gabriel Marcel asserts it, ""I love you" means: "I don't want you to die," "I don't love you anymore" will be understood as: "from now on, you can die, I'm indifferent to this." [55] "If the love of my father is indifferent to my mother, if the love of my mother is indifferent to my father, what shall happen to me?" interiorly exclaims the child who feels this death sentence could propagate to his own existence.

This anguish[56] will especially haunt him if one of his parents doesn't see him or only visits him in a very irregular and unforeseeable way, or does not pay sufficient attention to him, let alone actually abandons him—all this being often done for very complex reasons: shame of not being able to provide for the child's needs, true disinterest, personal immaturity, etc.

The first task of the parents consists in simply being aware of this suffering, recognizing it, not denying it, not seeking to justify it. Even if it costs them or questions them, they have the responsibility as parents to face reality. It is utopian and dangerous to try to spare one's child sorrow by pretending it does not exist.

Profoundly Distressed Parents

The child's acute existential crisis occurs at a time when the parents have little time to grant to their child because of the many constraints that they themselves must face: reorganizing the household, moving from home, changing schools, seeking employment, etc.

Most of all, the spouses who separate from each other are generally gravely weakened by their own divorce. Their rupture strikes at the heart of their life plan. It affects their vital assets. Each one of them must assume the end of a love relationship, the departure of a person who is sometimes still loved, the unavoidable guilt, the mourning of the ideal family, not to mention the more or less latent aggressions, violence and blackmails which sometimes contaminate the atmosphere. Each one must accomplish a painful interior journey with its moments of on-and-off denial, anger, relief, emptiness, disappointment, exaltation, accusation of oneself or the other, rancour, forgiveness, tranquillity, disgust, loss of self esteem, relief with a kind of rediscovered autonomy, depression, stress, guilt, well-being, frustration, questioning the meaning of one's own life and life in general, appeasement, giving up vain hopes, acceptance, reconstruction of oneself and new social relations.[57] Each one is in turn assailed by a nagging doubt that he dares not always make clear to himself: "Am I really lovable, being no longer loved? Am I capable of true love, when no longer loving? Am I worthy of being loved and loving?"

If the divorcing spouses are Christian, they may moreover be plunged into a real religious crisis: "Why doesn't God answer to my prayers? Why am I alone today? Why has Christ abandoned our family and us on our journey? Why such a silence? Why does he seem absent? What is my place in the Church now? Will I be looked at with suspicion, put aside, marginalized, especially if I decide a new union?"[58]

In short, parents who divorce—of which some will remarry[59]—usually have little time, strength and receptiveness to devote to their children in distress. They themselves cross "the valley of darkness," with their own lot of sufferings, agitations and pains. They themselves are in need of being helped. Such an observation does obviously not aim at judging those in difficulty, nor to deny the love they wish to lavish on their children. No, we just want to tackle the objectively difficult conditions which love must cut its way through.

This love begins with a real outer and inner receptiveness to the child. It is necessary to be present, at his side, as any other parent on earth. The child, inasmuch as he is a child, is entitled to that presence. He also will need it to meet the challenge imposed on him. For the child to remain a child, the adults must be adults, and do their utmost to behave as such.

Telling the Truth Humbly to Your Child

This receptiveness "of a heart which sees"[60] enables each parent to communicate in all honesty with the child, to find the words to explain the truth humbly and in a sober way, to give him the opportunity to ask questions. "We have decided to separate from each other for a number of reasons, some of which escape us. It is infinitely painful for you and also for me. I am deeply sorry. You are and will always be my beloved child. I will never abandon you. Know that you are absolutely not part of our couple's problem, which is a problem between adults. There is nothing you can do in this matter." The child has a vital need to hear these or other similar words. Otherwise, he would be compelled to guess by himself, to imagine the reasons for the split, to interpret the silence, to decipher the undecipherable. He simply is not equipped for such a task. He is a child, not an adult. If the truth is hidden from him—voluntarily or not—he risks remaining in a terrifying confusion. Only the truth, explained with love, has a chance to free him, little by little.

It is therefore necessary to speak with humble honesty, seeking the most appropriate words, gestures, and attitudes possible, without producing or divulging too many details, which is to say without burdening the young shoulders with weight they cannot bear. Total transparency is a destructive myth. Lucidity without love is blind and murderous. Not all adult truth is to be shared with the child, or adolescent. He does not need to assume the wanderings of one or both parents. The criterion for the words to pronounce has nothing to do with the well-being or the relief of the adult, but with the good of the child, who, at his given age, is equipped with such character, such force, such vulnerabilities. A delicate discernment without compromise is necessary.

From these hard to formulate words—nonetheless liberating for everyone in the end—the child will be able to undertake the difficult task of mourning his parent's marriage.[61] For many years, he will go through periods of denial, anger and revolt, bargaining, depression and acceptance.[62] He will be able to follow a pacification path.

In addition, the child must also be able to hear and perceive reassuring attitudes. "I am there! You can always count on me. I will surround you with my kindness and protection. Your father (or your mother) and I will try to answer in the best way any questions which are bugging you." The little child is dependent on all levels on the altruism of others to live. He cannot see his parents' divorce without fearing for his own safety. He has a vital need to feel that those who gave him life, even though destabilized, will remain stable and reliable, always able to take care of him. They will never fail in this task, and will never abandon him. Even if the parents are not truly able to face the situation—which children in their great sensibility never fail to note—it is right to take into account the need of the children for signs of protection to help them live with true confidence in the future.

Leading Your Child to Freedom through Listening

Listening

Talking is essential. Listening too! It is important for the child to put into words the events and emotions that affect him, naming the feelings he experiences. It is necessary for him to be able to find adults whom he trusts to express his fears, sorrows, grief, anger, rebellion, scandal, and despair: "My dwelling is plucked up and removed from me like a shepherd's tent; like a weaver I have rolled up my life"(*Is* 38 :12); or in his own language: "Who will take care of the dog? Will I have to love your new partner?" He needs to be listened to carefully in order to feel that he is listened to and understood. In other words, he needs you to listen to him with infinite patience and profound understanding of the heart. Whether he calls for it explicitly or not, he expects to be accompanied with the right words through the different stages of grief, to be helped by an actively attentive listener to situate this irreparable break and integrate it in his personal history and that of his family.

It is right and good not only that the parents should involve themselves in this way, but others as well, people whom you trust and if possible appropriate "discussion groups." Experience has shown that such mediations are extremely valuable.[63] The child can express himself in complete freedom, outside the family system, without the fear of worsening the situation or causing grief to his parents. Under receptive and competent guidance, he is surrounded by peers of his own age in the same situation. He feels accepted and recognized as a child, though as a child confronted with the enigma of divorce. He realizes that he is not alone and that what he feels is "normal" in his situation. He can listen to the stories from the others on a reality that is sadly familiar. He slowly leaves behind his confusion, together with the anguish and guilt attached to it. He is little by little able to step back from the immediate facts, finding some sense in the chaos that he endures by putting it into his own words, without necessarily understanding it all. He is gradually released from the negative part of his family history, all the more negative as it has happened early during his personal development. He can now reveal himself to himself, reconnect with the thread of his own life, be himself and become all the more in control of his own destiny.

It does not suffice to tell the child the truth. It is also necessary to allow him to appropriate this truth, to be able to think about it and to prepare to be ready to open the doors to his own future. Let us note that "it is necessary to pay particular attention to the child who doesn't seem to be affected, because denial is frequent: in the long run, denial can lead to shutting oneself into an inauthentic posture."[64] Moreover, the child very often avoids expressing his grief openly and directly. It is left up to the adult to delicately approach him and suggest a dialogue at the right time.

Learning to Respond

This growth in liberty is essential to become confident in a future that is partly marked by the irreparable. Divorce indeed affects the child to such a deep level, that it is and has to be reactivated, reinterpreted, and revised several times during his life: start of the new school year, home moving, birthdays, death of a beloved person, puberty, love affair, beginning of the professional life, marriage, birth of a child, children's marriage, or even as simple as an everyday event, for example visiting a place that brings back memories. In these moments—not necessarily all of them!—the person may live again, in another way, the painful enigma of his parents' divorce. He undergoes the slow and necessary construction of his evolving history in perpetual evolution, a history that can never ignore the mystery of its origin. Such toil is normal, healthy, brings hope, promise, life, and in a certain way, healing.

"What one has to be healed from," Bernadette Lemoine strongly underlines, "is not so much related to the wounds provoked by the separation, but the spontaneous, inaccurate and love-preventing reactions to these injuries, but which one may change in order to be able to construct love again."[65] It would be dangerous and illusory to believe that this "profound trauma"[66] and, in a certain measure, this offense could completely disappear one day. The most trying moments of existence, of which some were briefly mentioned above, are there to testify to this. The question is to learn how to react to them. From a psychological point of view, a vast field of resilience work opens here; and from a spiritual and ethical point of view, the adventure of freedom and love. The child must learn in time to over-determine "the determinism" of his situation.

Thus, when an adult, he will start his own family, he will be much more able to adequately respond to the psychological mechanism of "repetition." "We reconstruct past conflicts," observes Susan Forward, "because each time we hope to find a solution: 'This time, I will win the battle, I will succeed.'" [67] The child, then adolescent and adult, thus unconsciously recreates in his own life the conditions of the failure so as to overcome them victoriously—as he imagines in a sadly illusory way... "I myself will cause a split in my relationship, so as to prove to myself that I can now fix it."

Besides, this "repetition" can also find its origin in feelings of guilt that were not sufficiently heard, treated and deliberately fought. "I can't let myself succeed where my parents failed. I have no right to do so. As I feel guilty for their marital failure, I must pay the price for it and find a punishment that measures up to such a crime." How to understand this reaction?

Fighting Against the Child's Self-Accusations

On a playground, a 7-year-old child wearing a beautiful white sweater asks a priest: "Can God forgive me because of my sweater?" Surprised, the priest begins a dialogue and finally understands the sad drama accounting for this strange request. Eight months earlier, the parents violently fought over the famous white sweater that a small amount of chocolate had sullied. Slamming the door, the father left and has not resurfaced since then.

The child always feels responsible for the separation of his parents. Naturally egocentric, he believes that his father and mother did leave each other because of him, his mistakes, his incapacity to be what they wanted him to be. "He feels that it is his misconduct that leads his parents to leave *him*, instead of thinking that they themselves decided to leave each other."[68] He will then tend to make every effort to be forgiven. He could, for example, try to become impeccable, exemplary, so perfect that his parents would reunite. "The idea of perfection may even change into the idea that his own disappearance would be the best way to reconcile his parents."[69] The child might thus wish, be it consciously or not, to sacrifice himself to amend his parents' relationship at any cost, to find himself the solution even at the cost of his own development and life. And, as this ending will obviously never occur, he will live his continual failure as confirmation and proof that he is the cause of misfortune currently affecting his family.

Here is again a harmful reversal of generations. The child spontaneously places himself in the position of an adult, responsible for his parents. From an ethical point of view, it is up to them as parents to fight gently but firmly these feelings which harrow their child under the surface. "It's not your fault. It's our fault! Our separation has nothing to do with you. It's true that you unfortunately suffer some consequences, but it's not due to you." This truth must clear a path not only in the spirit of the child, but also in his heart, in the very center of his person.

Besides, "we must also exonerate parents," wisely observes Bernadette Lemoine, "without removing their responsibility . . . It is not a matter of supporting the behavior of parents who commit objective faults . . . If their behavior is condemnable, they themselves are not."[70] The father and mother generally feel guilty for their children. They don't know what to do to "compensate" for the wrongs and sorrows of their children. Some even feel they haven't the right to add new frustrations to previous ones, thus saying "yes" to all the requests of their child whom they now above all perceive as a victim.[71] The children—who are always quite insightful and a bit mischievous—are therefore tempted to use that status to get privileges: delaying bed time, increasing the time allowed to watch television, being offered "a little something" whenever they accompany their parents shopping. And they become even more successful because each parent fears a transfer of affection to the other parent.

Giving the Right Place to Your Child

Fairly recognizing the injuries of the child, being receptive to his distress, humbly telling him the truth, fathering him towards speech and freedom, fighting against the invasion of guilt, all these ethical tasks are clarified by the general principle discerned in our first discussion: give the child the place it deserves as a child.

This place is first and foremost *received*. It is first a gift, not a conquest. The child is objectively refused this gift when he is considered as non-existent or inversely when he is "adultized," "parentified," "parentalized," or "partnerized." Neither "the invisible child" nor the inversely "invaded child" is respected as a person, with his filiation and history.

The "invisible child" encumbers his parents who send him back and forth more or less like a tennis ball. He no longer has a real place in their new life. He becomes errant, sometimes even in the literal sense of the word. He travels hundreds of kilometres by train or plane to spend a weekend at the home of one or the other. He feels that he is in the way, that he is not desired: "My closet is my suitcase. Unpacking my bags, putting new sheets on the bed, this is pretty much how it is when I arrive. I can never rest. I am always moving. Others have replaced me in my parents' hearts. I have become for them a matter of tracking and trouble." These subjective feelings are unfortunately sometimes confirmed by facts.

On the other hand, the "invaded child" is encumbered by one of his parents—often his mother as seen in most cases as she usually gets custody of the children—or, more rarely, by both at the same time. When there is a divorce, "it happens that, little by little, in the new family blend which results, the child is asked to take the place of the missing partner and to feel concerned by anything that, in principle, chiefly belongs to his parents concern. . . . Not being able to be a child is ultimately the price he has to pay to fill that position."[72] Overwhelming her child by confiding unduly in him, sleeping beside him at night, relying on him to manage the home are among the signs of this profound disturbance. Sometimes under the guise of what seems to be "altruism," there is in fact a real kidnapping of childhood, or at least its diversion, or its confiscation. The adult tries to be consoled rather than to console, to be understood rather than to understand, to be loved rather than to love.[73] Often being himself in great suffering, he risks losing sight of the good of his child, using him more or less consciously, in his adult interest. This shady and harmful behavior is unfortunately likely to have no limits. . . The child loses status as a child. Instrumentalized, the child becomes a partner or parent of his parent. The relationship between generations is reversed.

The captured child and the invisible child therefore do not receive the place that is due to them within the family. In reality, they long to grow in the shade of their parents' marriage. They need "to be loved by someone who loves someone else," not to be either everything or nothing of those who take care of them. "You are my little prince whom I love with all my heart, but my king is Dad," responded with great finesse a young mother to her 5-year-old son. When the marriage bond is broken by divorce, it is important that each parent should continue to recognize the existence of the other parent—even their deposed king or queen—still giving him a place, even symbolically and also through the presence of a third party. He should at least refrain from insulting the absent spouse in front of the child.

Not Destroying the Absent Parent in the Heart of the Child

"Honor your father and your mother, so that your days may be long in the land that the Lord your God is giving you," commands the Decalogue (*Ex* 20:12; cf. also *Eph* 6:1–3). *Mutatis mutandis:* "honor the parent of your child so that he may have a long life on earth. Do not allow his heart to be turned into a battleground. Do not treat your child as a spy for your ex-spouse, as an accomplice to satisfy your revenge, as an ambassador of lies. Do not condemn him to struggle in insurmountable conflicts of loyalty. Never say ill of his father or mother, curse it not through words or actions, in open or covert ways. It would poison one of the two sources of the life of your child and thus poison him." Certainly, compliance with this command requires many hidden sacrifices and might order the endurance of many injustices and the returning of good when evil is received. Daily adherence can lead to genuine heroism. The fact is nonetheless true that such an attitude is all that is appropriate, just, right and therefore fruitful in the long term. It gives the child his due as a child.

Note that it does not necessarily imply abstaining from any judgments about the behavior or ideas of the absent spouse; it is rather a resolute refusal to enter into an attitude of condemnation against that person. Parents should strictly refrain from allowing their son or daughter to bear the weight of their divisions and their marital disagreements.

To refrain from bad mouthing one's former spouse is also to ensure that the child himself does not fall in these self-destructive patterns. Admittedly, he must sometimes be helped to distance himself from his father or his mother when they are especially "toxic" in the very words of Susan Forward.[74] But this vital separation between parent and child, sometimes sanctioned by the ruling of a court,[75] must retain a logic of life and goodwill. "Certain behaviors of your father or your mother are incomprehensible to you. Some of their actions might seem intolerable and morally indefensible. Which they objectively are. It is without a doubt necessary for you to distance yourself from him or her for a while. But don't curse him for all that. Do not condemn him." "For a child, a father is a father and a mother is a mother, persons who demand respect, even if one cannot agree with all their actions."[76]

Thus unconditional respect for both members of the couple, inasmuch as they are persons and parents, must be respectfully transmitted to the memory of the child. This point, although vital for the child, might easily be forgotten. The child must integrate himself into the history of the generations before him, with what was beautiful and grand, as well as what was painful and sometimes even tragic.[77] He needs to answer this dual question: "Who am I? Who do I want to become?" To discover and build his identity, to search for and find his place within human society, he cannot afford to overlook a recreation and a re-elaboration of his ancestors' history. It will also have an effect on his future fecundity: "What do I want to hand down?" If access to his family tree is partly denied or obscured, he will have the tendency to invent a mythical past, creating in his own mind an artificial family. If his genealogy is obscured or made partially unintelligible, he will be tempted to imagine a network of alliances and kin to escape a face to face confrontation with his parents. This imagined family tree has no past and therefore no hope for future. The child left at home after the parting of the "prodigal father"[78] should, wherever possible, try to recover the partially stripped legacy.

"Honor the memory of the mother or father of your child so that he may have a long life on earth," means therefore "honor the memory of the family of your child." The father or the mother is never *only* father or mother of his or her child. They come themselves from a father and mother, they themselves are brothers or sisters to others, as well as cousins, and so on. Let us however note that "to honor" is not a synonym of "to live at the mercy of." In certain situations, it makes sense to intelligently protect one's child from the harmful influence of a part of his family. But this legitimate and necessary protection in no way authorizes destructive criticism of these family members.

Seeking Out an Educational Agreement

A Fair Collaboration

This respect for the memory of the family, the constant will to avoid a path of destruction with the separated spouse should create "climatic conditions" favoring a good collaboration in raising the children. Of course, divorce is usually the result of many unresolved conflicts, absences, disputes, unspoken words, and mutual offences. An educative cooperation between the two former spouses, even if modest, must overcome many obstacles; moreover, it is often dependent on court decisions.[79] It is far from being simple! How to fairly find common ground, to communicate, while avoiding too much distance and at the same time not getting too close to the other?

Inaccurate intimacy during the encounters between separated spouses risks allowing the child to entertain the idea of his parents reuniting. Thus, all meetings between parents for birthdays, end of the year parties—because the parents get along—must be well thought out."[80] Divorce is ultimately incomprehensible to the child; he cannot help but interpret even a fleeting moment of peace between his parents as a sign of hope. In addition, an overly intimate relationship between them can also negatively impact the relationship with a new spouse, in the case where one or both are remarried. The idea of a "parental couple" which survives from the "married couple" is not without ambiguities from this point of view.

A fair cooperation between divorced spouses is nevertheless necessary for the good of the child. To abstain from speaking evil of one another is already an achievement, but it is not satisfactory enough. Parents, whenever possible, must endeavor to speak concordantly, a difficult task even for those couples that get along well. They are called to maintain consistency in education as well as, to keep up communications between them for this purpose, in order to make all the decisions of their child's life together. This challenge is great. The stakes are, too.

Even more important, the parents are invited to pursue a path to appease conflicts that still linger, moving towards the direction of forgiveness and reconciliation. In saying this we do not indiscriminately promote a resumption of common life, which may be in certain situations objectively impossible and even morally undesirable. No, from the point of view of the good of the children, with which our study is concerned, it is a question of relieving the agonizing struggle that plagues its victims. Like it or not, their hearts still inhabit their parents' broken or destroyed relationship. It is up to the parents to make their relationship—in this way a "home" for the children—viable by "a reorganization" of their antagonism, their offences, and their adult rivalries through steps towards forgiveness. The requirements of the "educational agreement" go that far. They allow the child to unify and to re-unify himself in the difficult conditions that face him.

The Danger of Confusion and Duplicity in Children

"I have two *Barbies*, I'm lucky, huh?" exclaims a 6-year-old child whose parents are divorced. Faced with the envy and amazement of her friend, she adds: "But you, you are luckier, you have only one *Barbie!*"[81] The child from now on is plunged into two different universes. She must continually adjust her behavior to the rules and practices of her two different households. "When I'm at dad's house, I can eat whatever I want out of the fridge; but not at mom's house." If the underlying educational references and ethical values are too divergent, even conflicting, the child may be overcome by confusion. In some cases it could even lead to a path of duplicity, in leading a double life and in shaping a dual character: the first corresponding to the universe in which her mother lives, the second corresponding to that of her father.

This confusion will be added to the one caused by the initial separation. It will become all the more harmful to the child as she is young. How shall she discover who she is, what her profound vocation is, if she never could experience anything other than the wrench of contradictory education? How will her conscience be formed if the first "models" which she observes are in fact themselves wrong models[82] and if moreover she could not even understand them as wrong? A too-young child does not know by herself the difference between good and bad. She must learn, discover and experience the good gradually through concrete personal standards, which is to say, through her parents' smiling and, if necessary, grimacing faces. At different stages of her maturity, she needs to be given points of reference and boundaries, to be encouraged in her works and efforts, to learn little by little justice, righteousness, faithfulness and self-giving. In other words, she needs to be brought up into her own humanity.[83]

An Education in Self-Giving

This fathering applies to all earthly parents. "The self-giving that inspires the love of husband and wife for each other," writes John Paul II,

> is the model and norm for the self-giving that must be practiced in the relationships between brothers and sisters and the different generations living together in the family. And the communion and sharing that are part of everyday life in the home at times of joy and at times of difficulty are the most concrete and effective pedagogy for the active, responsible and fruitful inclusion of the children in the wider horizon of society.[84]

In most cases, a divorce objectively denies this initial and normative self-gift despite the best efforts of the parents. How, in these conditions, can they consistently teach the good? Where and how will they integrate the rupture? "Dad and Mom haven't been faithful to each other, and therefore not either to me, or to my brothers and sisters. In whose name should I learn to live loyalty, trust, and self-giving?" The separation of the parents objectively induces a confusion and doubt within the child concerning the good to be sought and evils to be avoided, influencing the child's own moral capacity. His "muddled" interior state is reinforced by his desire to justify and to save his parents, against all odds. Jean-Claude Guillebaud goes so far as to speak of a "moral of divorce"[85] which is imposed by contemporary culture, i.e. a code of conduct based on the "values" stemming from the divorce: sincerity in relation to oneself, preferential option towards his own personal development, primacy of emotional issues.

Let us notice that, in 85 percent of divorce cases, the child is entrusted to the care of the mother. Fatherhood, very important in the ethical maturity of the person and the progressive integration of laws, is therefore lived intermittently or even not at all.

Faced with the internal turmoil created by this "moral of divorce," parents are invited to acknowledge, with humble loyalty, the truth of love and communion they have been unable to achieve in this crucial area of their lives. These words will be more credible and fruitful if they are practiced by each of the separated spouses at the same time. They will bear fruit, of which they are the premise, if the parents act accordingly, together when possible. Impossible mission? Certainly very delicate, such an undertaking is a duty of strict justice to the child. Through rendering him his due in as much as he is a child, the parents offer him a solid base, "to grow, become strong, and be filled with wisdom" (*Lk* 2:40).

CONCLUSION

There is no such thing as perfect parents. All, whether divorced or not, are called to treat their child as a child, not as an adult, and to desire them "in the same way that their creator desires them: for their own sake."[86] The seven points of reference elaborated in the second part concretely help to cut a path which each person may apply to his own situation. "I relieved your shoulder of the burden; your hands were freed from the basket" (*Ps* 81:5). Fathers and mothers must avoid every form of utilitarianism in their relationships with their children, all forms of monopolization and reduction of their children to means to be put into service of their interests as adults.

This is a beautiful and rewarding task. It is tough at times. Like other human relationships, the educational relationship needs to be saved and be presented to Christ, as our Savior and as the Beloved Son of the Father. "They were bringing small children to him . . . And he took them up in his arms, laid his hands on them, and blessed them" (*Mk* 10:16).

APPENDIX: THE CONTRIBUTION OF THEOLOGICAL ETHICS

Morality is often perceived as exercising a "ministry" of prosecution and conviction. Does it not recall the laws, and by consequence, does it not manifest mercilessly the gap between these laws and the behavior of people? Also, is there not a certain apprehension and even a certain shudder before hearing a moral discourse on "children of divorce"? Can any good be brought from it? Would it not be better to entrust this sensitive issue only to the guidance of psychologists, who without "judging," offer "effective" assistance, strategies for building and rebuilding oneself, and therapy centered on the patient's well-being? What is the specific contribution of theological ethics?

To respond to this question, it is necessary to "re-dimension" morality and leave behind the legalistic conception that has prevailed through the last six centuries. The legal approach necessary as it is, is neither the first nor the most important. Before prohibiting anything, ethics promote human freedom, which is accomplished in the truth of love, and all the values connected with them. The negative implications of morality are important, but come second. As it reads in the book of Genesis (*Gen* 2, 8:14), God first gives Adam and Eve the Garden of Eden: "You can eat all the trees of the garden" (*Gen* 2:16). He then adds: "But the tree of knowledge of good and evil, thou shalt not eat because the day that you eat, you surely die" (*Gen* 2:16).

Ethics are essentially at the service of life and of its growth, of good acts, of the exercise of liberties, focused on the complete good of the person, of his dignity and of his vocation. John Paul II writes:

> Precisely in this perspective, the Second Vatican Council called for a renewal of moral theology, so that its teaching would display the eminent vocation which the faithful have received in Christ, the only response fully capable of satisfying the desire of the human heart.[87]

"Then someone came to him (Jesus) and said: 'Master, what must I do to inherit eternal life?'" (*Mt* 19:16).[88]

Theological ethics penetrate a level of depth which psychology and other human sciences have neither the means nor the claim of reaching.[89] It possesses at the same time both an operational and contemplative aspect. It freely considers the human being in the original mystery of his liberty and his existential trajectory. It bears forth on this mystery an ecclesiastical view of faith, of hope and of charity in an eminently practical perspective.

Moral theology in fact is very interested in everyday life and the multiple decisions—big and small—that constitute the history of the persons, communities and societies. How, in the ordinary and extraordinary commitments of these liberties, do we allow Christ to "walk with each person the path of life"?⁹⁰ How do we humbly offer criteria of discernment, without giving pre-fabricated solutions, miracle recipes, which is to say without substituting the free choice of the acting subject? "Teach me wisdom and knowledge," implores the psalmist (*Ps* 119:66). Theological ethics is an operational science in the service of liberation, conversion, education, and promotion of the freedom of each person.

From these two points of view, both practical and contemplative, such a science has an infinite value to help divorced parents in their task as educators. "Give me understanding that I may live!" (*Ps* 119:144) "Enlighten me and I will be made to live!" The Holy Scriptures offer us invaluable light on this subject.

REFERENCES

1. "Obviously, separation must be considered as a last resort, after all other reasonable attempts at reconciliation have proved vain" (John Paul II, Apostolic Exhortation *Familiaris Consortio* (*FC*), 1981, 83).

2. Cf. Tony Anatrella, *Epoux, heureux époux. Essai sur le lien conjugal,* Flammarion, 2004, p.127–728: "Vaut-il mieux se quitter que se déchirer?.".

3. Children are quick to align themselves with the discourse of the adults whose esteem and affection they seek. Admittedly, they develop a certain personal autonomy in their perception and expression. But it does not leave them less relatively dependent and conformist in relation to the adult world.

4. Bernadette Lemoine, *"Maman, ne me quitte pas!" Accompagner son enfant dans les séparations de la vie,* Versailles, Ed. Saint-Paul, 2000, p. 201.

5. "You shall fear the Lord your God; him alone you shall worship; to him you shall hold fast, and by his name you shall swear." (*Deut* 10:20; cf. also *Deut* 4:4; 11:22; 13:5; 30:20; *Josh* 22:5; 23:8, *Ruth* 18:6, etc.).

6. Xavier Lacroix, "La dissociation entre conjugalité et parentalité," in AA.VV., *Quel avenir pour la famille. Le coût du non-mariage,* Bayard, 2006, p. 238.

7. "A person 'comes into the world,' but from where does he come? It would obviously be presumptuous to assume that the child himself is only the result of the union of two bodies, or even more so the sheer 'meeting' (is the word accurate here?) of two gametes. To be born from the conjunction of two people involves these desire, abandon and enjoyment that imply other dimensions and repercussions. Life is neither only biological nor an anonymous combination of objective processes." (Xavier Lacroix, *De chair et de parole. Fonder la famille,* Fayard, Paris, 2007, p. 43). "Human life is filiation, a reality rooted in the conjugal link." (cf. Xavier Lacroix, *Passeurs de vie. Essai sur la paternité,* Bayard, 2004, chapitre I).

8. Such is for example the starting point of the neuropsychiatrist Romain Liberman in his

study—already old—on the psychological consequences of divorce on the children : *Les enfants devant le divorce,* Presses Universitaires de France, Paris, 1979, p. 15–50.

9. *FC* 14. "The love between husband and wife and, in a derivatory and broader way, the love between members of the same family—between parents and children, brothers and sisters and relatives and members of the household—is given life and sustenance by an unceasing inner dynamisms leading the family to ever deeper and more intense *communion,* which is the foundation and soul of the *community* of marriage and the family. The first communion is the one which is established and which develops between husband and wife: by virtue of the covenant of married life, the man and woman "are no longer two but one flesh" (*Mt* 19:6, cf. *Gen* 2:24), and they are called to grow continually in their communion through day-to-day fidelity to their marriage promise of total mutual self-giving."

10. Cited by J. Eisenberg, *A Bible ouverte,* vol. II, *Et Dieu créa Eve,* Albin Michel, 1979, p. 155.

11. The theology of the gift recalls again the traditional doctrines of the "two ends" of marriage (union and procreation). The debate between the primacy of one or the other is thus renewed and to a certain extent exceeded in a personalistic dynamic. (Cf. Alain Mattheuws, *S'aimer pour se donner,* Lessius, Bruxelles, 2004).

12. Cf. Olivier Bonnewijn, *Ethique sexuelle et familiale,* Editions de l'Emmanuel, Paris, 2006, p. 48–81. André Léonard, has organized his ethical reflection in the field of sexuality around this fundamental principle: *Jésus et ton corps. La morale sexuelle expliquée aux jeunes,* Mame, Paris, 1996.

13. *FC* 14.

14. *FC* 14.

15. *FC* 38.

16. *FC* 38.

17. *Divine ressemblance. Le mariage et la famille dans la mission de l'Eglise,* Ed. Anne Sigier, Canada, 2006, p. 167.

18. "The divine 'We' is the eternal pattern of the human 'we,' especially of that 'we' formed by the man and the woman created in the divine image and likeness" (John Paul II, *Letter to Families,* 1994, 6).

19. "The Divine Persons create and sanctify the conjugal and familial relationships "within Christ." It is with him, through him and in him that the created relationships can be assumed in their own uncreated "relationality" to be sanctified and transfigured." (Marc Ouellet, *Divine ressemblance, op. cit.,* p. 99). "The sacramental mission of the family is to mediatize the love of Christ for his Church, that is to say the Trinitarian love for the world. The material for this mediation is the multiplicity of the everyday relationships of life in common, of sharing, of education and service to the community." (*Ibid.*, p. 97)

20. *Ibid.*, p. 97.

21. *Ibid.*, p. 163.

22. Paul VI, "Allocution aux Equipes Notre Dame," in *La Documentation catholique*, 1564 (1970), p. 504.

23. Jacques Arenes, "Le coût psychique du non-mariage," in AA.VV., *Quel avenir pour la famille?*, *op. cit.*, p. 206.

24. Reported by José Gerard and Cécile Richir, *Les enfants du divorce*, Ed. Feuilles Familiales, Dossier trimestriel N.F.F., Namur, 1993, p. 8.

25. Susan Forward, *Parents toxiques. Comment échapper à leur emprise?*, Stock, Paris, 2000, p. 86–68.

26. Jean-François Le Goff, *L'enfant, parent de ses parents. Parentification et thérapie familiale*, L'Harmattan, Paris, 1999; G. J. Jurkovic, A. Thirkield, R. Morrell, "Parentification of adult children of divorce: a multidimensional analysis," in *Journal of Youth and Adolescence* 30–0 (2001), p. 245–557.

27. Tony Anatrella, *Epoux*, *op. cit.*, p. 133.

28. Olivier Abel, *Le mariage a-t-il encore un avenir?*, Bayard, Paris, 2005, p. 39.

29. Xavier Lacroix, "La dissociation," *op. cit.*, p. 231.

30. *Ibid.*, p. 240.

31. "Since the first 'in vitro' fertilization (1984) and the first ovocyt gift (1988), for the first time in human history, the maternal role can be divided into three distinct women: the 'intentional' mother (who will raise the child), the 'genetical mother' (if need be, donor of the ovocyt) and the 'gestational mother' (term nowadays seen as fitting better than 'carrier mother')." (Geneviève Delaisi de Parseval, "Le temps des 'mères porteuses,'" in *Le Monde*, February 11:2008, p. 16; cf. equally ID., *Famille à tout prix*, Seuil, Paris, 2008).

32. Martine Gross, *L'homoparentialité*, PUF, "Que sais-je?", 2003, p. 120; Irène Thery, "PACS, sexualité et différence des sexes," in *Esprit*, November 1999, p. 139–981. For a critical reading of this new concept, see Xavier Lacroix, article "Homoparentalité," in *Lexique des termes ambigus et controversés sur la famille, la vie et les questions éthiques*, under the direction of: Conseil Pontifical Pour La Famille, Téqui, Paris, 604 ss.

33. Xavier Lacroix, "La dissociation," *op. cit.*, p. 245.

34. "In a modern family, one is first of all a parent; filiation comes first. The matrimonial situation is only second to it." (J.-P. Rosencsveig, in *Le monde*, September 21st, 1995). "This half-century identifies the family as based on the child and not on the couple any more." (Irène Thery, *Le démariage*, Odile Jacob, Paris, 1993, p. 330). "We are witnessing a transfer of the indissolubility of marriage towards filiation." (Irène Thery, "Le démariage et la filiation," in *Dialogue*, 1998, 141, p. 11–17). "Today, it would be filiation that would constitute a family. To found a family would be giving birth to a child, to acknowledge him, to give him a name." (Xavier Lacroix, *De chair et de parole*, *op. cit.*, p. 35). Cf. also Catherine Labrusse-Riou, "La filiation en mal d'institution", in *Esprit* (December 1996); Jean-Claude Guillebaud, *La tyrannie du plaisir*, Ed Seuil, Paris, 1998, p. 451–159. Guillebaud wonders about the impossible task for filiation to lean on a mainly emotional conjugality.

35. John Paul II, *Amour et responsabilité*, Stock, Paris, 1985, p. 32.

36. *Letter to Families*, 9. "Man is the only creature on earth whom God willed for its own sake," also confirmed by Vatican II (Pastoral Constitution *Gaudium et spes*, 1965, 24).

37. *FC* 38.

38. *FC* 38.

39. France QUÉRÉ, cited by Xavier Lacroix, *De chair et de parole*, op. cit., p. 46.

40. *FC* 36.

41. *FC* 38.

42. "Hoping against hope, he believed that he would become 'the father of many nations', according to what was said, 'So numerous shall your descendants be'" (*Rom* 4:18).

43. Conseil Pontifical Pour La Famille, *L'éducation sexuelle des enfants*, Droguet-Ardant, Mame, Paris, 1996, 37, p. 57. This assertion concerns non divorced parents. It can be extended to all sacramentally married parents.

44. John Paul II, *Letter to Families*, 1994, 4.

45. Bernadette Lemoine, *"Maman, ne me quitte pas!,"* op. cit., p. 204.

46. Cf. Marie Desplechin, Irène Thery, *Recomposer une famille, des rôles et des sentiments*, Textuel, Paris, 2001; Claire Garbar, Francis Theodor, *Les familles mosaïques*, Paris, Nathan, 2003.

47. *FC* 36.

48. Vatican Council II, *Gaudium et spes*, 22, 2.

49. Xavier Thevenot, *Une pensée pour des temps nouveaux*, Editions Don-Bosco, Paris, 2005, p. 14.

50. "Loneliness and other difficulties are often the lot of separated spouses, especially when they are the innocent parties. The ecclesial community must support such people more than ever. It must give them much respect, solidarity, understanding and practical help" (*FC* 83). Among these difficulties, there is obviously that of education.

51. "It is urgent therefore to promote not only family policies, but also those social policies which have the family as their principle object, policies which assist the family by providing adequate resources and efficient means of support, both for bringing up children and for looking after the elderly, so as to avoid distancing the latter from the family unit and in order to strengthen relations between generations" (John Paul II, Encyclical Letter *Centesimus Annus*, 1991, 49).

52. John Paul II, Encyclical Letter *Redemptor hominis*, 1979, 10; cited in *FC* 18.

53. At the psychological level, cf. Jacques Arenes, "Le coût psychique du non-mariage," op. cit., p. 208–810.

54. Tony Anatrella writes as a psychotherapist: "It is because the parents love each other that the child feels loved. He builds his identity using the couple's relationship as a basis. That is

why it is not right to tell a child: "Mum and dad are separating because they don't love each other anymore, but they will keep on loving you." This message is nonsensical to the child who can only answer according to his own logic: 'If you don't love each other anymore, you cannot love me anymore.'" (Tony Anatrella, *Epoux, op. cit.*, p. 129).

55. Xavier Lacroix, "La dissociation," *op. cit.*, p. 239.

56. At the psychological level, the separation of the parents is grafted on other separations that the children already lived through, more or less successfully, during their existence. It thus reactivates certain wounds and their attached anguish.

57. Cf. on this subject Rosie Boucaud and Jacques Poujol, *Le divorce. Dépasser les blessures, construire l'avenir,* Ed. Empreinte temps présent, La Bégude de Mazenc, 2007, p. 11–11.

58. "Let all divorced and remarried men and women know that the Church loves them, that she is not far from them and suffers from their situation. Remarried divorcees are and remain her children. The Church sees their suffering and the grave difficulties in which they struggle. She also sees their children from a previous marriage: deprived of their birthright to live with both their parents, they are the first victims of these painful events" (John Paul II, "La pastorale des divorcés remariés. Discours prononcé devant la XIIIème assemblée plénière du Conseil pontifical pour la famille," in *L'Osservatore romano,* 25 janvier 1997, 3). Cf. also André-Mutien Léonard, *Séparés, divorcés, divorcés remariés, l'Eglise vous aime,* Editions de l'Emmanuel, Paris, 1996.

59. A remarriage mobilizes a considerable amount of additional energy, from a spiritual, intellectual, psychic, and material point of view.

60. Benedict XVI, Encyclical *Deus caritas est,* 2005, 31.

61. In certain cases, this work can also require the mourning of a particularly pathogenic relation, with one of the child's parents or both. If the child needs a father and a mother to construct himself, this cannot be done at any price.

62. These stages of mourning were clarified by Elisabeth Kübler-Ross within the framework of accompaniment of the dying.

63. Among these experiments, let us point out for example those carried out by Costanza Marzotto for the children ("Appartenere alle due stirpi: i gruppi di parola per figli di coppie separate," in *Studi interdisciplinari sulla famiglia,* XXII [2007]) like those mentioned by Lynn Cassella-Kapusinki for teenagers (*Now What Do I Do? A Guide to Help Teenagers with Their Parents' Separation or Divorce,* Acta Publications, Skokie, 2006).

64. Tony Anatrella, *Epoux, op. cit.*, p. 130.

65. Bernadette Lemoine, *"Maman, ne me quitte pas!," op. cit.*, p. 204. 65; "The child's unconscious mind will never accept the tearing of his two roots. This explains why, at the symbolically important moments of his life (birthdays, wedding, success,...), he wishes for both his parents to stand beside him" (Rosie Boucaud and Jacques Poujol, *Le divorce, op. cit.*, p. 63).

66. Bernadette Lemoine, *"Maman, ne me quitte pas!," op. cit.*, p. 201.

67. Susan Forward, *Parents toxiques, op. cit.*, p. 89.

68. Rosie Boucaud and Jacques Poujol, *Le divorce, op. cit.*, p. 68.

69. *Ibid.*, p. 68, note.

70. Bernadette Lemoine, *"Maman, ne me quitte pas!,"op. cit.*, p. 201–102.

71. According to Jean-Claude Guillebaud, parental and social culpability towards the children tend to victimize them. They become victims of everything and everybody, including their parents. A "right of the child" emerges as opposed to the "parental rights" (*La tyrannie du plaisir, op. cit., p.* 460–062: "L'idéologie des droits de l'enfant"). Cf. also Irène Thery, "Nouveaux droits de l'enfant, la potion magique?," in *Esprit* (mars-avril 1992).

72. H. Schrod, "Enfant roi et divorce," H. Schrod, "Enfant roi et divorce. La séparation des parents n'est qu'un élément parmi d'autres," in *L'enfant-roi, victime ou tyran ?*, revue d'action *L'Observatoire* 45 (2005).

73. Reversal of the prayer of St. Francis. "In such a situation, it is not exaggerated to say that the parent acts like a badly loved child, considering his own child like an adult capable of giving him comfort and love. We must understand that it is the adult that must procure the emotional care and the child that must receive it. We have to recover as soon as possible when we feel unable to meet the child's need" (Ross Campbell, *Comment vraiment aimer votre enfant*, Orion, Richmond, Québec, 1979, p. 89–90).

74. *Parents toxiques. Comment échapper à leur emprise?, op. cit.*

75. A court can certainly offer a precious help in protecting and promoting the good of the child, but it has no right to corner a child into solemnly choosing the parent with whom he would want to live. It is for the responsible adults to decide where the child should live, while listening to his sufferings and his joys. Besides, as Bernadette Lemoine notes it: "When, after an intensive but cruel questioning, we manage to make the child admit that he 'prefers' his father or that he 'prefers' his mother, it often only means that he prefers a way of life, habits, a house, his school or his friends, not the parent himself" ("*Ne me quitte pas!,*" *op. cit.*, p. 73).

76. Bernadette Lemoine, *"Ne me quitte pas!,"* *op. cit.*, p. 202.

77. Cf. Eugenia Scabini e Raffaella Iafrate, *Psicologia dei legami familiari*, Il Mulino, Bologna, 2003.

78. Cf. cited above in our reading of the prodigal son (*Lk* 15:11 ss.).

79. Cf. Joan B. Kelly, "Developing beneficial parenting plan models for children following separation a divorce," in *Journal of American Academy of Matrimonial Lawyers* 19 (2005), p.101–118; "Children's living arrangements following separation and divorce: Insights from empirical and clinical research," in *Family Process* 46 (2007), p. 35–52.

80. Nathalie Ponet, "L'impact de la séparation du couple sur les enfants," in *Bulletin trimestriel d'information et de documentation du Centre de Recherche de la Médiation*, January-February 2008, p. 28.

81. Reported by José Gerard and Cécile Richir, *Les enfants du divorce, op. cit.*, p. 8.

82. Today, children of divorce find refuge in the "model couple" of their grandparents. Nowadays, the marital stablity of the grandparents is even in question. What will be the consequences for the children?

83. Cf on the subject AA.VV., *Il cammino della vita: l'educazione, una sfida per la morale,* presented by Juan José Pérez-Soba and Oana Gotia, Latran University Press, Città del Vaticano, 2007.

84. *FC* 37.

85. *La tyrannie du plaisir, op. cit.,* p. 453.

86. John Paul II, *Letter to families,* 1994, 9.

87. Jean-Paul II, *Veritatis splendor, op. cit.,* 7.

88. "For the young man, the *question* is not so much about rules to be followed, but *about the full meaning of life.* This is in fact the aspiration at the heart of every human decision and action, the quiet searching and interior prompting which sets freedom in motion." (*Veritatis splendor,* 7)

89. Cf. Vincent Laupies, "Logique de conversion et logique de guérison," in AA.VV., *Vie spirituelle et psychologie,* under the dir. of J.-N. Dumont and T. Anatrella, Le Collège Supérieur, Lyon, 2004, p. 153–363.

90. John Paul II, *Redemptor Hominis, op. cit.,* 13.

II A Pastoral Approach

A Pastoral Care Plan for Children of Divorce

José Noriega

What do parents see in their child? And what does the child see in his parents?

If, for his parents, the child is the memorial of being one flesh, parents are for the child a memorial of an origin, a foundation, a source: something he is not given automatically, but is offered in the most wonderful way possible, since it is thanks to his parents he has come into being. So then the child, seeing his origin, will be able to see himself as "loved for himself" and welcomed into a communion of persons, as the fruit of a love, a gift within a gift.

The memory that each man has of his birth implies, therefore, his ability to open up to gratitude, with the perspective of one who sees in reality his own goodness, his loveableness: that what surrounds me is a friend, precisely because from my very beginning, there was a particular love. In this way, every man, in memory of his beginning, may realize that he is a son, and in the parenthood of his mother and father will recognize the Fatherhood from which all paternity on earth gets its name. In memory of the Original Beginning, that first act of love of the Father, every man finds meaning in his life and his vocation: to recognize himself as child, to become a spouse and thus to arrive at paternity.

However, it is quite common that for many people the memory of their beginning is not so clear, in as much as those who procreate, the parents, live an ambiguous love or even a love that has been fragmented, wounded, broken.

José Noriega is Vice President and Professor of Moral Theology at the Central Session of the Pontifical John Paul II Institute for Studies on Marriage and Family, Vatican City.

The child then, looking to his origin, would see a love, a source, but a source which has ceased to flow. It becomes difficult for the child to find himself in that origin because it lacks continuity. The love that is found in his beginning, tying his parents into a singular unity, no longer exists and those people are now gone in different directions. Divorce implies an interruption of that period of love when the stream that flows down the mountain of life is seen to be broken, shortened, interrupted. The foundation that we were given in that communion, from which we came into being ceases to be the source of our life and the person is then seen to be suspended in air without ties to his origin.

Here then is the essential difficulty that the tragedy of divorce presents to children. It is the removing of their foundation, leaving the person in fear before his existence, unprotected in the face of fate. In this moment the reality that surrounds him is no longer a friendly one, but rather becomes ambiguous and threatening. Without wanting to, the parents wounding the bond of love between them also wound the presence of hope in the child. By divorcing, they break the link between the stream and the source, separating that reality from the child. The drama that involves the existence of every man begins to be obscured through the willed absence of those who were there at its beginning.

But is it possible to heal the wounds of life if we are far from our roots, our origin? Only if human fatherhood were to be a weak love that generates merely by chance, then that font of love might indeed stop flowing, and then we would be left to fate. But the human fatherhood that is present in that origin is the mediation of another parenthood, the Fatherhood of the Father. That human communion that makes it possible is a mediation of another communion, the Trinitarian communion, which sustains all and guides all to its fullness. That fullness of communion with God the Father, Son and Holy Spirit, is an origin and a destiny that marks the entire passage of life and that, beyond our fragileness, leads us to the good.

Beyond the fragmentation of our lives, fragmentation caused by us or by others, can a common thread be found that weaves together the fabric of one's history? But how can one's own broken life-story be helped and interpreted when such a great and intimate suffering is present? Here lies the importance of understanding the role of the great variety of human mediations in which there is the memory of the Beginning. Fatherhood is certainly a unique mediation, but it is not the only one. In this sense it becomes essential to understand the mediation of human communion that takes place in groups and how the mystery of the expressed word may help to decipher the mystery of one's own life. This is a path which involves a journey of growth and corresponds to sacramental development.

This section of the book seeks to show the paths already explored in work with children and to highlight the paths and means to help them discover the memory of the Beginning. In this they may see themselves as begotten children, able to discover the foundation to look back on, that allows them to face their destiny with hope to become spouse in order to become father.

REFERENCES

1. Cfr. H. Arendt, *Love and Saint Augustine*, University of Chicago Press, Chicago 1996, 51–52 see the excellent commentary by S. Kampowski, *Arendt, Augustine and the New Beginning*, Eerdmans, Grand Rapids (MI) 2008, Cap VB.

2. Cfr. L. Melina-J. Noriega-J.J. Pérez Soba, Camminare alla luce dell'amore. I fondamenti della morale cristiana, Cantagalli, Siena 2008.

Building A Ministry With Children of Divorce: Obstacles & How to Overcome Them

Lynn Cassella-Kapusinski

Divorce is one of the most significant problems affecting our world as well as our Church. In the United States, 43 percent of first marriages end in separation or divorce within 15 years (Centers for Disease Control and Prevention, 2001). In most European countries, this rate is between 20 and 30 percent within a period of 15 years from the marriage formation (Andersson, 2003).

In the United States, Catholics have been found to be neither more nor less likely to get divorced than anyone else (Archbishop Joseph E. Kurtz, Chairman of the USCCB Subcommittee on Marriage and Family Life, responding to research from the Center for Applied Research in the Apostolate, October 2007). This is especially disturbing, considering the effects divorce can have on the well-being of children and their families, on subsequent divorce rates of both children and their parents, and on alienation from the Church. The stressful nature of divorce, along with the prolonged process of change and adaptation that accompanies it, has been found to increase the likelihood of adverse behavior and to affect the psychological well-being in children. While substantial debate continues regarding the extent of these adverse affects, numerous research studies have documented that many children are negatively affected by their parents' divorce in the short term (e.g. Amato & Keith, 1991a; Chase-Lansdale, Cherlin & Kierman, 1995; Hetherington & Stanley-Hagan, 1999). Some children also experience these negative effects in the long term (Amato & Keith, 1991b; Chase-Lansdale et al., 1995; Wallerstein

---

Lynn Cassella-Kapusinski is President and Founder of the Faith Journeys Foundation, Inc., Ellicott City, MA (www.faithjourneys.org)

& Lewis, 1998), such as an increased divorce rate for themselves. Additionally, the probability of separation or divorce for a second marriage during the first 10 years was found to be 39 percent in 1995 (Centers for Disease Control and Prevention, May 2001 report).

Moreover, issues involving divorce and remarriage have been found to be the number one cause for alienation from the Church. According to research in Mitch Finley's book, *It's Not the Same Without You: Coming Home to the Catholic Church* (Doubleday, 2003), some Catholics still believe that divorce means a person is excommunicated from the Church. Others do not understand the Church's annulment process or find it an unreasonably difficult or painful one.

The critical question becomes: What can we, as a Church, realistically do to help heal the wounds of separated and divorced families while also helping them to bring God and Jesus Christ into their struggle and to grow in their understanding of Church teachings?

I am very passionate about this topic, primarily because I am a child of divorced parents and one who has been fortunate to "beat the odds." I know how challenging this adversity can be for young people because I lived it. I also know from my personal experience how necessary it is to follow the model of Jesus in order to rise above it. Even though the Kingdom of God is not fully here yet, we—the children of divorced parents—like all people, can begin to benefit from the effects of Christ's coming into the world. As Jesus said to his disciples, "Whoever wishes to come after me must deny himself, take up his cross and follow me" (Mt 16:24). "For the Son of Man will come with his angels in his Father's glory, and then he will repay everyone according to his conduct" (Mt. 16:27). Through the groups, retreats and publications of my nonprofit foundation, Faith Journeys (www.faithjourneys.org), I have been working for years to present this redemptive message in an engaging way for young people while helping them work through the emotions associated with their parents' divorce and develop healthy coping skills.

THE FORMATION OF MY CALLING

My calling to help children from separated and divorced families was born from my childhood experiences. My parents had a high-conflict marriage, eventually separating when I was 11 years old. Yet, even as a young girl when my fears became greatest, I heard what seemed to be God's voice, reassuring me that someday, somehow, life would get better. It was not wishful thinking or escapism, but a hope-filled confidence that I credit to God's grace.

After the separation, my dad moved out of state and was not involved in my life in an active way. Even though my journey into adulthood was not an easy one, I did not become one of the statistics so often associated with children from divorced and, particularly, fatherless homes. For example, I never had a behavioral or chemical dependency problem. Nor was I ever at risk of dropping out of school, running away from home, or committing suicide. Instead, with God's grace, I was able to use my parents' divorce as a positive motivator that enabled me not only to excel in school but also "get marriage right."

I have continued to ask, what enabled me to beat these odds when so many children from divorced families have not? What message did I grab hold of that appears to elude the grasp of others? Time and time again, I come back to faith and the teachings of the Church, both of which grounded and afforded me considerable strength and support throughout my journey.

An additional critical factor was living with a parent who had good coping and parenting skills. This relationship with the residential parent plays a central role in a child's adjustment. In particular, research shows that a supportive and authoritative parenting style encourages optimal adjustment among children from divorced, as well as intact, families (Hetherington et al., 1999; Katz & Gottman, 1997).

Having a safe place to express my grief was also necessary for my healing. For me, that safe place was a very small support group that I formed with my older brother. Even though it was made up of only the two of us, it helped me tremendously because it normalized my loss and, as a result, helped me feel less alone.

BENEFITS OF GROUP WORK

This strong underpinning of relief is one of the key benefits of group work, particularly for children from divorced families. In reducing their sense of isolation, a group also helps to reduce accompanying feelings of inferiority that may result in perceiving themselves as not "good enough" because they do not have an intact nuclear family. In hearing other members share feelings and concerns similar to their own, young people often feel more in touch with the world as well as themselves.

Peer support is also a component of group work, especially in adolescent groups where young people may be more likely to reach out and help one another. This type of opportunity can provide them with a meaningful role, increase their self-esteem, and help them live out the value of serving others. Young people may accept observations and suggestions from another group member more readily than from the group leader as well.

In one of my groups, for example, Justin, a 16-year-old, was attempting to back up his answer of "false" to the true/false statement, "you have to feel grief in order to heal." As he was struggling to clarify his thoughts, Mark, a 15-year-old, jumped in and said he thought the statement was "false" as well because "everyone grieves in their own way." After affirming Mark's statement as being true, I clarified the meaning of the true/false one and posed some negative consequences that can result when people do not express grief. Justin began to buy into this new insight, sharing that he thought his step mom had not "dealt with her grief," yet he remained largely silent while Mark sat quietly with an irritated look on his face. Matthew, a 17-year-old in the group, then broke the silence and shared that he had "bottled up his feelings" in the past but no longer does so because it causes him to feel more stress and lash out at the wrong people. As he shared, Mark sat up in his seat and Justin went on to say that his dad "kept things bottled up" and that he "didn't want to be like that." The boys responded more readily to the personal sharing of Matthew than my suggestions, and they began to model themselves on this aspect of his journey as well. Had it not been for Matthew's sharing and reaching out as their peer, the other group members might not have grasped this important tenet fully enough.

Group work offers many other significant benefits, including psychoeducation, the learning of healthy coping skills, and acceptance into a social group which, of course, plays a significant role, especially for adolescents. Additionally, while outcome research regarding specific group treatments is limited, a survey of more than 40 years of research shows an abundance of evidence that group approaches are associated with clients' improvement in a variety of settings and situations (Bednar & Kaul, 1978, 1979, 1994; Bednar & Lawlis, 1971; Kaul & Bednar, 1978, 1986).

OBSTACLES IN BUILDING A GROUP PROGRAM

Developing and maintaining a successful faith-based group program for youth, however, requires a host of factors to come together. Perhaps the most important factor is utilizing facilitators who are adequately trained in group counseling, child and adolescent development, and general clinical areas. Facilitators should also have specialized knowledge about pastoral counseling as well as an understanding of the unique pastoral needs and other concerns of children and adolescents from divorcing families.

A successful program also requires anticipating obstacles and building in safeguards to overcome them. The following are the most common obstacles I have encountered in running groups and retreats for young people through my nonprofit foundation, Faith Journeys.

Obstacle #1: Recruiting a Sufficient Number of Young People

The majority of young people, especially those in middle school and high school, will not want to participate in group work because, for them, it feels like going to the dentist. They know it will likely hurt. In addition, to cope with difficult feelings and transitions, the young person may have learned to use unhealthy responses such as blaming others, withdrawing, and the like. Participating in a group or retreat will challenge those outgrown coping skills and nudge young people toward confronting their painful feelings, both of which takes them out of their "comfort zone" in many ways. As a result, they may show resistance about joining the group, and parents often give into this resistance (see the next section).

To overcome this obstacle, some programs make their group a general "grief group" and open it up to young people who are experiencing other losses, such as the death of a loved one or a parent's military deployment. However, this is not recommended because, while these losses have similarities to those experienced by children from divorced families, the losses are more dissimilar than similar. As a result, children can fail to identify with one another which will jeopardize the group's cohesiveness and cause it to be less effective. Greater identification and support among group members, especially early in the group, have been associated empirically with more favorable outcomes (Yalom, 1995).

Children will already have a tendency to compare themselves to others in the group, even when they are all from divorced families. Highlighting additional differences among them by inviting children experiencing other losses will exacerbate this tendency.

This interaction between group members is illustrative. For one of my after-school groups which consisted of all boys, I allowed Justin to join upon the request of the school guidance counselor. Although not from a divorced family, Justin was grappling with similar confusing and difficult losses. His mother had died several years ago, and he had been living with his grandparents ever since because his father had a drug addiction. During one of the sessions, Jason, another boy in the group, complained about the possibility that his mother might get divorced a second time, and that he would have to "go through this divorce stuff all over again." Upon hearing this remark, Justin blurted out quite angrily, "at least all of you have parents. My mother is dead, and I never see my dad because he's a drug addict. I don't have a mother or a father." While Jason's sharing was helpful in encouraging Justin to get in touch with his anger, his involvement thereafter highlighted more of his differences, rather than his similarities, with the other boys. He was acutely aware of one major difference, in particular: Neither of his parents was emotionally available to him. It is arguable how much Justin benefited from his participation in the group as a result.

This situation also raises an important point about the uniqueness of the grief that children from divorced families experience. They struggle with resolving open-ended and, often, unclear losses. These divorce-related losses are very different than other losses such as death of a loved one, for example. In bereavement, a person is dead. The loss is final. However, for children with separated or divorced parents, while something gets lost in their relationships, something also remains. One parent moves out of the home, so a child may not see that parent as much. That same parent may start dating or become overwhelmed by personal problems, either of which takes attention further away from the child. Yet, the parent remains a parent, and the child is left alone in determining what that role now means. Their uncertainty about their parent's place in their life freezes the grieving process.

Obstacle #2: Parents May Not Understand the Value or Need for This Program

Divorced and separated parents may be inclined to give into their children's resistance about joining a group. This is understandable when you look at the reasons why this can happen:

1. Parents are often at their limit in many respects and simply do not have the energy to engage in another battle.

2. Parents may also have a very strained relationship with their children, which makes them reluctant to insist that their children join a group. These parents may have an indulgent or neglectful parenting style as well and, as a result, let discipline slide more than they should. So, the children's wishes often win out, even when not in their best interests.

3. Other parents are in denial about the fact that their children are hurting. It may be too painful for these parents to admit that their choices have caused difficulties for their loved ones, so they may overlook or minimize the effects of the divorce.

4. Or the parents may have arrived at a comfortable place with the breakup, and mistakenly assume that their children's healing will require a similar amount of time. These parents often lack information about the grieving process of children along with the factors involved in resolving that grief.

Any one of these reasons can detour parents from understanding how a group program can benefit their child as well as his or her need for it. This obstacle underscores the importance of offering educational programs for divorced and separated parents on a regular basis.

Obstacle #3: Finding Adequately Trained Facilitators

The success of your program will be due largely to the effort you put into selecting and training facilitators. Utilizing facilitators who have relevant experience and training is very important because it helps to ensure that your group will reach its full therapeutic potential. It also helps to ensure that your group will be run in an ethical manner. This means that the facilitator will know how to maintain appropriate boundaries with young people, and that he or she will also know what measures to take in crisis situations such as a child who expresses a desire to hurt himself or another. An experienced facilitator will also be better equipped to screen participants and refer those who would be better served by individual therapy or a psychotherapy group.

It can be difficult to recruit qualified facilitators, however, if you lack the financial resources to pay them. One option that can help noticeably in this regard is to utilize graduate counseling students who are fulfilling their clinical requirements for graduation and, as such, would not require payment.

Your program will still have additional expenses, however, such as developing marketing materials, postage, paying a staff member to handle registrations and so on—which leads to a fourth major obstacle.

Obstacle #4: Finding Adequate Financial Resources to Run Your Program

Obtaining grant money for group work can be a difficult as well as a very time consuming process, not only in writing the grant applications but also given the time it takes for a grant to be awarded. Additionally, if you want to include a spiritual and/or religious component in your group, the number of appropriate funders will narrow even further. Many funders are reluctant to fund the same program on a repeated basis as well.

One way to combat this obstacle is to charge higher program fees, which is reasonable if you run your group as a *psychoeducational* group rather than just a support group. However, a higher fee can significantly limit the number of young people you reach, since many separated and divorced families often have limited financial resources. The only way they may be able to afford mental health services is through their insurance program and, while some insurance companies pay for group therapy, this benefit only applies if the group facilitator is a licensed professional which your organization may not have access to.

Another expense in running a group program is finding a suitable and affordable curriculum to utilize, which leads to the last common obstacle.

Obstacle #5: Finding a Suitable and Affordable Curriculum

Group programs currently available for children from divorced families offer their curriculum only as part of a "start-up kit." These kits range from $500 or 319 Euros to approximately $1,000 or 639 Euros. Not only are they costly, but their curricula contain serious flaws as well. For example, some include teachings that are contrary to the Catholic Church, and others are very generalized "grief programs" that fail to address the unique challenges and concerns of children from divorced families and which, as mentioned, hinder group cohesiveness as a result.

A MODEL FOR GROUP WORK WITH SEPARATED AND DIVORCED FAMILIES

Given these difficult obstacles, how can we, the Church, develop a successful ministry program for separated and divorced families? The model I propose involves a "building process" where families are exposed in a small way to this outreach with more intense programming offered as time moves along. This is analogous to learning to swim where one starts at the shallow end of the water then, gradually, makes their way into deeper water as they grow more comfortable.

Step #1: Educational Workshop for Separated and Divorced Families—with Parish and School Personnel Invited Also

I suggest starting with an educational workshop for separated and divorced families and inviting parish and school personnel as well. Why include all these people? Research has found that the initial positive effects of intervention programs tend to diminish over time, to the extent that environmental supports to maintain the child's gains are lacking. Therefore, programs that involve parents and other important adults in the child's life are likely to be more beneficial (Ramey and Ramey, 1998). Parental involvement is especially important to the success of early intervention programs, given the dependency that children have on their parents. We also need to remember that young people spend a large amount of time in school and are likely to show their main reactions to divorce in a school setting such as the classroom.

The purpose of this workshop is to help parents as well as children better understand young people's reactions to parental separation and divorce, their needs in working through this loss, and how to help in their healing, adjustment and growth. It also gives a good opportunity to announce your upcoming ministry programs and conduct pre-registrations for them.

Step #2: A Healing Retreat for Separated and Divorced Families

Once parents have a greater understanding of their child's needs and concerns in working through the separation or divorce, they may become more open to seeking help for their child as well as themselves. This one-day, family retreat provides an excellent opportunity for taking this next step. It consists of brief, informal talks and small group sharings for both parents and children with each group meeting separately to process similar topics in coping with and growing from separation and divorce.

My foundation has led retreats for youth in conjunction with the Diocese of Pittsburgh, PA and the Diocese of Harrisburg, PA, and has found them to be a non-threatening, compassionate way of showing families that the Church is there and still cares about them, even while viewing divorce as a deep wound to the natural moral law. This pastoral outreach, therefore, serves as a real and active way for the Church to show loving mercy and trust in the capacity for recovery. Pope Benedict XVI reaffirmed the importance of this merciful love in his April 2008 address to our International Congress during which he said, "Yes, the Gospel of love and life is also always the *Gospel of mercy,* which is addressed to the actual person and sinner that we are, to help us up after any fall and to recover from any injury." During this address, Pope Benedict XVI also reminded us of what John Paul II said during his homily when inaugurating the new Shrine of Divine Mercy in Krakow: "This fire of mercy needs to be passed on to the world. In the mercy of God the world will find peace" (17 August 2002, p. 8).

In addition to being tailored to the needs and concerns of separated and divorced families, this retreat should also contain Catholic facets. For example, during lunch time, individual confessions can be offered for both adults and children. And, throughout the sessions for the youth, Church teachings on marriage and divorce, what annulment means, and other important topics such as forgiveness and the child's image of God can be explored.

This retreat opportunity can also generate a lot of publicity which will help in getting the word out to a large number of families, many of whom may no longer be attending Mass or reading the church bulletin or Catholic newspaper. I found the secular newspapers, as well as the Catholic ones, to be especially interested in highlighting the youth retreat. So, know that, in promoting this event, you will likely find a lot of media outlets that will recognize the good you are doing and will want to help you in reaching families.

The reporters I spoke with were also very interested in the topics being addressed, which was encouraging as well. I typically organize the day retreat so that the small group discussions address three or four main topics. Also included are fun, theme-specific activities which emphasize important points and enable the young people to bond with one another.

What curriculum did I use? Because I have found no suitable curriculum available from both a Catholic and a pastoral counseling perspective, I have written my own which is available in my books, *Now What Do I Do? A Guide to Help Teenagers with Their Parents' Separation or Divorce* (ACTA) and *Making Your Way After Your Parents' Divorce* (Liguori).

Making Your Way After Your Parents' Divorce has been endorsed by Archbishop Wuerl of the Archdiocese of Washington, D.C., and the foreword for the book was written by Reverend Theodore Hesburgh, C.S.C., President Emeritus of the University of Notre Dame. This book is written for college age students and young adults.

Now What Do I Do? has also been endorsed by Archbishop Wuerl of the Archdiocese of Washington, D.C. and Archbishop O'Brien of the Archdiocese of Baltimore. It won an award from the Catholic Press Association in 2007. All of the book's questions and activities have been tested in groups for ages 12 to 18. In addition, the book has the unique distinction of being written from my perspective as both a child of divorce and pastoral counselor. As such, the material not only stems from personal authority, but also incorporates a faith-based dimension along with a traditional counseling approach. An accompanying facilitator's guide is also available and can be ordered directly through my foundation, Faith Journeys. It includes practical instruction on running groups and over 40 activity ideas to supplement sessions. A curriculum for parents and elementary school aged children is also available through Faith Journeys.

Launching a retreat program and sustaining it will require a strong, ongoing marketing effort. Given your staff, availability, and financial resources, you may only be able to offer this one program, either on a yearly basis or perhaps every few months. If so, it's a good idea to offer a follow-up activity for the young people who attend your retreat as well as their parents. You can do this one month after the retreat during which you have a meeting to "check in" and see how the families are doing. You can offer this "check in" on a monthly basis thereafter as well.

What I have found after leading retreats for U.S. dioceses, however, is that both parents and children want to continue the group work. Even though many of the young people initially do not want to attend a retreat, they eventually experience some healing from it, plus they have met other young people in similar situations whom they want to keep interacting with as well. So, I encourage you to build on this work and offer an ongoing group program, if possible (see step # 4).

For young people as well as their parents, this option of a group may be more appealing than individual counseling, given its stigma. Plus, while it certainly can be helpful, individual counseling may not be necessary in most cases. This is because, while divorce and remarriage are added stressors for children, the majority do not experience significant adjustment difficulties. Research has shown that 20–25 percent of children in divorced or remarried families have significant adjustment problems, compared to 10 percent in intact families (Hetherington, Bridges and Insabella, 1998). In other words, while divorce or remarriage doubles a child's risk, the majority of young people do not experience significant adjustment problems.

Once your recruitment for a weekly group program is underway, you will want to start actively screening and training potential facilitators. How many facilitators will you need? I recommend that you have two facilitators (one male and one female) for each small group of six to eight young people, with at least one facilitator in each group being an experienced facilitator. Always err on the side of recruiting more, not less, facilitators as some might not be able to commit to all the days and times of your group meetings.

Step #3: Training Program for Group Facilitators

Perhaps the most important tool in facilitating groups is the facilitator's ability to establish solid relationships with the young people. In order to promote growth with those in your group, this person should also be committed to growth and reflection in his or her own life. This means you will want to look for persons who have a sincere interest in the welfare of young people, and who are also courageous and willing to model and teach desired behaviors. Good facilitators are also open and self-aware, and have a strong enough ego to cope frankly and nondefensively with criticism.

These personal qualities, however, are not enough to facilitate effectively. Basic counseling skills specific to group situations are also needed. A broad range of mental health professionals would have the necessary skills and training to run a group in an effective manner, such as counselors, social workers, psychologists, and psychiatrists. Graduate students in counseling or psychology who have completed courses in the helping relationship, counseling theory and practice, psychopathology, human development, and professional and legal ethics can also be good candidates. As mentioned, for their clinical internship requirements, graduate students need to obtain clinical hours which can help your recruitment efforts appreciably. If the student does not have experience facilitating groups, however, you will want to pair him or her with an experienced facilitator so that the student can refine these skills under appropriate supervision.

Prior to starting your group, you will also want to have training for facilitators.

In addition to reviewing developmental issues, the grieving process of children, stages of group development, and helping strategies, this training would instruct on guidelines for assessing and reporting suicidal behavior and potential physical or sexual abuse of minors. These situations may never arise, however you will want to err on the side of caution and detail your requirements in these situations.

Step #4: Weekly Group Programs for Young People with Parents Included

The last step in your outreach program will be offering a weekly group for young people. In your marketing materials, you will want to use the term "discussion group" or, if offering your group as part of a school program, you might want to call it a "club" or a "class." Even though your group will be much more given all the processing that occurs, these terms are much more inviting, especially for young people, than if you call your group a *psychoeducational* group" or even a "support group." For college students, an attractive option is to offer a more general "changing families" group where students can share difficulties in handling various stresses and concerns at home while living away.

If possible, I recommend offering the group for young people as an afterschool program at a Catholic school. Attachment to school has been found to be the strongest non-family factor predicting adolescent mental well-being (Rodgers & Rose, 2002). In addition, utilizing a school location also helps recruitment considerably since guidance counselors and teachers often recommend students for the group and can be a support to parents in the process. Another good option is to hold the group at a centrally located parish.

Another decision you will need to make concerns the registration fee. As mentioned, if offering a *psychoeducational* group, you will be able to charge a higher fee which, in turn, will enable you to utilize more qualified facilitators, do more marketing for your program, plus have additional money for supplies. *Psychoeducational* groups in the United States currently charge as much as $180 or approximately 115 Euros for a 6-week session. I have consistently found that parents value a group program more when they pay a reasonable amount for it, versus getting it for free or a very low cost.

Another decision concerns for which ages to offer your group. I recommend that you start by focusing on one age group. Then, once you have built that group successfully, it becomes much easier to expand your program and treat other age groups. However, if you have sufficient facilitators, you may want to offer your group program for more than one age group and, ideally, for every young person in the family.

What age group should you treat first? I suggest starting with adolescents or, more specifically, ages 12 to 18 (with separate groups for middle schoolers and high schoolers), for a variety of reasons. The most pressing reason stems from the fact that children from divorced homes have a much higher rate of divorce themselves later in life. Researchers tell us that, in the United States, 60 percent of women whose parents divorce get divorced themselves while this percentage is 35 percent for men (Davis, 1985). By reaching out to pre-adolescents and adolescents, you would be working to stop this trend in two very important ways. First, you would be helping them to heal and therefore not carry unresolved grief into their future relationships and, secondly, you also could use your group as an opportunity to instruct them on healthy relationships as well as the Church's teachings on marriage. Adolescence is an ideal age to present this information because many adolescents either have an interest in dating or are starting to date, but not yet dating seriously. This developing interest can make them easier to reach than young adults, for example, who may already have a committed dating relationship.

Another important reason for starting with adolescents concerns the added stress that adolescence brings for many families. These years are often the most challenging and trying for both parents and children, given the extent and rate of the adolescent's physical and psychological changes. In addition, parents may be in need of extra support during this time as they experience their children separating more from them in attempts to carve out their niche in the world.

The advanced cognitive development level of adolescence, as compared to those in middle and late childhood, is another benefit of working with this age group. According to Piaget, at approximately age 11, children move into the formal operational stage of cognitive development which allows them to think in abstract and more logical terms. They begin to entertain possibilities for the future and are capable of considering concepts like heaven and love as well. As a result, at this age, it can be helpful to explain divorce in religious terms and encourage them to formulate abstract conclusions about the divorce and, thereby, learn that much more from it.

As mentioned, if interested in offering a group program for ages 12 to 18, you may want to utilize my workbook, *Now What Do I Do? A Guide to Help Teenagers with Their Parents' Separation or Divorce*. It contains curriculum for a 10-session group program for ages 12 to 18. This book is the *only* resource currently available that treats these difficulties from both a Catholic and counseling perspective. In addition, the book also incorporates vignettes of my experiences as a child of divorced parents which add an important relational dimension and authority, and help young people honor and explore their own journeys.

RECOMMENDED FORMAT FOR A YOUTH GROUP PROGRAM

How can you utilize this resource in your group program? I recommend organizing your group program into two, six-week sessions, referred to as Part I and Part II. This format allows you to address each chapter of *Now What Do I Do?* in order while also including two wrap-up sessions for the entire family. Part I should cover chapters 1 through 5, corresponding to sessions 1 through 5, with a family wrap-up session being held during session 6. Similarly, Part II should address chapters 6 through 10, which would correspond with sessions 7 through 11. A closing ceremony with the parents and children as well as any extended family members would be held during session 12.

The program can then be marketed as two, six-week sessions that the young people register for at the start of each series. This format gives them, as well as their parents, an opportunity to "test out" the group before committing to all 12 sessions/weeks. Most families will be more comfortable committing to a shorter, six-week time period and will be more likely to commit to both series as a result. What I have consistently found in running groups is that, after the Part I group, the overwhelming majority of young people want to continue.

Another important reason to offer a longer program is that research across four decades has found that program intensity leads to program success (Ramey and Ramey, 1998). In other words, programs that include more meetings, more hours, and so on, are more effective. Moreover, parents and children who participate more regularly and actively show greater positive results as well.

RECOMMENDED FORMAT FOR INDIVIDUAL SESSIONS

Each session should be $1^1/_2$ hours in length with meetings taking place on the same day and during the same times each week. For children in elementary school, you may want to reduce the session length to 1 hour, given their more limited attention span. A small group sharing serves as the core of each meeting. For middle schoolers and high schoolers, this sharing is preceded by private time to complete three to five questions and/or exercises in a chapter, which you designate. For children in elementary school, you will want to use various play therapy techniques and activity sheets to supplement the small group sharings.

No matter how you start this "work component," you will need to complement it with fun, creative activities that either precede the small group sharing, follow it, or both. These activities serve as fun and effective ways to emphasize main points regarding the weekly topic. The activities also provide informal, "bonding time" that is critical for the youth's enjoyment and learning as well. A listing of over 40 theme-specific, activity ideas is available through the *Facilitator's Guide for Now What Do I Do?* which can be ordered directly through my foundation. This guide also includes additional, practical instruction on running a group program for young people.

THE IMPORTANCE OF INCLUDING PARENTS

Research across four decades shows that regular and active participation by parents is one of the main principles that guides successful early intervention programs (Ramey and Ramey, 1998). Pope Benedict XVI also affirmed the important role that parents, in particular, play in their children's adjustment to separation and divorce. During his April 5, 2008 address to our International Congress, *Oil on the Wounds*, he said,

"Supportive pastoral attention must therefore aim to ensure that the children are not the innocent victims of conflicts between parents who divorce. It must also endeavor to ensure that the continuity of the link with their parents is guaranteed as far as possible, as well as the links with their own family and social origins, which are indispensable for a balanced psychological and human growth."

What are some practical ways to include parents? As mentioned, if offering a retreat, you can offer an educational workshop for the family, either prior to the retreat or soon afterwards. If offering a weekly group program, at a minimum, I recommend offering three sessions that include parents: the introductory, educational workshop and wrap-up sessions at the end of each five-week series.

The introductory session, as mentioned, helps all family members better understand young people's reactions to parental separation and divorce, their needs in working through this loss, and how to support them in their grieving. During this introductory session, it is also important to help parents gain a better understanding of how a child's developmental level affects their grieving journey and, hence, how children will rework and process the breakup at higher levels as they mature. Because of this reality, it is important to stress children's needs for ongoing support in working through the loss, not only during the immediate crisis stage of separation but during the long-range period of the divorce as well.

The purpose of the wrap-up sessions is to present the main points that the youth discussed during the prior five weeks, and to give general feedback on the difficulties they shared (for example, being put in the middle of their parents' arguments, feeling pressured to "choose sides" between parents, not having adequate time with a non-residential parent, etc.). For divorcing parents who lack good coping skills and fail to notice the resulting effect on their children, these sessions often provide important and necessary "wake-up calls." During these wrap-up sessions, instruction should also be included on divorce-related difficulties so that parents receive some guidance and support for resolving them. In addition, it is important to allow time for open discussion so parents can process their concerns and explore their own grief. You will also want to have information available on local counseling resources, while stressing that a better adjusted parent can provide a more supportive framework for fostering their child's grief work.

Another option is to hold a separate group just for parents, which meets on the same days and at the same times as the children's group. This group would help parents learn about the grieving process of children and how to support them through it; it also allows parents to discuss strategies for strengthening their family as they work through divorce-related changes and problems. A parent curriculum that accompanies the workbook, *Now What Do I Do?*, is available from the Faith Journeys Foundation.

In addition to increasing the effectiveness of your children's group, involving parents is also an excellent way to show young people that "they are not the problem in the family." Adolescents, in particular, can become very resentful if their parents do not have to participate and do work themselves. During one of my groups, Steven, a 17-year-old who had become very argumentative with his teachers and complained of his mother's over involvement, was very vocal about this point when he said, "my mom is the one who needs the therapy. She really needs to get a life." Steven's remark illustrates the importance of viewing a child's symptomatic or problematic behavior as multi-determined and arising out of a family context versus from within a single "sick" person, hence the need to involve as many family members as possible in your intervention program.

CONCLUSION

One of the profound gifts of this ministry is that it gives us a direct and immediate way to instill healthy attitudes about moral suffering to children from separated or divorced families as well as their parents. In his apostolic letter, *Salvifici Doloris,* John Paul II said that suffering "seems to belong to man's transcendence: it is one of those points in which man is in a certain sense 'destined' to go beyond himself, and he is called to this in a mysterious way" (11 February 1984, p. 1).

We need to emphasize to young people, in particular, the extraordinary example of Jesus, who showed us that the only way out of pain is through it. In so doing, we can make it clear for them that—if they, too, embrace suffering—it will not triumph over them but, instead, lead them toward good. Realizing this truth will help them draw closer to Jesus in a very real way and find meaning in their suffering.

Specifically, we need to ask young people: What are you learning from your pain? Are you learning something that helps you grow and choose "life?" Or are you learning something that holds you back and encourages you to "give up" on yourselves and others?

The second question we need to ask them is: How is suffering changing you for the better? We need to teach young people that there are two ways to approach suffering and loss. One leads to meaning or choosing "life." The other leads to meaninglessness or choosing "death."

Meaningless suffering, as we know, is marked by thinking, "Poor me. Life is unfair. I'm bad. I'm powerless." Instead of accepting suffering, young people try to dump it. They may act out towards others—or towards themselves by using self-destructive behaviors.

Meaningless suffering basically occurs when young people think of themselves as "victims." They're down on life and themselves. Meaningful suffering, though, is marked by growth. It enables young people to move past that "poor me" attitude and recognize that—although things are really tough right now—they have power and the ability to make good choices. They realize their hurts won't last forever, and they accept help from others. When suffering is handled like this, it creates greatness inside them.

REFERENCES

Amato, P.R. & Keith, B. (1991a). Parental divorce and adult well-being: A meta-analysis, *Journal of Marriage and the Family*, 53, 43–58.

Amato, P.R. & Keith, B. (1991b). Parental divorce and adult well-being: A meta-analysis, *Psychological Bulletin*, 110, 26–46.

Andersson, Gunnar. February 2003. *Dissolution of Unions in Europe: A Comparative Overview*. Rostock, Germany: Max Planck Institute for Demographic Research.

Bednar, R. L., & Kaul, T. J. (1978). Experiential group research: Current perspectives. In S. L. Garfield & A. E. Bergin (Eds.), *Handbook of psychotherapy and behavior changes: An empirical analysis* (2nd ed., pp. 769–815). New York: Wiley.

Bednar, R. L., & Kaul, T. J. (1979). Experiential group research: What never happened. *Journal of Applied Behavioral Science*, 11, 311–319.

Bednar, R. L., & Kaul, T. J. (1994). Experiential group research: Can the cannon fire? In A. E. Bergin & S. L. Garfield (Eds.), *Handbook of psychotherapy and behavior change* (pp. 631–663). New York: Wiley.

Bednar, R. L., & Lawlis, F. (1971). Empirical research in group psychotherapy. In A. E. Bergin & S. L. Garfield (Eds.), *Handbook for psychotherapy and behavior change* (pp. 812–838). New York: Wiley.

Center for Disease Control and Prevention (2001). First marriage dissolution, divorce, and remarriage: United States. Bramlett MD, Mosher WD. *Advance Data from vital and health statistics;* no. 323. Hyattsville, Maryland: National Center for Health Statistics. hhttp://www.dcd.gov/nchs/data/ad/ad323.pdf

Chase-Lansdale, P. L., Cherlin, A. J., & Kierman, K. E. (1995). The long-term effects of parental divorce on the mental health of young adults: A developmental perspective. *Child Development*, 66, 1614–1634.

Davis, James A. 1985. General Social Surveys, 1972–1985: Cumulative Codebook. Chicago: National Opinion Research Center. Hetherington, E. M., Bridges, M., & Insabella, G.

M. (1998). What matters? What does not?: Five perspectives on the association between marital transitions and children's adjustment. *American Psychologist,* 53, 167–184.

Hetherington, E. M., & Stanley-Hagan, M. (1999). The adjustment of children with divorced parents: A risk and resiliency perspective. *Journal of Child Psychology and Psychiatry,* 40, 129–140.

Katz, L. F., & Gottman, J. M. (1997). Buffering children from marital conflict and dissolution. *Journal of Clinical Child Psychology,* 26, 157–171.

Kaul, T. J., & Bednar, R. L. (1978). Conceptualizing group research: A preliminary analysis: *Small Group Behavior,* 9, 173–191.

Kaul, T. J., & Bednar, R. L. (1986). Experiential group research: Results, questions, and suggestions. In S. L. Garfield & A. E. Bergin (Eds.), *Handbook for psychotherapy and behavior change* (3rd ed., pp. 671–714). New York: Wiley.

Kurtz, Joseph E., Archbishop. (October 2007) A Response to the Research. Response to the research from the Center for Applied Research in the Apostolate. Washington, D.C.: CARA.cara.georgetown.edu/Response.pdf.

Ramey, C. T., & Ramey, S. L. (1998). Early intervention and early experience. *American Psychologist,* 53, 109–120.

Rodgers, K. Bl, & Rose, H. (2002). Risk and resiliency factors among adolescents who experience marital transitions. *Journal of Marriage and Family,* 64, 1024–1037.

Wallerstein, J. S. (1983). Children of divorce: Stress and developmental tasks. In N. Garmezy & M. Rutter (Eds.), *Stress, Coping and Development in Children* (pp. 265–302). New York: McGraw-Hill.

Wallerstein, J. S., & Lewis, J. (1998). The long-term impact of divorce on children: A first report from a 25-year study. *Family and Conciliation Courts Review,* 36, 368–383.

Wallerstein, J. S. & Blakeslee, S. (2004). *Second Chances: Men, Women and Children a Decade after Divorce.* Boston: Houghton Mifflin.

Yalom, I. D. (1995). *The theory and practice of group psychotherapy* (4th edition). New York: Basic Books.

An Educational Initiative Addressing Children of Divorce in the Church

ANA MARIA ANASTASIADES, M.D.

"The future of humanity passes by way of the family."[1]

This simple yet profound and prophetic statement captures the crucial importance of the family in the continuation of the human species, of human society, and of the human spirit during its sojourn through the history of time. Although humanity all over the world is composed of different cultures, different societies, and different spiritual belief systems, the nuclear family defined as a male husband/father and female wife/mother and their natural and/or adopted children remains the most common basic traditional family unit. The changes in the last 30 years have seen a dramatic increase in divorce, cohabitation without marriage, children born outside of marriage, unnatural contraception, abortion, gender identity confusion, same sex unions, single parenting by choice, either heterosexual or homosexual; to name just a few of the changes. According to the latest European statistics, *Eurostat 2006,* one out of every two marriages ends in divorce, in more than half of Europe, with Spain, United Kingdom, Germany, France, Sweden, Finland, and Denmark, leading the way.[2] Canada, Australia, and New Zealand, and the United States also report rates above or just below the 50% mark. In sheer numbers, divorce in the United States has involved at least 1 million children *each year* since 1973.[3] Children born outside wedlock have risen to more than 50% of all children born in Spain, France, Sweden, Denmark, and Netherlands.[4] Needless to say, these statistics are staggering and very worrisome.

Ana Maria Anastasiades, M.D., is Chief Child Psychiatrist, Diagnostic Center for Child Assessment & Therapy, Nicosia (Republic of Cyprus).

Unfortunately, the consequences of these statistics are far reaching. Recent reports and studies that have followed children of divorce for 25 years[5] and up to 30 years[6] after the fact, have found that many of these individuals continue to suffer in their own lives from the wounds created by the divorce of their parents. Many baptized Catholics leave the Church when they divorce, primarily because they no longer feel welcome, also out of shame, out of not understanding or not knowing how the Church can help them, or not understanding the Church's position on civil divorce, remarriage, or the procedure for seeking an annulment. Unfortunately, the children of these divorced parents also lose touch with the Church and the Sacraments for similar reasons and many abandon practicing their faith and continue to suffer.

> "In perhaps the most poignant finding of the study, of those young adults who were regularly attending a church or synagogue at the time of their parents' divorce, two thirds say that no one—neither from the clergy nor from the congregation—reached out to them during that critical time in their lives, while only one quarter remember either a member of the clergy or a person from the congregation doing so . . .One important study found that Catholic and moderate Protestant children of divorce are more than twice as likely to leave religious practice altogether, and conservative Protestants are more than three times as likely to do so . . .The stricter Catholic theology on divorce can make some Catholic children of divorce feel unwelcome at church. As one young man said, "It seemed pretty clear that if you're from a divorced family, you can't be Catholic anymore." It is not true that Catholic children of divorce can no longer be Catholic, but the misconception is not uncommon."[7]

The pontificate of Pope John Paul II, Servant of God, (1978–2005) saw the rapid dissemination of the culture of death, and the plagues of divorce and abortion in post-modern western societies. It is no coincidence that both of these plagues have reached epidemic proportions at the same time. As early as 1981, he wrote *Familiaris Consortio, The Role of the Christian Family in the Modern World*. In 1994, he delivered *Gratissimam Sane, Letter to Families for the International Year of the Family*. There have been numerous documents and speeches addressing the indissolubility of marriage, the importance of the family in the lives of children and for the good of society; calling the clergy to minister to couples in crisis, to the divorced and remarried, and to the children from previous and current marriages. The recommendations and *Con-*

clusions of the Fifteenth Plenary Assembly of the Pontifical Council for the Family, Rome, October 17–19, 2002 are entirely devoted to addressing the response of the Church to divorced persons, the remarried, and the children of divorce. Pope Benedict XVI has continued the appeal for educating youth in virtues and values, to inspire a search for the meaning of truth in their lives, in order to combat the materialism, relativism, and eroticism present in western culture today that erode relationships and the family, particularly in his recent letter to the Romans on the urgency in education.[8]

Concrete implementation of programs and support groups for divorced adults has been initiated by individual parishes sporadically in many dioceses. However, pastoral outreach to children of divorce has been scarce and mostly referral to local secular community support groups or international secular support groups such as RAINBOWS[9] (USA, CANADA, UK, NZ, and Australia) which is primarily focused on helping children deal with loss, not specifically the divorce of parents.

Given the current state of affairs regarding the reality of divorce in postmodern western societies, and the awareness of the Catholic Church of these facts, the task of this presentation is to describe a multidimensional educational initiative which would enable the members of the Church, clergy, religious and laity, to reach out to children of divorce of all ages. First, we will look at a brief review of the highlights from relevant Church documents addressing the importance of the family, the plague of divorce, the need to minister to the divorced and remarried, especially the children, and present a closer look at the conclusions of the 15th Plenary Assembly of the Pontifical Council for the Family. Then, in order to develop a practical response to the directives of the Church, we will look at a composite child development model from a family systems perspective; and, using this reference tool, which also allows a framework to understand the impact of divorce on children, we can structure, in combination with the directives of the Church, a practical multidimensional educational initiative which can be implemented.

THE CHURCH SPEAKS: RELEVANT CHURCH TEXTS

There have been many references and appeals to address the rapid increase in divorce from the Church, primarily during the pontificate of John Paul II, Servant of God. The critical importance of the family as the "domestic church" and source of nurture and love for raising children has also been extensive. Of particular richness, the following texts are especially illuminating:

John Paul II, *Familiaris Consortio:* "Role of the Christian Family in the Modern World," 1981.

The Holy See, "Charter of the Rights of the Family," 1983.

Pontifical Council for the Family, "From Despair to Hope: the Family and Drug Addiction," 1991.

Pontifical Council for the Family, "The Rights of the Family and Pastoral Care of Families," 1993.

John Paul II, *Gratissimam Sane:* "Letter to Families for the International Year of the Family," 1994.

John Paul II, *Evangelium Vitae:* "The Gospel of Life," 1995.

John Paul II, Address to Pontifical Council for the Family: "Pastoral Care of the Divorced and Remarried," 1997.

Pontifical Council for the Family, "Pastoral Care of the Divorced and Remarried," 1997.

Pontifical Council for the Family, "The Family and Human Rights," 1999.

Pontifical Council for the Family, "Conclusions of the 15th Plenary Assembly of the Pontifical Council for the Family," on the topics of Divorce, Children of Divorce, and Pastoral Action, 2002.

The limits of this presentation prohibit an extensive consideration of each of these documents; however, the presenter will highlight the directives presented in *Familiaris Consortio,* the 1997 address "Pastoral Care of the Divorced and Remarried," and the 2002 "Conclusions of the 15th Plenary Assembly of the Pontifical Council for the Family." The phrases that appear in bold and/or italics are placed by the presenter as keys which will help form and guide the educational initiative.

John Paul II begins *Familiaris Consortio* with the importance of the family, and the need for the Church to understand its role and its situation today. Following are some highlights which are relevant to the call to help all families, especially the divorced:

"The *Church ought to apply herself to understanding* the situations within which marriage and the family are lived today, in order to fulfill her task of serving." (n. 4)

. . .the family is "the first and vital cell of society" (n. 42)

"Thus the *fostering of authentic and mature communion between persons within the family* is the first and irreplaceable school of social life, and example and stimulus for the broader *community relationships marked by respect, justice, dialogue and love* . . .it makes an original contribution in depth to building up the world, by making possible a life that is properly speaking human, in particular by *guarding and transmitting virtues and values"* (n.43).

"The Church's pastoral action must be progressive, also in the sense that it must *follow the family, accompanying it step by step* in the different stages of its formation and development" (n.65).

Referring to priests:

"Their responsibility extends not only to moral and liturgical matters but to personal and social matters as well. They must support the family in its difficulties and sufferings, caring for its members and helping them to see their lives *in the light of the Gospel* . . .*Priests and deacons,* when they have received timely and serious preparation for this apostolate, must unceasingly *act toward families as fathers, brothers, pastors, and teachers,* assisting them with the means of grace and enlightening them with the light of truth" (n. 73).

Concluding:

"Today with the synod, I earnestly call upon pastors and the *whole community of the faithful to help the divorced,* and with solicitous care to make sure that they do not consider themselves as separated from the Church, for as baptized persons they can, and indeed must, share in her life" (n. 84).

"No one is without a family in this world: *the Church is a home and family for everyone* . . .*The future of humanity passes by way of the family"* (n. 86).

Important highlights of the address given by John Paul II on January 24, 1997, to the Pontifical Council for the Family on "Pastoral Care of the Divorced and Remarried":

"The Church cannot be indifferent to this distressing problem, which involves so many of her children . . . .The *Church, mother and teacher,* seeks the welfare and happiness of the home, and when it is broken, for whatever reason, she *suffers and seeks to provide a remedy,* offering these persons pastoral guidance and complete fidelity to Christ's teachings . . .The Church sees their suffering and the serious difficulties in which they live, and in her motherly love *is concerned for them as well as for the children of their previous marriage:* deprived of their birthright to the presence of both parents, they are the first victims of these painful events. It is first of all *urgently necessary* to establish a pastoral *plan* of preparation and of timely *support for couples at the moment of crisis* . . .A very important aspect *concerns* the human and Christian *formation of the children born of the new union* . . .A special demanding but necessary task concerns the other members who belong, more or less closely, to the family. With a closeness that must not be confused with condescension, they should *assist their loved ones, especially the children* who, because of their young age, are even more affected by the consequences of their parents' situation."

The Conclusions of the 15th Plenary Assembly of the Pontifical Council for the Family, 2002, summarize the consequences of divorce on children, and propose a guide of principles by which to develop pastoral care of marriages and also formation of children. This document is of particular relevance and will form the backbone of the educational initiative.

Long term negative effect of divorce:

". . . in the numerous studies dedicated to this topic, many experts emphasize that *divorce upsets* all the family members, profoundly disturbs the *relationship between parents and children in the crucial years* in which the personality is formed, and causes them to lose the symbolic reference points offered by the family environment. The child has to find his bearings in new family relationships which cause him upheaval and suffering. *For the child,* his/her *parents' divorce* will be the *most important and painful event in the years of his growth,* the event that affects him/her most deeply. The consequences of divorce on the child are manifold, profound and permanent. Some will only surface in the long term.

"Therefore it is not surprising to note that *divorce often causes* such phenomena in children as *falling behind at school, the temptation to crime, drug use, personal instability, relational difficulties, fear of commitments, profes-*

sional failure, alienation, as the experts in these matters prove. Statistics also show that the children of divorced couples have greater *difficulties* than others in forming a *stable conjugal relationship* and that *divorce is more frequent among them.* In fact, separation and especially divorce, cause considerable damage to children and mark them for the rest of their life."

Formation for pastoral care of marriages:

"This demands specific pastoral attention, with the involvement of priests and laity. Pastoral care requires a concentration of reflection and formation at the parochial and diocesan levels. Pastoral care will be prepared by a *satisfactory formation of future priests* in the seminary.

Three aspects of this pastoral action can be distinguished:

- *to prevent*
- *to accompany*
- *to reconcile and to start over again.*

This preparation must be *remote, close* to the event and *immediate.* The remote preparation begins in childhood, in the home where the children are born, where they are opened to affection and love, following their parents' example."

Parish formation of the young:

"*In the period between the sacrament of Confirmation and the sacrament of Marriage, in the schedule of youth activities, parishes should organize special catecheses on the themes of commitment in marriage, in the family and for life.*"

"The preparation for marriage of engaged couples must include an increased insistence on the definitive commitment they will be making before God and men. It is on these lines that it will be possible to place an emphasis on the promise to be kept and their responsibility for their own actions. *Psychologists, educators or Christian couples should help young people discover genuine love in themselves, with all that this implies in the way of feeling, attachment, passion and also reason.* By underlining these points, the Church will make her message on responsible parenthood understood and better received. *During this preparation, special formation has to be given to children who come from broken homes.*"

Formation of children from broken homes:

"The emotional upheaval suffered by children of separated couples who suddenly find themselves with a single parent or in a "new" family, poses a challenge for bishops, catechists, teachers and all who are responsible for the young. The number of these children is growing constantly. Despite their capacity for adaptation, the children often suffer and find it difficult to trust others. Educators must help them. It is not a question of replacing their parents but of collaborating with them. It is a matter of enabling their children to express themselves, to rediscover their confidence and to learn forgiveness. This can be done in the context of their family life, of friends' homes, of movements for children and youth, of Christian guidance teams and on the occasion of catechesis."

We will return to these directives after having looked at the developmental model of a child within his family, and developed a framework for understanding the impact of divorce.

IMPACT OF DIVORCE

Part 1: Normal Childhood

To understand the impact of divorce, it is necessary to have a basic understanding of how a child grows and develops within his family, his environment, and the world around him. We will use a composite developmental model, originally used by family systems therapists. First, we will look at the "spheres of influence" in the Domains of Childhood[10], the corresponding ages when these spheres develop with their respective challenges, then use the same model as representing the psychosocial development proposed by Erik Erickson.[11]

In the chart on the following page, Domains of Childhood, each circle represents a "sphere of influence" or domain, and each relates to the other, but not in a continuous or linear fashion, but through levels of inclusion. The innermost sphere represents the child, as he is born to his two married parents[12] with his own genetic uniqueness, constitution, character, and temperament.

The nuclear family, consisting of parents and siblings, is the first to impact the child.

As the child grows, the "sphere of influence" includes the extended family, grandparents, aunts, uncles, cousins. All these relationships interact with the child and influence the growth and development of the child.

The sphere below represents the child within his family interacting with the outside world. This is well underway by the time the child enters primary school, and continues to expand through his secondary school years. Neighbors around his home play a role, involvement in his Church, friendships also become more important. Mores and values in the ceremonies and rituals of family life become more important and become incorporated into the makeup of the child.[13]

At the same time, if a child has health problems, such as diabetes, asthma, or is handicapped in some way, his interaction with the world is affected. If the parents are unemployed, or change employment, which affects where the

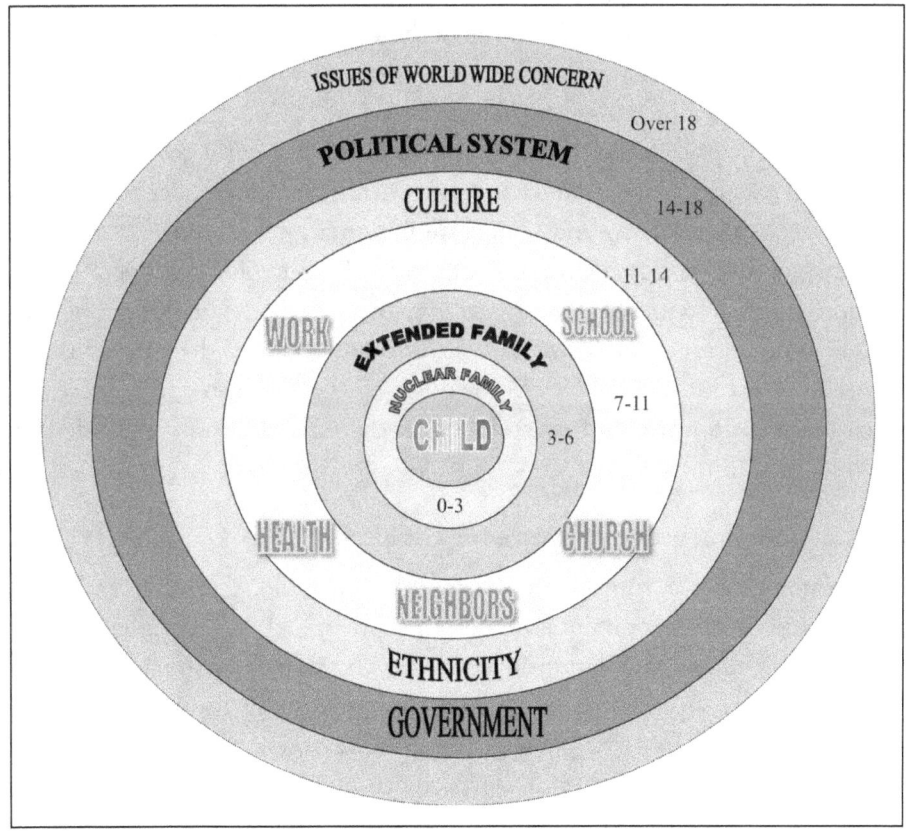

Domains of Childhood

family lives, that too affects the child and is incorporated into his development. As the child approaches adolescence, ages 11–14, the local culture and ethnicity play a larger role; the child builds his self esteem, his sense of belonging.

As puberty unfolds, awareness and interest in the workings of society become more important; the child is interested in how he fits into the world; he looks more to his peers for reference; he has begun to separate from his parents, seeking what he wants to do with his future, his own relationships, and how he will define himself.

Using this simple schematic tool, we can also overlay the psychosocial development proposed by Erikson, the 8 Ages of Man,[14] to this diagram, although we will only cover the first five of the eight ages. The child's first task is to accomplish the development of trust in other persons, being loved, during his first year of life (trust vs. mistrust). Of course, this can only be accomplished by the interaction of the child in a relationship with another person, such as a parent, who will love the child, and provide for his every need. Next, comes the development of boundaries, physical neuromuscular control, "yes and no," language, all reinforced by the nuclear family (autonomy vs. shame and doubt). As the child expands his world to the extended family, increased socialization occurs, and with it, the emergence of self-confidence, competitiveness, and cooperation (initiative vs. guilt). During the primary school years, the child is eager and willing to learn, cooperate with friends, group activities, sports, all the way through to the beginning of adolescence (industry vs. inferiority). Well into adolescence, the teen is asking himself, "Who am I?" "Where do I belong?;" along with this comes increased need for peer approval and over-identification with ideals of peers (identity vs. role diffusion).

Part 2: Consequences of Divorce for Children

Divorce causes a rupture in the world of a child. As we have briefly reviewed in our developmental model, the core of a child's world is his family; and that means his relationship with *both* his parents, and siblings. Normally, the parents provide a loving, and emotionally nurturing environment in which the child learns to be loved, and to love, to trust in relationships, to feel good about himself; to not worry about putting food on the table, or earning money to keep the house running and functioning; to not worry about providing medical care, or resolving differences between his parents.[15]

With divorce, the focus of the intact family is no longer the raising and educating of the child—now marital conflict and separation take center stage. When parents separate and divorce, the "unit" of "parents" no longer exists.[16] They become two separate people, and the child has to redefine and adjust his parent-child relationship to two individuals who are not emotionally or physically available to him, like they were before the divorce. This loss affects children of different ages in different ways. Parental conflict reduces the parent's effectiveness as caretaker and disciplinarian because anxiety, anger, and economic stress render the parent less tolerant and less emotionally present and may also have long-term effects on parenting capacity.[17] The effect of divorce on young children under the age of six carries a heavy burden because of the impact so early in their development.

> Children of primary years should be consolidating their parental attachments, capacities for intimacy, and trust in order to develop social competence . . .Such competence prepares them for school and peer relationships, and eventually for love relationships. Impulses come under self-control, and behavioral consistency develops, if the child feels safely connected to his parents and other family members. Children are never too young to be impacted by divorce and the subsequent decisions about their care. The developmental needs of preschool children are typified by their wish to be cared for and protected by the significant familiar adults who keep their world stable. Ongoing parental conflict destabilizes children and can evolve into significant emotional and behavioral difficulties . . .Children are preoccupied with personal safety, both physical and emotional . . .security of routines, schedules, and kept promises . . .Attention to details and predictability of schedules, transitions, and continuity of caregivers become especially important because of the relatively brief history of a functioning parental coalition.[18]

One recent situation in the presenter's experience as a consultant provides an interesting illustration. Two 7-year-old girls were referred for psychiatric evaluation by the elementary school because of persistent fighting, screaming, and finally aggression, in the classroom. The girls were hitting each other, and throwing their belongings on the floor, being disruptive in class, and alarming and upsetting the other children in the classroom. These two children had begun the school year as friends, but their relationship had deteriorated over the past four months, culminating in physical aggression for the last several days. The writer was called to evaluate the first child, and below, is her drawing of her "family." When she gave the writer the drawing, she apologized, because there were "more people in her family," but she ran out of room to draw them.

Proceeding from the center, in the center is the child herself, and next to her is her older sister. In the next level, is her mother on the left, her father on the right, with his brother, her uncle, next to him. Further out are two aunts on either side, then one cousin on the left, and two more cousins on the right. The last figure on the left is the paternal grandmother with her walking cane. The details in the drawings were advanced for a child of seven, and her concept of her "family" was clearly connected beyond her "nuclear" family. When asked about her relationship regarding the other child in question, this child did not know why the other girl was always "angry" with her. "I was not doing anything, and she would start yelling at me. And when she hit me, I hit her back."

Without seeing the other child in question, the presenter could not conclusively make a recommendation. The "parents" of the second child refused to have their daughter evaluated and the child was removed from the school. It was then revealed that the "parents" had divorced right before school had started, and this little girl, the only child, living with her mother, had moved into this neighborhood to "get away from the father's family." No doubt this little girl was going through her own loss and grieving, perhaps even denial, regarding the situation of her own parents' separation and divorce. Without knowing the details of the second child, it is very interesting to note that the

one piece of information, "getting away from father's family," may have been "The" very reason she was always angry with the first child who always had her family present and involved. No further intervention was needed with the first child; there were no incidents of any irregular behavior or altercations for the rest of the academic year.

When parents divorce, some children feel that their childhood is lost. "The day my parents divorced is the day my childhood ended."[19] The world is newly perceived as a far less reliable, more dangerous place because the closest relationships in their lives can no longer be expected to hold firm. More than anything else, this new anxiety represents the end of childhood.[20]

> Unlike children who lose a parent due to illness, accident, or war, children of divorce lose the template they need because of their parents' failure. Parents who divorce may think of their decision to end the marriage as wise, courageous, and the best remedy for their unhappiness—indeed, it may be so—but for the child the divorce carries one meaning: the parents have failed at one of the central tasks of adulthood. Together and separately, they failed to maintain the marriage. Even if the young person decides as an adult that the divorce was necessary, that in fact the parents had little in common to begin with, the divorce represents failure . . .this failure in turn shapes the child's inner template of self and family. If they failed, I can fail, too. And if, as happens so frequently, the child observes more failed relationships in the years after divorce, the conclusion is simple. I have never seen a man and a woman together on the same beam. Failure is inevitable.[21]

Children of divorce have significantly more adjustment and achievement problems; more difficulties with social relationships and authority figures; problematic relationships with mothers and fathers; lower academic achievement; more aggressive, impulsive, behavior; more likely to engage in antisocial behaviors; more likely to use alcohol, cigarettes, marijuana, and engage in promiscuity.[22] Depression in adolescents is associated with a variety of environmental stressors, including divorce, marital conflict, poor quality of relationships with parents, personally stressful life events and negative peer and social relationships.[23]

> Young adults whose parents divorced during childhood, compared with never divorced children, have more pregnancies outside of marriage, earli-

er marriages (a risk factor for later divorce), poorer marital relationships, increased propensity to divorce, and poorer socioeconomic attainment. Parent-child relationships also appear quite vulnerable, in that adult children of divorce show less affection for their parents, have less contact with them, and engage in fewer intergenerational exchanges of assistance compared with never divorced adult children.[24]

Another illustrative situation is that of the following family. The presenter was asked to evaluate a 17-year-old young man referred by the high school because the teen had become withdrawn over the last couple of months, not turning in his homework, failing several classes, and found to be irritable and easily angered, particularly during soccer practice. The previous academic year he had done well, considered to be bright by his teachers, and talked about going to college and pursuing a business career. He did not have any medical problems, and was not involved with illicit drug or alcohol use. The mother, the young man, and his three siblings came for the evaluation. The father could not come because he was away on a business trip. The young man is the oldest, at 17, the next son is 12, the next child is a daughter, age 8, and there is another daughter age 5. At the time of the consultation, there were no reported problems with the other three children, nor had there been any problems reported or expressed in the past. The parents had divorced when the son was 15 and the father married another woman the week after the divorce was final, and had the sons take part in the religious service. The father and his new wife bought a house one block away from the mother, and continued to see all four children regularly, sometimes even twice weekly.

Each child was asked to draw a picture of his family. Following are the drawings; the black line which is visible in the middle of the pages is due to an artifact of the scanner. The first drawing is that of the young man. We will look at all of them before arriving at some conclusions.

Starting from the far right and going from right to left is the mother, the 17-year-old himself, then his younger brother, and the two sisters, in succeeding age order. Notice that the figures are large, the largest being himself, standing next to his mother. There is very little detail in the drawing. The only figure with a smile is the littlest sister. All the children are dressed the same. The facial expressions appear to be those of bewilderment. Notice that neither the mother nor the two brothers have hands. And the sisters have only one hand each. There is no father in this picture; if you did not know

An Educational Initiative Addressing Children of Divorce in the Church

that the person drawing the picture did not put a "father" in the drawing, you would easily assume the figure next to the mother, is the father. He may indeed be playing a role very similar to the role his father played before the divorce, "parentification."[25] Let us look at the other pictures.

The drawing by the younger brother, the 12 year old, is shown next. He is the one smiling with the orange shirt on the left. The mother is the first figure on the right.

The two sisters are the figures with the pink shirts, and the last figure standing behind the mother and the 9 year old sister is the older brother. There is no father in this picture. The figures are small for the size of the paper. The details of the drawings include hands, fingers,

feet, and colored clothing. Notice that the older brother has no smile, no color to his shirt, and his hands are behind the mother and the sister.

Next is the drawing of the 9 year old sister.

This drawing shows the daughter in the center with the black hair, the mother above her, with the two brothers on either side and below the mother. The littlest sister is on the right of the 12 year old brother. The details of the drawing are appropriate for a 9-year-old except for the arms and hands. Notice that the mother has her arms crossed, without hands, just two black lines; the oldest brother has his arm lines going to his pocket; the 12 year old brother has one arm line extended as does the daughter herself, and her other arm line is in her pocket. All figures have smiles. Of particular interest is the curling blue coils which surround and envelop the group. Again, there is no father in this picture.

The drawing on the following page is by the youngest, the 5 year old, and it's truly an interesting drawing.

The 5 year old has not only drawn her family, but has named each one of them, and a new person has been added, the mother's boyfriend; he teaches athletics in a high school, therefore the nick name "coach." The littlest figure is the 5 year old, Angela.

Notice that her head is even with everyone else in the "family" and her name is above, everyone else's is below. Being young or little is no obstacle to thinking you are just as important as everyone else! Standing next to her is her oldest brother, the 17 year old, Will. Next to him going towards the right is the mother, mama. Next to the mother is the older sister, Teresa. The

following figure is the boyfriend, "coach," who is next to the 12-year-old brother, Philip, who is last on the right. Details in this picture are advanced for her age; notice arms, fingers for everyone; colored clothing, feet, noses, and smiles. Again, there is no father in this picture.

Needless to say, there are many factors contributing to the young man's difficulties. If we look back on page 115 at the "Domains of Childhood" we can see that at 17, this young man is at a developmental stage where he is very cognizant of the greater involvement of the political and governmental systems in society. Also, as we have mentioned before, at the same time in Erikson's psychosocial ages, at 17, this young man is looking to form his identity, who he wants himself to be and his aspirations for his life. There are conflicts in his world and incongruities that he is trying to sort out, and they are preoccupying his time. The relationship with his father, is nothing like what he would have wanted; represented by his absence in the picture. His own position next to his mother, has taken the place of his father; a burden for which he needs a large chest and back to carry. The lack of hands in two of the drawings is significant. To the young man, it's as if he feels incapable of doing anything; he has no hands. That feeling is also considered to be expressed by his brother and his mother. It is also interesting, that the younger brother, who went to great lengths to draw hands on everyone, put his troubled older brother in such a position as to not have hands; either sensing his brother's frustration, or willfully pushing him out of the circle of the other members of the family. The 9-year-old sister also drew figures without hands, and her mother's arms crossed. Another interesting element in the drawing are the blue curling circles enveloping the family group—like a tension coil filled with anxiety, locking them in, or the world out. In her domain of development, the most significant milestone is connecting with the world outside home; her school, friends, church. According to Erikson, the age of industry vs. inferiority, where she is beginning to be less involved with her family and moving out; it seems that she is trapped in or by her family circle, keeping the world at bay. The youngest child, the 5-year-old, in her world of socialization and incorporating the extended members of the family, has extended her world to include the new boyfriend, but, again, very troubling is the absence of her father whom she regularly sees. Remarkable too, in this the age of development where she is learning self-confidence, and competitiveness, she draws herself "up there" with everyone else in her family world, equal to them even though she knows she is physically smaller than they are.

It is remarkable that these children see their father weekly, sometimes twice weekly, and none of them included him in their drawing of their family. They each drew their pictures independently at separate locations and even so, none them put their father in. This supports the evidence in the psychiatric literature indicating "that no direct relationship exists between the amount of time a child spends with the less seen parent and the child's adjustment, a finding echoed in the joint-custody literature."[26]

> Father contact is linked to child adjustment when the quality of the relationship between parent and child, rather than the quantity of time spent together, is examined. More likely than not, greater amount of time spent together translates into increased involvement in the child's activities, a greater sense of the child as a person, and consequently, a warmer parent-child relationship. Some children report very positive feelings about parents with whom they spend relatively little time . . .The critical determinant clinically is whether they feel known, loved, and fundamentally important to the parent's emotional life.[27]

The previous vignette represents one of many stories of children adjusting to the divorce of their parents. The art work provides clues into the world of the children from their own point of view. These are only a beginning, a point in time in which to start trying to understand how a particular child lost his way on the journey towards acquiring the skills and development needed to become a confident, independent and loving adult.

The impact of divorce on children is extensive and varied. Each age carries its own wounds and burdens. As the child matures to the next sphere of development, he must re-integrate the traumas, wounds and gaps from the past in the light of the new skills or insights that he has acquired. Unfortunately, this process also brings with it internal imbalance and disturbance.

There are effects of divorce that children of all ages experience, even though their behavior and reaction to these effects are age-dependent. All children experience a sense of "loss," anger, sadness, grief. Some children blame themselves for their parents' divorce; others deny that their lives have changed or that their relationship will change with their nonresident parent. They experience a loss of self esteem, shame, guilt, rejection by family, parents, and grandparents. Children who come from a faith-based background can feel rejected by God, abandoned in their time of need.[28] Members of the clergy don't reach out to these children, or their divorced parents, so they do not feel welcomed and stop practicing their faith.[29]

Other unfortunate consequences are the effects on children, after the divorce of their parents, of having to manage the new boyfriends and girlfriends of their parents. Remarriage brings a new configuration to the family; new siblings may also be included. There is a period of adjustment in remarried families that can last for several years. More than half of second marriages also end in divorce–another major trauma for the children.

AN EDUCATIONAL INITIATIVE

Webster's International Dictionary defines the word "educate":

—from Latin: *educere,* which means "lead forth, lead out;" to provide or assist in providing knowledge of wisdom, desirable qualities of mind or character, moral balance, or good physical health or general competence.

In order to *lead* someone, besides knowing where you are going, you have to *"accompany"* the person as well. So, in reality, "to educate" means to accompany someone, leading him forth towards the truth. Therefore, an "educator" accompanies a person, walks with him, leading him towards truth, and in doing so, gives of himself, begetting a mutual exchange between him and the one who walks with him towards the truth. As Christians, we do this with an attitude of charity, hope and faith.

Let us return to the directives of the Church presented in the first section. We can summarize them in nine directives:

1. The Church must be progressive. "It must follow the family, *accompanying it step by step* in the different stages of its formation and development."

2. Between Confirmation and Marriage, in the schedule of youth activities, parishes should organize special catecheses.

3. The Church should assist with "fostering authentic and mature communion between persons within the family, relationships marked by respect, justice, dialogue and love . . . in particular by guarding and transmitting virtues and values."

4. Priests' responsibilities include "satisfactory formation received timely; they must unceasingly act toward families as fathers, brothers, pastors, and teachers, assisting them with the means of grace and enlightening them with the light of truth."

5. Help the divorced and remarried to feel and consider themselves part of the Church; assist their loved ones, especially the children.

6. Provide timely support for couples in crisis.

7. During marriage preparation, special formation has to be given to children who come from broken homes.

8. Collaborate with parents; children need to express themselves, rediscover their confidence and learn forgiveness; use friends' homes, movements for children and youth, Christian guidance teams, and even the occasion of catechesis.

9. Three aspects of this pastoral action can be distinguished:
   - *to prevent*
   - *to accompany*
   - *to reconcile and to start over again.*

This preparation must be *remote, close* to the event and *immediate.*

In formulating a "how to" response to these directives, keeping in mind our definition of "educate," we find that the most significant common denominator is "to accompany;" the members of the Church must be present, accompany and lead forth, walking towards healing and Truth, in charity, hope and faith. The Church, as Mater et Magistra, must truly "educate."

We can group the directives into three categories:

1. Formation of the clergy, religious, and laity

2. "To accompany" the children of divorce;

3. "To accompany, to prevent" the occurrence of divorce.

Part 1: Formation of Clergy, Religious and Laity

In order for the priests, religious and laity to be able to *"accompany,"* educate and lead, they themselves need education regarding the impact of divorce on children, and what they as religious members of the Church can do to help them. They also need to have a basic understanding of human development and the importance of the family to that development which includes the physical, emotional, cognitive, behavioral, moral and spiritual. The Apostolic Constitution of the Institute for Studies on Marriage and Family founded by John Paul II in 1981 states the purpose:

> . . . This is done so that the truth of marriage and the family may be given ever closer attention and study and so that lay people, religious and priests can receive scholarly formation in the study of marriage and the family both in a philosophical-theological way and from the point of view of the human sciences. . .[30]

Formation can be expanded in the Institutes to include teaching a multi-dimensional approach to child development, and also the consequent impact of divorce for these children, their siblings, and their child-parent relationships. Understanding of the family life cycle, as it pertains to normal families, divorced families, remarried and step families, and unfortunately, re-divorced families is necessary for persons who will work in family ministry for the divorced and remarried, and children of divorce. As we continue to look at the educative initiative, we will see an expanding role for the parish and the pastor in this regard.

Part 2: To Accompany: Practical Considerations

2.1. Reaching Out in Individual Situations

In order for the Church to reach out to these children of divorce, it is necessary to have programs, and projects, led by individuals who understand the developmental life of a child, and how that has been impacted, interrupted, derailed, or blocked, by the consequences of his parents' divorce. These individuals can include a priest or religious person, and of course, laity. Recalling our "domains of childhood" spheres, and the center being the child, followed by his nuclear family, extended family, etc., it is interesting to note that the social doctrine of the Church of "subsidiarity" can also be represented by the same diagram.[31] The service and helping of families should be delivered by those closest to the families in order to preserve the integrity and dignity of the individuals and thus, local parishes should work directly with the families and be places of welcome to help children of divorce. The principle of "solidarity" with these broken families can also be applied.[32] These situations need to be carefully decided upon on a case by case basis, and the parish priest/pastor would oversee this decision.

There can be a parish team of loving adults, including mental health, and legal professionals which can assist the parish priest in supporting these children, and also keep communication open with both parents if possible, and even the grandparents. If grandparents live in the vicinity, and they are willing and interested, they can be a tremendous asset to the children of divorced parents. Of course, the matter of being in cooperation with the custodial parent is paramount, but enlisting the grandparent to help with caretaking when the parent is necessarily not able to be present provides a continuity of known persons to the child, especially younger ones who very much depend on and need trusting, reliable and consistently dependable relationships. The child needs to be connected more than ever, not to be alone with the burden of his sadness, anger, disappointment, and a parent who is not emotionally available to him. Depending on the configuration of the parish team which could help these divorced families, a "solidarity of spirit," a gentle presence of compassionate faith, can also be of comfort and support to these parents and children.

Mentoring programs in the parish can be of enormous help to children of divorce. A "Big Brother" or a "Big Sister" program which pairs up an older child of divorce with a younger one from the same parish, helps both children in their development. The older child has "been there and done that," has continued to progress in his healing, while the younger child has barely begun his walk towards healing and peace. Together, through their interaction, walking together in charity, hope and faith, they can help each other, and the formation of the relationship is another support for each of them.

When a group or individuals from a parish, or the parish priest personally minister to a divorced parent, it is important for these persons to have in mind the concept of suffering and loss that the divorced parent and his children are experiencing. By this same token, it is equally important to be aware of when this suffering reaches the point of needing professional psychological or psychiatric help. Depression in the parent and/or child is one such situation. The parent may be withdrawn, down, uninterested in tending to the child, unable to work, have appetite disturbances, not able to sleep, feeling helpless, hopeless and/or worthless. Any person, who persistently remains in this kind of a state for more than 3–4 weeks, needs the attention of a psychiatrist, psychologist, or both.

In children, depression may manifest in different ways. Seriously depressed youngsters experience disturbing symptoms beyond the range of normal sadness; the child may become withdrawn, complain of headaches, stomachaches, or other physical problems; he may become anxious, particularly when separating from his parent, refusing to go to school. The child can also behave aggressively, become fearful, withdraw from family and friends, become moody, not interested in friends, have difficulty concentrating at school, refusing to do school work.[33] Feelings of worthlessness, anger or guilt may lead to suicidal thoughts or ruminations about death. Any combination of these behaviors or symptoms should alert the parishioner and/or priest to advise the parent that the child may need professional help.

Older children, teenagers can also be in need of professional help. Warning signs include feelings of helplessness, hopelessness, and worthlessness; being uncharacteristically listless or dull; withdrawing from friends; loss of appetite; looking dirty and disheveled, not bathing or taking care of his hygiene; refusing to talk to people, moodiness, aggressive behavior, loss of interest in school, inability to concentrate, excessive sleeping; drinking alcohol or doing drugs to "numb" himself; self-injurious behavior; suicidal thinking and/or planning.[34] Teenagers from divorced parents, and teenagers in high conflict marriages, or high conflict litigation, have an increased incidence of attempting and committing suicide.[35] Again, the parishioners working with, or helping adolescents showing these behaviors, need to alert the parents of these teens to the possibility of needing professional help. Financial difficulty may be involved, or a parent in denial of any problems with his adolescent may also complicate the referral. If at any time, the parishioner believes that the adolescent is in danger of hurting himself or someone else, he should immediately call for help. These are more difficult situations, and proceeding with parental knowledge and consent whenever possible is advisable and preferable.

Some other problems that may be encountered which also need professional intervention and interaction with other agencies, involve truancy, mental illness of the child or the parent, and serious medical illness.

Substance abuse and drug abuse are additional problems which need professional attention. Alcohol, illicit drug use, prescription drug abuse, can involve the divorced parent or his child. Parental violence, physical abuse or sexual abuse of the other parent or child or children, needs immediate professional attention for all parties involved. Interventions with other systems, such as law enforcement, may be necessary to physically protect a child, children, or a spouse. Safety is a paramount issue, and must be provided first, before any further intervention can take place. Promiscuity and teenage pregnancy also can become a difficult problem requiring further referral to professional services.[36] Any parishioner who is involved with reaching out to children of divorce and their parents needs to be aware of these problems.

2.2. Reaching Out in Group Situations

Helping children of divorce with group work is of great benefit to these children from different perspectives. Let us look at the different types of group work that can be used or provided in the parish community.

Support Groups. These types of groups can address a variety of goals. They do not need professional therapists, and can be run by caring, educated laity or led by the parish priest or deacon. The purpose of this kind of group is to provide a safe forum for different children to come together and share their experiences in the effort to encourage and support other children in the same or similar situation. Role modeling of appropriate communication, affirmation, listening, and empathizing can be demonstrated by the group leaders. This gives children time away from school and parents, to express themselves without worrying about the reaction of their parents. This is especially true of younger children, who frequently feel that they are in some way to blame for the divorce of their parents.[37] Many children do not want to say that they feel bad or sad because they don't want the parent feeling worse than he/she already does.[38] Elementary school children are often concerned about continuing to have friends, and participating in extracurricular activities which may have been curtailed because of the divorce. The experience of traveling back and forth between the homes of the two parents is also a topic which the children learn not to discuss with either parent; these support groups help very much to open the door for the child to see that he is not alone, and that other children experience similar conflicts. Saying "hello" to one parent always means saying "goodbye" to the other parent, and this too is painful.[39] The experience of being caught between loyalties to each parent and being put "in the middle" when one parent verbally berates the other parent through the child is a painful and confusing one. The group leaders can facilitate other children in the same group sharing their experience and in that way each child does not feel alone with his worries in his own world. These groups can be divided developmentally, in age groups, and should not be larger than 8 to 10 children. They can meet weekly for an hour, and can run for 6–8 weeks, and then begin again. It is up to the parish to decide if the group can be "open" or "closed." If it is open, a new child can join the group at any time; if it is closed, a new child can join the group only when the cycle is finished, and a new one begins.

Play is a very important developmental need for children. Groups which allow children time to "play," either freely or in an organized manner, help the child in his internal processing. In the preschool years their play is characterized by an increasingly sophisticated ability to think, imagine, and pretend. Children express their fantasies and wishes in their play; they also practice socialization, learn to respect others, take turns, resolve conflicts, play by the rules. During play they express themselves, they rehearse their "solutions" to their present problems or disturbing thoughts; they retreat into a world where they control the outcomes, repeating scenarios over and over again.

> Play is a critical aspect of a child's social and moral development. It forms the basis of learning where you fit into the world of equals, how to share and when not to share, when to put up your dukes and when to run. These are all things that grown-ups can't teach. You have to learn them yourself. Unstructured play—where children build forts or tree houses to keep out the adults—is especially important. It enables a child to take a step toward independence and into the world of peers. It's the basis for honing leader-

ship skills, for learning not to cry, not to run home to Mommy, but to trust yourself. It's climbing a tree by yourself and learning how to test the branch before you put your foot on it. Imaginative play is the basis for creativity and fantasy life.[40]

By the time children are in elementary school, their play is more organized, competitive, with elaborate rules, and they learn to practice, delay gratification, and plan ahead. Play allows children to understand human interaction and the roles and responsibilities of the individual and group in society.[41]

Skill building groups. Leading and conducting these groups require some training of the group leaders. Children of divorce can use and be helped by learning skills which improve their communication and listening; skills which teach conflict resolution with role playing and problem solving. Appropriate modeling, practicing and giving feedback are very important for these children, particularly because of the marital conflict that they have experienced. Children are sensitive to the unverbalized resentments and frustrations of their parents. Their feeling of being a burden upon their parents decreases their feelings of self-worth. Children's self-esteem can be enhanced through opportunities to gain competence, particularly in areas of everyday living and also in developing positive social skills. Another important skill is learning stress management at the child level; children living with stressed parents become stressed themselves, and coping skills to deal with stress can help. Various tools can be used with children, such as drawing, drama, role playing, games, and team oriented work.

It is important to emphasize that parents, even though divorced, continue to play a very large and important role in their children's lives whether they are physically present or not. Building skills for cooperation enhancement and effective communication can only help and improve their parent-child relationship and in return, help the continued development of their children. Divorced fathers in particular can benefit very much by learning parenting skills to improve their relationship with their children.

Another application of skills building which also impacts children of divorce, are parenting skills in a family with stepparents and stepsiblings. The boundaries are very different in step families, and children naturally resist the imposition of the new stepparent in their life, and in the life of their biological parent.[42] Children are afraid of "losing" their parent to the new spouse, or losing the parent's love which must now be shared with new, rival, siblings. Helping this group of remarried parents can only help the adjustment of their children.

Group Therapy for Children. Group therapy for children requires professional psychologists, counselors, and therapists. In a parish setting, this would have to be arranged by the professional in conjunction with the organizing or requesting group of the parish. Usually these types of groups are conducted in centers for mental health services, universities, or even public schools.

Part 3: To Accompany, to Prevent: Practical Considerations

In *Familiaris Consortio,* John Paul II, Servant of God, said "the Church's pastoral action must be progressive, also in the sense that it must follow the family, accompanying it step by step" (n. 65). The Church has seven sacraments, five of which most Catholics receive before they are 30 years old—Baptism, Holy Eucharist, Reconciliation, Confirmation, and Matrimony. The Pontifical Council for the Family in its "Conclusions of the 15th Plenary Assembly" recommends: "In the period between the sacrament of Confirmation and the sacrament of Marriage, in the schedule of youth activities, parishes should organize special catecheses on the themes of commitment in marriage, in the family and for life." Why stop there? Why not "expand the connections" to all the Sacraments? The development of a child begins with his birth and continues through to his early adulthood; late teens for some, and early twenties for others. The Church can very well *accompany the family step by step* by expanding its connections to the sacraments, and include the "in-between" the sacraments to remain "connected" to the family. Let us look at some "practical considerations" as to how this can be done.

EXPANDING THE CONNECTIONS TO THE SACRAMENTS

Baptism

From the moment a family comes into the Church to baptize their first child, the Church community must continue to be in "active" contact with these new young families. There are several ways this can be done. One easy and interesting activity is for the parish to offer parenting classes for new parents, including basic child development, what to expect in the first year of the life of their child. Most new parents are eager to learn how to be the best of parents, and so are willing to listen and talk to others. Another very important activity that can take place is for the parish to match up new parents with parent couples who are further along in their family life, maybe have a second child already, or their first is 4–5 years old. This couple can "mentor" the new parents, not only for the sake of managing and learning about parenting, but moreover to "learn by example" how to keep their "marriage," their spousal relationship alive and well and loving under the stress of having a new baby and the change in their lives which this brings.

Along these lines, there can be a parish group for "new mothers," a support group where new mothers come together with some older mothers to share and talk about their experiences and help one another. The older teens of the parish can offer "child care" during these meetings, so that the mothers can participate without worrying or needing to arrange babysitting. Also, what would be very helpful is a "new father's" group. Men need to feel like men, want to be loving and caring fathers and husbands. A support group with new fathers and some older fathers would be of tremendous help. Another group which can be a great resource for new families is grandparents. Of course the new families have their own extended families, but because of the mobility of people due to jobs and opportunities, they may be far away from their natural grandparents. The parish can pair up the new families who are physically far from their grandparents with someone in the parish who may be a widow or widower, or live far away from their own grandchildren. The baby boomers are in their 50's and 60's, and many are still active; they can be a tremendous resource.

The point of all this outreach and connecting is "accompanying the family step-by-step" in reality, and spiritually, and socially. The parish is a living, breathing, active community. It is a family, part of the family of the Church. Making these connections with other people in the parish extends relationships, and it's by these Christian relationships and friendships which evolve that people remain connected.

Holy Eucharist, Reconciliation

By the time the new baby becomes old enough to go to school, the new family may already have a second child. The parish community has supported the new family and they have formed a connection with the parish and its priests, and through them, the family of the Church. Now the child moves into another sphere of influence, the school setting. The child interacts with more children; if he is not in a Catholic school, he meets other children who do not share the same faith. This makes things more difficult for the child because this is the age of becoming aware of "conscience" of learning good and bad, right and wrong; he has learned empathy, how to put himself in someone else's shoes.[43] This is also the time for parents to be pointing out by example and by word, virtues and values. The parish can offer a seminar for parents on how to teach Christian virtues and values. The same can be done for children, prior to their preparation for these two Sacraments.

Since this is the time in development when children themselves branch out and begin to develop friendships in school, with neighbors, within the parish community (Domains of Childhood), and learning about the world around them, (industry vs. inferiority [Erikson]), this is a good time to start the children involved in group activities such as youth groups, hiking and outdoor projects; exploring parks, environmental projects which benefit the community. Community service should begin at this time too, such as visiting the sick in the hospital, old persons who are shut-ins, helping out with charity work. Doing these things within the parish community reinforces the value of the "corporal works of mercy." Children learn cooperation, respect for others, companionship, the value of rules, the satisfaction of accomplishing something that will help someone else. These things can be included along with the regular catecheses for these two Sacraments and continue until they begin formation for the next sacrament.

Confirmation

Developmentally, these children are entering puberty, and beginning adolescence, the sphere of influence where culture, ethnicity, rituals and ceremonies are important. Friendships too gain more priority. Certainly, as their own bodies are changing, this is an excellent time to begin teaching about Christian sexuality. The parish priest and/or pastor can have a meeting with parents of those children preparing for Confirmation, and discuss with them how they wish to proceed. In following the principle of "subsidiarity," as mentioned before, this is best done with those closest to the children, which are the parents. Relationships, peers, and discipline need to be discussed from a Christian perspective of virtues and values. Faith formation continues in group activities such as social skills building; role playing; how to handle peer pressure; how to resolve conflicts. Youth group activities such as team sports and learning good Christian sportsmanship are valuable. More outdoor hiking with members from the parish, especially the priest, helps form bonds informally and creates an atmosphere open to sharing and contemplating, even prayer. Karol Wojtyla was an advocate of outdoor exploring with young people. Community service should also be expanded, with more involvement, and perhaps even leading younger children in activities.

Parents with children in this age group should also be supported by older parents, stay in contact with them, listen and learn from them how to deal with teens in terms of: supervision, friends, privileges, and sibling rivalry. The parish can continue to offer seminars; the priest can also be more involved as a role model and guide in this education.

From Confirmation to Matrimony

These are critical years to "accompany the family step-by-step" and to accompany the teens. The secondary school years need continued formation, leadership, mentoring and practical experiences with other youth who live their faith. This period of time can continue well into the late teens and early twenties. Peer support is extremely important as parental influence begins to recede as part of normal development. Issues of respect for life, for individuals, differences, conflict resolution, political and governmental responsibility need discussions in the light of faith and leadership. Mentoring is a valuable tool. The parish can arrange for older teens to take up mentoring younger teens in group activities. A "big brother" and "big sister" program can connect the older teen with the younger teen, and offer a new friendship which is based on respect, faith, and helping each other. Judith Wallerstein, a 30 year veteran of research on children of divorce writes:

> But when so many people have never seen a good marriage, we have a moral obligation to try to intervene *preventatively* . . . In my opinion, a better time to begin helping these youngsters is during mid-adolescence, when attitudes toward oneself and relationships with the opposite sex are beginning to gel. Adolescence is the time when worries about sex, love, betrayal, and morality take center stage. Education for and about relationships should begin at that time, since if we do it right, we'll have their full attention . . . Churches and synagogues and social agencies might provide a launching place . . . As an opening gambit, "how do you choose a friend?"

A group of teenagers considering this problem could be drawn to the important question of how to choose a lover and a life partner—and even more important, how not to choose one.44

Robert Coles, Pulitzer Prize winner, child psychiatrist, Harvard Medical School professor, and lifetime observer, researcher, and listener of children writes:

> Teenagers are looking for something to believe in, that's what is going on. When they become cynical and fault-finding, that tells you something. They've got a conscience working inside them—or they wouldn't have the slightest interest in finding fault with anyone, anywhere!. . . They seek, a kind of moral companionship from an adult or two, be it a parent, teacher, a relative, a friend's kin–whomever they can find who is ready to "level" with them. . .45

Pope Benedict XVI, on the occasion of speaking to the Roman clergy in February of 2007 answered the following in response to a question asked by a priest:

> The youth must truly be a priority in our pastoral work, because they live in a world so far removed from God. [...] Young people are in great need of accompaniment to be able to find this road. I am able to say—even though I live far enough away from them that I am not in a position to offer any concrete ways to do so—that the key truly seems to me to be, over and above all else, accompaniment. They must see that it is possible to live their faith in these times, that it is not something that belongs only to the past, but also to the present, that it is possible to lead a Christian life and thereby find the good.

The Holy Father spoke about the priority of accompanying youth as a way to help them along the path of faith. They need this companionship to see and understand that walking in faith can indeed be done.

In the area of Christian sexuality and respect for life, at all ages, it is critical to offer examples and mentoring during this time. Particularly it is the relationships that these young people forge with those who lead them forth towards truth that will keep them on the path of faith. Continuing more community service as part of mentoring is important, such as Habitat for Humanity, which is more of a commitment from the young person, but a very valuable experience.

In accompanying the family, step by step, prayer is of greatest importance.

If it is true that many families have given up prayer, it is also true and encouraging that many others have freshly taken up the habit of praying for their future and for the future marriages of their children, putting everything in the hands of the Lord of the Covenant. Indeed, as the Holy Father recalls, "the family that prays together stays together" (*Rosarium Virginis Mariae*, n. 41).

Matrimony

The preparation for the Sacrament of Matrimony is vital as well as critical.

Current preparation for marriage is quite extensive in some parishes, and not so involved in others. A real education in the theology of the body, understanding the commitment of marriage, for the family and for life is sorely needed. Special education should be given to young people coming from divorced families.

> It's in adulthood that children of divorce suffer the most. The impact of divorce hits them most cruelly as they go in search of love, sexual intimacy and commitment. Their lack of inner images of a man and a woman in a stable relationship and their memories of their parents' failure to sustain the marriage badly hobbles their search, leading them to heartbreak and even despair.[47]

A carefully planned education for adult children of divorce needs to be a part of the pre-marriage preparation.

Another valid and useful tool for young newlyweds is a "mentoring couple." This approach has been implemented in different ways in the United States and also in Australia. A Protestant group "Marriage Savers" has implemented a program to protect, preserve, and promote marriage. They, together with ministers, train mentor couples to be of support, example, witness, and friendship to couples preparing for marriage and throughout the marriage. One Catholic diocese in Evansville, Indiana, adopted the program for its diocese in 1997, and in the years from 2003–2005, the filings for divorce in their diocese dropped 20 percent. At the same time, the rate of marriages went up 16 percent.[48] In Australia, the Pastoral and Matrimonial Renewal Center has a program called "Embrace" which has three different setups with mentoring couples for engaged couples to do their pre-marriage preparation.[49] The program was started by one of the leaders of World Wide Marriage Encounter, Father Charles Gallagher, S.J.[50] This program is also under development in the UK, and available under the title "Preparing to Live in Love" in parts of the United States, including areas of Pennsylvania, New Jersey, New York, Michigan, Indiana, and Hawaii.

> "Preparing to Live in Love" is an extraordinarily effective sacramental preparation program that offers a practical application of John Paul II's Theology of the Body presented through the witness of a young couple who is intentionally trying to live out the sacrament of matrimony with an attitude of other-centered generosity. The course is powerfully experiential and teaches practical skills in the ideal adult learning setting, one couple working with one couple, in the home.[51]

As part of the expansion of connections to the sacraments, accompanying the family step-by-step also means when families are in trouble, and that includes couples in crisis. John Paul II, Servant of God, in his address to the Pontifical Council for the Family on January 24, 1997, said: "It is first of all urgently necessary to establish a pastoral plan of preparation and of timely support for couples at the moment of crisis."

Practical considerations involve persons who can help the couples who are having difficulty. If there have been mentoring families along the way with this couple, those persons can intervene. If that is not the case, the priest can talk to the couple, listen, and decide what or who in the parish can reach out to them besides himself. Counseling, conflict resolution, even Marriage Encounter[52] may help the couple. The necessary point is to "not abandon" them, even, in the worst case, when they seek a separation; the connections in the parish should continue to be present to them, in action and prayer. If the couple or the individuals move away from the parish, the priest should contact a parish in their new neighborhood and have them "connect" with someone there who can continue to help them.

CONCLUSION

The Church has spoken, calling her members to respond urgently to the present pain of her children who are suffering from the rupture of their families. In order to respond to the call, we need a multidimensional approach. We need to understand the role of the family in the life of a child. The

Domains of Childhood provide a schema, another tool, to put into perspective normal child development over time; the milestones that are attained as the child passes from one age to another; the formation of character, morality, and social awareness that every child needs to experience in order to know himself; the relationships that help him to know himself, so that he can make a gift of himself to others, in friendship, love, and respect. With this background, we can then appreciate the wounds caused by the loss of the integral parental unit in the world of the child.

> These children face risk factors in their development, including the likelihood of living below the poverty level, greater potential for developing attachment disorders in early childhood, and manifesting clinical symptoms such as antisocial behavior and school dropout in adolescence. As these data further indicate, they have many fears, and they often doubt even now whether their parents will marry again, and by identification, whether they will marry when grown. Yet they also often have a sophisticated understanding of the differences in their parents' capacities to parent or function well emotionally.[53]

> Much research has been done, but the general conclusion seems to be that divorce does not have consistent effects across the board for all children at all ages. Older children may have the ability to be more sensitive to family conflict and, therefore feel more pressure to intervene between their parents. That is the downside, but on the other hand, they are beginning to develop more emotional resources and refined skills at this time in their lives to help them cope. The younger the child, the less risk they run of being able to intervene in conflicts between their parents, but it is clear they have fewer cognitive resources to make sense of the events and emotions that they are witnessing and experiencing, also creating risk to the child. Children of all ages seem to experience a sense of loss and shame, denial and profound sadness, self-blame, and powerlessness . . . .it is clear, after reviewing many of the major studies, that how a specific child will deal with divorce entails understanding that child's strengths and weaknesses and the demands of the individual situation.[54]

We need a multidimensional educational initiative to respond to the call of the Church. This initiative begins with the formation of priests and religious so that they are prepared, understand, and have real tools in their hands to help these children, to be present to them, to walk with them, to mentor them, to provide a trusting, dependable, consistent relationship that will "accompany" them, lead them forth and "educate" them in their path towards truth. The John Paul II Institute for Studies on Marriage and Family is in a position to "lead forth" the Church in her need to prepare clergy, religious and laity with formation in this part of family ministry.

In order to be present and "accompany" these children, we need to look at what they need to go through in order to heal; the pain, the suffering, the loss, the anger, the blame, the guilt.

> First, reinforcements that sustain the child's sense of being loved and treasured can be bolstered by extended family contact and neighborhood and community connections. Interventions should foster these broader supports for the child's healthy dependent needs.[55]

Through the parish family community, support groups and skill building groups can be established, linking children of divorce to other children, letting them know they are not alone. Staying at home on the computer and playing computer games or on the television and playing video games does nothing for the child but make his time pass without necessary human interactions. Also, unsupervised internet use increases the risk of falling prey to pornography. Outdoor group activities led by a loving parishioner and/or the parish priest can provide necessary role modeling, and example to these children. It is in the nature and nurture of "relationships" that children grow, and find their way. Lynn Cassella-Kapusinski points out:

> In working with teens, it's critical to remember that they require years, if not decades to work through the grief and problems resulting from their parents' separation or divorce. This is because their healing is intertwined with their ongoing personal development and maturation.[56]

A great effort must be placed towards supporting families, the parents, their loving spousal relationship, helping them with authoritative parenting, teaching the faith, Christian virtues and values. Every person and child needs to hear, know and feel that he or she is loved by God. We must *"accompany to prevent"* further serial or intergenerational divorce. We need to enlist the entire parish family community in support of families; with a sense of solidarity and following subsidiarity. Older parent couples need to mentor younger parent couples; older couples need to mentor newlywed couples and engaged couples; older children need to mentor younger children. Again, it's about relationships. *Following the family step-by-step* can be done by expanding the connections to the sacraments that follow the life of the family. The parish family community can take part in the development of this expansion, and keep the connections of faith alive and active. Social skills, conflict resolution, marriage building skills, all need to be active parts.

> In studies of divorce, the most consistent support was found for the role of family conflict rather than for parental separation in the development of emotional problems in children. In fact, high-conflict intact families scored lower in psychological adjustment than divorced families.[57]

Several research studies reported in psychiatric literature show that there is a correlation between the marital relationship before the separation and the parent-child relationship that affects the ability of the children to adjust to the separation of their parents.

> Recent studies investigating the impact of divorce on children have found that many of the psychological symptoms seen in children of divorce can be accounted for in the years before divorce.[58]

Even those children, who seem to survive the divorce of their parents fairly well, sacrifice something of themselves in exchange.

> James Anthony termed the "resilient" child in 1987, and noted, however, that these children maintain distance in interpersonal relationships even after having become successful as adults. Thus, he pointed out that a sacrifice is made for the resiliency exhibited in childhood. Anthony's trade-off theory derives from searching for the sources of resilience primarily within the child, with the environment regarded as either not contributing, as providing stress that must be confronted, or at best, as offering only modest support. Rutter, who included multiple environmental factors in his inquiries, commented that two factors seem to be associated with resilience in the face of adversity: "secure, stable, affectionate relationships and the experiences of success and achievement."[59]

There is also evidence showing that supporting parent-child relationships in divorce situations helps the child adjust and also helps the parents. Efforts to reach out to these individuals must continue.

> When custodial parents provide appropriate emotional support, adequate-

ly monitor children's activities, discipline authoritatively, and maintain age-appropriate expectations; children and adolescents are better-adjusted compared with divorced children experiencing less appropriate parenting.[60]

Much work needs to be done in the time between the sacrament of Confirmation and Matrimony. The ground work for learning a Christian sexuality needs to start at the beginning of adolescence. The children of divorce who are approaching their own marriages need special care and attention to help them look at the commitment of marriage and the meaning of their experience of the divorce of their parents. This may be painful, but it will help them gain insight into their own motivations and dynamics in their relationships.

> It is not by sidestepping or fleeing from suffering that we are healed, but rather by our capacity for accepting it, maturing through it and finding meaning through union with Christ, who suffered with infinite love. (Benedict XVI, *Spe Salvi* n. 37.)

Continued support for engaged couples and newlyweds cannot be understated. These relationships serve as examples of interpersonal giving and sharing, in faith, and hope and love.

In the end, it's really a matter of love. The love that heals, "that is patient, love that is kind, is not self-seeking, but rejoices over truth, bears with all things, believes all things, hopes all things, endures all things." (*1 Cor* 13: 4–7)

> The hymn to love in the First Letter to the Corinthians remains the Magna Carta of the civilization of love. In this concept, what is important is not so much individual actions (whether selfish or altruistic), so much as the radical acceptance of the understanding of man as a person who "finds himself" by making a sincere gift of self. A gift is obviously, "for others": this is the most important dimension of the civilization of love.[61]

The first thing every child needs to know is that he is loved by God. The fact that you exist, means God loves you—he knew you before you had a name, as he said to the prophet Jeremiah: "Before I formed you in the womb, I knew you; before you were born, I sanctified you" (Jeremiah 1:5). This is where we begin our educational initiative. If circumstances and choices made by their parents have caused children of divorce to suffer, we must be present to them, "accompany" them on the path towards love once again. In the words of Lynn Cassella-Kapusinski, herself a child of divorce:

> This newfound strength was born out of my growing relationship with God and the space I made for the Spirit to guide me. The more I opened myself to God, the more I was led and, with each step, I discovered greater self-love because I was discovering God's love for me in a profound way.[62]

Man's great, true hope which holds firm in spite of all disappointments can only be God—God who has loved us and who continues to love us to the end . . . (Benedict XVI, *Spe Salvi*, n. 27).

The Christian's program—the program of the Good Samaritan, the program of Jesus—is a "heart which sees." This heart sees where love is needed and acts accordingly. (Benedict XVI, *Deus Caritas Est* n. 31).

BIBLIOGRAPHY

Bedard, V. Rabior, W. *Catholics Experiencing Divorce, Grieving, healing and learning to live again*, Liguori, MO 2004.

Benedict XVI, *Deus Caritas Est*, Libreria Editrice Vaticana, Vatican City 2006.

Benedict XVI, *Spe Salvi*, Libreria Editrice Vaticana, Vatican City 2007.

Bolgar, M.D., R., et al, "Childhood Antecedents of Interpersonal Problems in Young Adult Children of Divorce" in *Journal American Academy of Child & Adolescent Psychiatry*, 34:2 (1995) 143–150.

Cassella, L., *Making Your Way After Your Parents' Divorce,* Liguori Lifespan, Liguori, MO, 2002.

Cassella-Kapusinski, L., *Now What do I do? A Guide to Help Teenagers with Their Parents' Separation or Divorce,* ACTA Publications, Skokie, Illinois, 2006.

Centro Di Ricerche Per Lo Studio Della Dottrina Sociale Della Chiesa, Universita Cattolica del Sacro Cuore, *Dizionario di dottrina sociale della Chiesa, Scienze sociali e Magistero*, Vita e Pensiero, Milano 2004, 87–93.

Coles, R., *The Moral Intelligence of Children: How to Raise a Moral Child,* PUME Penguin Group, New York, 1998, 218 pages.

Coles, R., *The Spiritual Life of Children*, Houghton Mifflin Company, Boston, 1990.

Combrinck-Graham, L., *Giant Steps: Therapeutic Innovations in Child Mental Health,* Basic Books by Harper Collins Publishers, 1990.

Combrinck-Graham, L., *Children in Family Contexts, Perspectives on Treatment*, The Guilford Press, New York & London 1989.

Counts, C., et al, "Family Adversity in DSM-IV ADHD Combined and Inattentive. Subtypes and Associated Disruptive Behavior Problems" in *Journal American Academy of Child & Adolescent Psychiatry*, 44:7 (2005).

Cuffe, M.D., S., et al, "Family and Psychosocial Risk Factors in a Longitudinal. Epidemiological Study of Adolescents" in *Journal of the American Academy of Child & Adolescent Psychiatry*, 44:2 (2005) 121–129.

Dulcan, M., "Reviews in Child & Adolescent Psychiatry," in *Journal of the American Academy of Child & Adolescent Psychiatry*, 37 (1998).

Erikson, E., *Childhood and Society*, W.W. Norton &Co. In., New York 1963.

Folensbee PhD, R., "What about the Kids? Raising Your Children Before, During, and After Divorce by Wallerstein & Blakeslee" book review in *Journal of the American Academy of Child & Adolescent Psychiatry*, 43:11 (2004) 1450–1451.

Gardner, M.D., R., *The Boys and Girls Book About Divorce,* Jason Aronson Inc., Northvale, New Jersey & London 1992.

Ginsburg, H., Opper, S., *Piaget's Theory of Intellectual Development*, Prentice Hall, Englewood Cliffs, New Jersey, 1988.

Gould, PhD, MPH, M., et al "Separation/Divorce and Child and Adolescent Completed Suicide" in *Journal American Academy of Child & Adolescent Psychiatry*, 37:2 (1998) 155–162.

Hammen, PhD, C., et al, "Family Discord and Stress Predictors of Depression and Other Disorders in Adolescent Children of Depressed and Nondepressed Women" in *Journal of the American Academy of Child & Adolescent Psychiatry*, 43:8 (2004) 994–1002.

Jansen, W., "Children and Divorce: How Little We Know and How Far We Have to Go" in *Michigan Bar Journal*, 9 (2001) 50–53.

Josephson, M.D., A., *Child and Adolescent Psychiatric Clinics of North America: Current Perspectives on Family Therapy, Volume 10, Number 3*, W.B. Saunders, Philadelphia, PA, 2001.

Licamele, W., "Lost Childhoods: The Plight of the Parentified Child," Book Reviews, in *Journal of the American Academy of Child & Adolescent Psychiatry*, 37:8 (1998) 895–896.

Kelly, PhD, J., "Children's Adjustment in Conflicted Marriage and Divorce: A Decade Review of Research" in *Journal of the American Academy of Child & Adolescent Psychiatry*, 39:8 (2000) 963–973.

Macgregor, C., *The Divorce Helpbook for Teens,* Impact Publishers, Atascadero, CA, 2006.

Marquardt, E., *Between Two Worlds, The Inner Lives of Children of Divorce,* Three Rivers Press, New York, 2005.

Melina, L., *The Identity, The Mission, The Project, 2007,* Pontifical Lateran University, Vatican City 2007.

Miller, M.D., G., "The Unexpected Legacy of Divorce: A 25 Year Landmark Study Wallerstein, Lewis, Blakeslee" book review in *Journal of the American Academy of Child & Adolescent Psychiatry*, 41:3 (2002) 359–360.

Nomura, PhD, Y., et al, "Family Discord, Parental Depression, and Psychopathology in Offspring: Ten-Year Follow-up" in *Journal of the American Academy of Child & Adolescent Psychiatry*, 41:4 (2002) 402–409.

Piaget, J., Inhelder, B., *The Psychology of the Child*, translated from the French by Helen Weaver, Basic Books, Inc., New York, 1969.

Pilowsky, M.D., D., et al, "Family Discord, Parental Depression, and Psychopathology in Offspring: 20-Year Follow-up" in *Journal of the American Academy of Child & Adolescent Psychiatry*, 45:4 (2006) 452–460.

Pontifical Council For The Family, *Enchiridion on the Family*, Pauline Books & Media, Boston, 2004.

Pruett, M.D., K, *Child and Adolescent Psychiatric Clinics of North America: Child Custody, Volume 7, Number 2*, W.B. Saunders, Philadelphia, PA, 1998.

Pruett, M.D., K., "The Importance of Fathers: A Psychoanalytic Re-evaluation by Trowell and Etchegoyen" book review in *Journal of the American Academy of Child & Adolescent Psychiatry*, 43:4 (2004) 502–503.

Pruett, M.D., K., Pruett, PhD, M., "Only God Decides: Young Children's Perceptions of Divorce and the Legal System" in *Journal of the American Academy of Child & Adolescent Psychiatry*, 38:12 (1999) 1544–1550.

Pruitt, M.D., D., *Your Adolescent, Emotional, Behavioral and Cognitive Development from Early Adolescence through the Teen Years*, HarperCollins Publishers, 1999.

Pruitt, M.D., D., *Your Child, What Every Parent Needs to Know About Childhood Development from Birth to Preadolescence*, HarperCollins Publishers, 1998.

Rice, PhD, F., et al, "Family Conflict Interacts with Genetic Liability in Predicting Childhood and Adolescent Depression" in *Journal of the American Academy of Child & Adolescent Psychiatry*, 45:7 (2006) 841–848.

Rodgers, B., Rodgers, T., *Adult Children of Divorced Parents, Making your Marriage Work*, Resource Publications, Inc., San Jose, CA, 2002.

Singer, D., Revenson, T., *A Piaget Primer, How a Child Thinks*, Plume by Penguin Books, New York, 1996.

Stillwell, M.D., B., et al, "Moral Valuation: A Third Domain of Conscience Functioning" in *Journal of the American Academy of Child & Adolescent Psychiatry*, 35:2 (1996).

Wallerstein, J., Blakeslee, S., *Second Chances, Men, Women and Children a Decade After Divorce*, Houghton Mifflin Company, Boston & New York, 1996.

Wallerstein, J., Blakeslee, S., *The Good Marriage, How & Why Love Lasts*, Warner Books, New York & Boston, 1996.

Wallerstein, J., Lewis, J., Blakeslee, S., *The Unexpected Legacy of Divorce; The 25 Year Landmark Study,* Hyperion, New York, 2000.

Zimmerman, PhD, J., Thayer, PhD, E., *Adult Children of Divorce,* New Harbinger Publications, Inc., Oakland, CA, 2003.

REFERENCES

1. John Paul II, *Familiaris Consortio,* The Holy See, Citta del Vaticano, 1981, no. 86.

2. http://epp.eurostat.ec.europa.eu.

3. Marquardt, E., *Between Two Worlds, The Inner Lives of Children of Divorce,* Three Rivers Press, New York, 2005, xiv.

4. Ibid.

5. Wallerstein, J., *The Unexpected Legacy of Divorce: The 25 Year Landmark Study,* Hyperion, New York, 2000.

6. Marquardt, E., *Between Two Worlds,* Three Rivers Press, New York, 2005.

7. Ibid., 155–557.

8. Benedict XVI, *Letter to Romans on the Urgency in Education,* Zenit, Jan 21, 2008.

9. www.rainbows.org/.

10. Combrinck-Graham, L., *Giant Steps,* Basic Books by Harper Collins Publishers, 1990, 45.

11. Erikson, E., *Childhood and Society,* W.W. Norton & Co. Inc., New York, 1963.

12. For the sake of clarity, specificity and simplicity, "married parents" will heretofore be defined as the heterosexual male and female natural biological parents joined legally and/or religiously in matrimony. It is definitely a sad sign of the times that this definition has to be stated and protected.

13. Combrinck-Graham, L., *Giant Steps,* Basic Books by Harper Collins Publishers, 1990, 52.

14. Erikson, E., Childhood and Society, W.W. Norton & Co. Inc., New York, 1963, 273.

15. Marquardt, E., *Between Two Worlds,* 24.

16. Ibid., 22–28.

17. Pruett, M.D., K, *Child and Adolescent Psychiatric Clinics of North America: Child Custody, Volume 7, Number 2,* W.B. Saunders, Philadelphia, PA, 1998 279.

18. Pruett, M.D., K., Pruett, PhD, M., "Only God Decides: Young Children's Perceptions of Divorce and the Legal System" in *Journal of the American Academy of Child & Adolescent Psychiatry,* 38:12 (1999) 1544–4550.

19. Wallerstein, J., Lewis, J., Blakeslee, S., *The Unexpected Legacy of Divorce,* 25.

20. Ibid., 27.

21. Ibid., 34.

22. Kelly, PhD, J., "Children's Adjustment in Conflicted Marriage and Divorce: A Decade Review of Research" in *Journal of the American Academy of Child & Adolescent Psychiatry*, 39:8 (2000) 963–373.

23. Hammen, PhD, C., et al, "Family Discord and Stress Predictors of Depression and Other Disorders in Adolescent Children of Depressed and Nondepressed Women" in *Journal of the American Academy of Child & Adolescent Psychiatry*, 43:8 (2004) 994–4002.

24. Kelly, PhD, J., "Children's Adjustment in Conflicted Marriage and Divorce: A Decade Review of Research" in *Journal of the American Academy of Child & Adolescent Psychiatry*, 39:8 (2000) 963–373.

25. Licamele, W., "Lost Childhoods: The Plight of the Parentified Child," Book Reviews, in *Journal of the American Academy of Child & Adolescent Psychiatry*, 37:8 (1998) 895–596.

26. Pruett, M.D., K, *Child and Adolescent Psychiatric Clinics of North America: Child Custody, Volume 7, Number 2*, W.B. Saunders, Philadelphia, PA, 1998, 277.

27. Ibid., 278.

28. Cassella, L., *Making Your Way After Your Parents' Divorce*, Liguori Lifespan, Liguori, MO, 2002, 49.

29. Marquardt, E., *Between Two Worlds*, 149.

30. Melina, L., *The Identity, The Mission, The Project, 2007*, Pontifical Lateran University, Vatican City 2007, 11.

31. Centro Di Ricerche Per Lo Studio Della Dottrina Sociale Della Chiesa, Universita Cattolica del Sacro Cuore, *Dizionario di dottrina sociale della Chiesa, Scienze sociali e Magistero*, Vita e Pensiero, Milano 2004, 87–73.

32. Ibid., 77–75.

33. Pruitt, M.D., D., *Your Child, What Every Parent Needs to Know About Childhood Development from Birth to Preadolescence*, HarperCollins Publishers, 1998, 329.

34. Pruitt, M.D., D., *Your Adolescent, Emotional, Behavioral and Cognitive Development from Early Adolescence through the Teen Years*, HarperCollins Publishers, 1999, 209–910.

35. Gould, PhD, MPH, M., et al "Separation/Divorce and Child and Adolescent Completed Suicide" in *Journal of the American Academy of Child & Adolescent Psychiatry*, 37:2 (1998) 155–562.

36. Kelly, PhD, J., "Children's Adjustment in Conflicted Marriage and Divorce: A Decade Review of Research" in *Journal of the American Academy of Child & Adolescent Psychiatry*, 39:8 (2000) 963–373, 967.

37. Pruett, M.D., K., Pruett, PhD, M., "Only God Decides: Young Children's Perceptions of Divorce and the Legal System," 1544–4550.

38. Cassella, L., *Making Your Way After Your Parents' Divorce*, Liguori Lifespan, Liguori, MO, USA 2002, 67–79.

39. Marquardt, E., *Between Two Worlds*, 168.

40. Wallerstein, J., Lewis, J., Blakeslee, S., *The Unexpected Legacy of Divorce*, 19.

41. Pruitt, M.D., D., *Your Child, What Every Parent Needs to Know About Childhood Development from Birth to Preadolescence,* HarperCollins Publishers, 1998, 130.

42. Ibid., 416.

43. Coles, R., *The Moral Intelligence of Children: How to Raise a Moral Child,* PUME Penguin Group,. New York, 1998, 105.

44. Wallerstein, J., Lewis, J., Blakeslee, S., *The Unexpected Legacy of Divorce*, 304.

45. Coles, R., *The Moral Intelligence of Children*, 156, 162.

46. Benedict XVI, "L'incontro con il clero romano," *Roma Sette, Supplemento di Avvenire,* 2007 Feb 25th.

47. Wallerstein, J., Lewis, J., Blakeslee, S., *The Unexpected Legacy of Divorce*, 298.

48. www.marriagesavers.org.

49. www.embrace.org.au.

50. www.wwme.org/.

51. www.pmrcusa.org/PLL%20Home.htm.

52. www.wwme.org/.

53. Pruett, M.D., K., Pruett, PhD, M., "Only God Decides," 1544–4550.

54. Jansen, W., "Children and Divorce: How Little We Know and How Far We Have to Go" in *Michigan Bar Journal,* 9 (2001) 50–03.

55. Pruett, M.D., K., Pruett, PhD, M., "Only God Decides," 1544–4550.

56. Cassella-Kapusinski, L., *Now What do I do? A Guide to Help Teenagers with Their Parents' Separation or Divorce,* ACTA Publications, Skokie, Illinois, 2006, 171.

57. Cuffe, M.D., S., et al, "Family and Psychosocial Risk Factors in a Longitudinal Epidemiological Study of Adolescents" in *Journal of the American Academy of Child & Adolescent Psychiatry,* 44:2 (2005) 121–129.

58. Ibid, 963.

59. Combrinck-Graham, L., *Giant Steps: Therapeutic Innovations in Child Mental Health,* Basic Books by Harper Collins Publishers, USA 1990, 38.

60. Kelly, PhD, J., "Children's Adjustment in Conflicted Marriage and Divorce: A Decade Review of Research" in *Journal of the American Academy of Child & Adolescent Psychiatry,* 39:8 (2000) 963–373.

61. John Paul II, *Gratissimam Sane:* "Letter to Families for the International Year of the Family," 1994, n14.

62. Cassella, L., *Making Your Way After Your Parents' Divorce*, 12.

"Voice Groups" for Children of Divided Families

Costanza Marzotto

> *I hate separation
> because there are always
> shouts and criticisms*
> —Marco, 9 years old, Voice Group, 2008

PREMISE

The word identifies us as subjects when we come into the world. To name a child is to distinguish him from oneself and from others. The word permits us to exist, it links us to others, gives us membership, founds our identity, situates us in a family, a genealogy, and inscribes us in the most vast group of the social community. The baby, a distinct subject and separate from others, exists only if he is articulated as so, possessing his own word in reference to others—an expression of his life as a subject.

To try to keep the child apart, for the purpose of protecting him from the conflict and a sense of culpability, is wrong, because excluding him cuts off any possibility of constructing a sense of what is happening around him. Besides, a baby is capable of intuiting what is happening between his parents. It is necessary to remember that that which is not verbalized cannot take form, or be anchored in reality. This provokes feelings of anxiety, confusion and helplessness in the baby.

My hypothesis is that the "social body," in its turn, has the responsibility

---

Costanza Marzotto is a psychologist and family mediator for the Clinical Psychology Service for Couples and Families, Università Cattolica del Sacro Cuore, Milan (Italy).

of making available a place and time for children of divided families to put into words the experience of divorce that the family body is going through: otherwise the risks of suffering, hardship, illness or even simply reproducing/recreating fragile bonds will accompany these subjects for generations and will weaken our communities.

From the studies that have been conducted, we know that adults who have experienced the separation of their parents even 30 to 40 years in the past, still recall the event as one of the most dramatic points in their lives.

The *Voice Group* is a homogenous group of 4 to 10 children between the ages of 6 and 12 which meets four times a month for two hours each time. The goal is to begin a process in which every subject, having the experience of a bond with their peers and reliable adults, can come to realize that the "division" of the parental couple is a long, complex journey that involves many players and that brings suffering, but of which one "can always speak!"

We know, in fact, that for the youngest children the trauma of the separation is amplified if a sufficient explanation is not given for the parents' breakup. The difficulty of making sense of the separation has a perturbing effect on the children. The absence of communication between parents and children sharpens the expressive difficulty and generates a climate of great insecurity. In this state, the child is at risk of conjuring phantasms and representations/images that are much more terrifying than the reality. The hypersensitivity provoked from the intensity of these emotions induces the child to seek the protection of the adults (on whom he depends), and avoid displaying his anxiety, uncertainty and the needs he experiences.

I have chosen to communicate my reflections along with some of the words of the children of divided families found in the groups conducted by our team based out of the Center for University Studies and Research on the Family (*Centro di Ateneo Studi e Ricerche sulla Famiglia*) at Sacred Heart, the Catholic University of Milan. Our basis was formed by Professor Marie Simon of the University of Grenoble, France, who used a model of work that was developed over many years by Lorraine Fillion in collaboration with the Tribunal of Montreal in Canada.

As Simon writes, "naming these events and difficulties renders them workable for the children, accessible for possible internalization. Outlining the boundaries of their family space, the child is permitted to place him/herself in the singularity/uniqueness of his/her history. Putting the word into circulation allows them to reconstruct their history, favoring the recollection of the absent persons, helping the child to distinguish between absence and mourning, that is, between the momentary separation and the irrevocable separation of one of their parents. The *Voice Group* proposes a space dedicated to the healing and safeguarding of the family bond. The word is at the crossroads between the thought and the act, the change should therefore pass through it" (Marzotto, 2007).

THE UNEXPECTED CRITICAL EVENT:
IN ORDER THAT A DRAMA DOES NOT BECOME A TRAGEDY

According to the "symbolic relation" approach (Scabini and Cigoli, 2000), it is not just the difficulties at the level of the couple's interactions (less time for the healing of the bond, less energies to invest in the family) that render the divorce painful, but also the symbolic significance of the event—that is, the place that the child fills between generations, the function that the child accomplishes for his parents and for the two families, the maternal and the paternal. The critique of divorce is linked to the dimension of debt and credit that the child fills in the multi-family scenario, to the "mission" that the child was called to carry out in his kinships that will remain unfulfilled or suspended after the separation.

These are the most recurrent questions in the children's discourse within the group: What meaning do my father and my mother give to their relationship with me? In what place does everyone put me in the relationships with my biological parents and with the new partner? What position do I occupy in the intergenerational interlacing?

As I note in the research on children, that which harms the children is not only the breakdown of the union of the "divine couple," the beginning of the separation between those who generated them—accomplishing an act possible only by God—but also the persistence of the conflict before and after the division of the two family houses.

"I don't want the problem of screaming to be resolved by shouting over the phone! We children get scared!" (Alessandro, 9 years old).

Living in an environment where both verbal and physical violence between parents exist, is one of the major sources of harm for the children; but also to feel that the paternal function or maternal function is discredited puts children in a conflict of loyalty, where their desire is to remain connected as much to the father as to the mother, to the paternal grandparents as to the maternal. Even if only 31 percent of children suffer from grave disturbances connected to the division between the parents, for many of them, in the first two years after the division between dad and mom, a series of difficulties in their bodies and their behavior can be verified (Canziani, 2000). And because they feel trapped in a guilty place, stuck between two opposing sides, they feel like they are always living in a war, as Marco, 7 years old, portrays in his drawing.

The questions which we have sought to answer with the *Voice Group* are: how can the children of divided families be helped in order to be able to transition beyond the critical event of "the separation of the parental couple" and to save their confidence in these bonds and their own self-esteem? How can they continue to have access to the father and the mother, be able to feel a part of both extended families, the  maternal and paternal families, and not feel "caught in the middle" of the conflict? How can adults continue to be generative and transmit to the new generation the gift of the sense of being supported by the social community?

The experience of *Voice Groups* represents a gift for the community and for the parents of children of divorce to empower them to deal with the pain.

> Even if you think that we do not suffer, it may be that while you shout, we are in our bedrooms with our heads under the pillow so that we don't hear you, our eyes closed, we cry uncontrollably, with our hands over our mouth so you don't hear us, but even so, between your screams and your troubles, you will not hear us anyway. Your concerns however will never be as grave and serious as ours. Don't think that we are naive and that we don't understand, on the contrary! (Lucia, 12 years old)

These young people have doubts about the love of their own parents and are full of very painful memories. Speaking permits them to find a way out by establishing useful relationships (Cigoli, 2008).

NEEDS OF THE CHILDREN OF SEPARATED/ DIVORCED COUPLES

In a synthetic way, we can summarize the needs of the children of the separated as the need to be heard, the need to be informed, the need to be reassured, and the need to have access not only to the two parents, but also the two genders (masculine and feminine), and the two extended families.

These fundamental necessities manifest themselves, for example, in the need to be authorized to love both the parents for the construction of the mind. Alex, thus, formulates his desire to have his mom say, "OK, from now on, if you happen to want to stay to eat with your dad in the afternoon, I will give you permission without getting angry, and without finding an excuse to say no!" The need to be reassured of the continuity of affection causes this to be written in a letter from the group: "But will you both continue to love me? I wish you would tell me that you are friends and that you still love each other."

It is unbearable for children to feel the other parent being denigrated. "When dad says that mom is stupid, I don't know who to believe anymore" (Elena, 8 years old). But, above all, the absence of the mutually supportive parents moves some children to have serious learning, behavior and sexual identification problems.

On the other hand, many children come to their groups talking about new partners and feel the need to ask that the separated parent not be replaced with the new companion. Otherwise, the pain is renewed every visit and becomes so unbearable that it can move them to refuse to go to the home of dad or of mom. "I wish that dad would say that he and his girlfriend will not become serious, but also I wish dad, to give an example, would not always take into consideration his new fiancée."

But the ability to speak about what happens in the family is seen by some children as prohibitive and risky. It is what Carlo, 9 years old, appears to reveal when he was asked to complete a drawing depicting a ring with two points . . .

When invited to comment in the group about his drawing, Carlo added a small salutation for his parents "hi dad and mom" and tried to calm the group by saying that the person he drew will never speak again. He and his brother were waiting to know what the judge and social services had decreed regarding their future.

It is true, as well, that participation in the group offers the children of the separated an opportunity to discover and name the advantages of the separation: first of all, the possibility of no longer having to live between screams and scenes, but also of being able to receive a weekly allowance and, as Emmanuel (8 years old) says, "If you ask me, separation has its advantages, such as that I can stay with the parent that I like more."

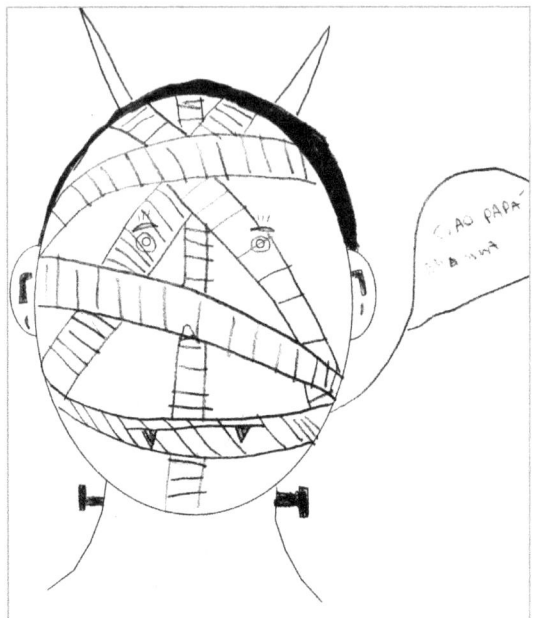

He even manages to write: "You love me more since the separation. You give us more toys and sometimes more money! Being separated, you fight less!"

Those Who Are Not Heard

The emotive commitment to manage the rivalry/delusion in the confrontation of the separated husband and wife renders some parents deaf and mute, while others become obsessively devoted to the education of the children. Both are situations in which the ear of the adult is closed and the mouth of the adult speaks of things that are not interesting (sometimes parents think they should illustrate to the children all of their hardships of heart, which are of no interest to the children). In this case, it is useful for them to say in the group:

> Dad, I don't want your girlfriend to take the place of mom and for her to come live with us . . . Dad, I want to live alone with you and not with mom! Why? Because with you, I live better, feel better, I eat better and I love you more!

This dangerous affirmation is possible to share with their companions and once they have expressed their feelings, they find it easier to talk about them again at home with a courage renewed by the support of the group.

"I wish that mom would not suffer so much!" As numerous studies show, the risk is high among separated parents of putting the children in the "grown up" position of comforter, confidant of the "abandoned" or "guilty" parent. Sometimes the maturity of the children surpasses that of the adults, rendering them excessively weighed down with responsibility. Francesca (11 years old) says to her father,

> But dad, you are a little "strange" and you know it; you have already married twice and twice you've left; don't you wonder whether there is something that should be modified in you? I don't know what, but there must be something and even you say that to me, so I beg you, try to understand what it is!!!

Reconsider Hope

"Mom and dad: you may have made some mistake, some errors, but you can always fix them and, as with a car engaged in the fourth gear, you can always reverse!"

One of the most widespread expectations among children of the separated is the reconciliation of the parents. Even four or five years after the divorce and the appearance of new partners, the children continue to hope and think that it is within their power to rekindle the romance. As we will see later, the role of the adult that conducts the group is to restrict the ability of the children and relieve them of the "heavy" dream of such a possibility.

The Criteria of Admission

A tragedy for a child is the loss of access to both parents. They feel the need to side with one parent over the other and feel they are not allowed to love dad as much as mom. For years, specialists have considered it sufficient to identify one parent as "fit" for the placement of the minor. Even with strong conflicts, it is indispensable for the children to have access to both families, the maternal and the paternal, regardless of the choice of the adults. To know oneself to be loved by the parental couple that survives the divorce of the conjugal couple is the great challenge put forward by our team of technical counselors for the judge, family mediators and conductors of voice groups centered in the relational symbolic model (Cigoli et. al., 2000).

Participation in the *Voice Group*, authorized by the signature of the father and mother, symbolically permits access to a place where children are able to speak of both families of origin with liberty and where both the parents are in attendance, during the last hour of the last encounter, for the reading of the letter of the group.

THE RESOURCE OF THE WORD SPOKEN IN GROUP

The bonds of the group can become a positive resource, if at the heart of it the group welcomes and elaborates on the multiplicity of emotions coming from the internal world and external world, if there is a place in which it is possible to "share" aspects of life such as sympathy for dad's new companion, banished by mom, or the feeling of emptiness at home since dad left.

In particular, a group performs its function if the child is free to pause in a play area, in a creative area where nothing concrete is produced, not the fantasy of the future and the memory of the past. Above all, for the only child (the majority of children of separation), solitude can have the gravest effects. Without a place to understand through a word, a drawing, or a game, that which is happening internally, a child cannot approach the change. At best, he can passively conform himself to the will of the adult and adapt himself, but at a steep price.

Through the diverse activities and the spoken and written word, the work of the group with the children is developed within and through the thought and allowing truthful communication, the exchange of experiences, the aquisition of others' knowledge, and the creation of a personal strategy to confront the new situation. In this way, the child's energies will shift towards learning and his mind will be freed from concerns regarding the family situation, loved ones who have suffered, and the weight of the unspoken.

The advantage of the group's work is in the fact that the children of the separated are not "confined" to an introspective observation. But within the inter-subjective space they can speak of the emotions, the fears, and the conflicts in a less dangerous way than in a one-on-one relationship. At the same time, they can observe the changes in time and the reactions of their contemporaries to arrive in their turn to offer questions about themselves and their own family (Marzotto, 2007).

THE ADVANTAGES OF DIVERSITY

The heterogeneous composition for age and sex of the group with children between ages 6 and 12 years permits assembling children of diverse ages who are living different phases of the divorce itinerary (one parent has just left the home; the judge has given the sentence; a parent is living with another partner; another sibling has been born; they have discovered that they have a half-brother).

In the group, the children are given permission to speak of an unspeakable event, of the separation, of the dislike they have for the end of the idyll of the couple. On the occasion of the second encounter, every participant can bring something from home that holds significance for the group. Francesca has chosen to bring "one of the games from when my parents were together. I have put them all in a box. . . I decided to bring this, because it is a reminder of when I was small." Alessia brings the photo album from "when dad and mom were still together."

THE FUNCTION OF THE ADULT GUIDE

In the midst of a group of children who understand the experience of parental separation, what is the purpose of *a third person*? The question concerns all of us adults who carry different titles in being the trusted outsider to whom a child can say certain unspeakable things. As educators, priests, catechists, and psycho-social professionals helping children of separation, we have certain fundamental responsibilities. For example, we must make known to minors that they cannot be the ones to decide the life of the adults, that they are not responsible if their parents, or grandparents, argue and insult each other. Even more so, the adult conductor of the voice group—confronted by the children's desires to choose which parent to live with, to hinder the father and the mother from having other children with the new partner, to be the referee in the dispute—has the task of reordering the ability of the children and helping them to distinguish that which is within their responsibility from that which is within the adults'. Great interest arises among participants after the ruling of the judge, a third authority that decides above all!

A peculiarity of the *Voice Group* is that it is not conducted by psychotherapists who treat a symptom, but by adults who are reliable and prepared to help facilitate the symbolic expression lived by the child of the separated (on the linguistic, narrative, pictorial, and musical levels).

HELPING TO MAINTAIN A DUAL BELONGING IN THE MATERNAL AND PATERNAL FAMILIES

The help of books expressly written for children according to their age, with beautiful and fun images and with simple and realistic texts, permits them to confront this theme of a "lost war" a "diabolical battle" (as is written in the drawing of Francesco, 9 years old). It seems, in fact, that many children of separation have given up and resigned themselves to living within only one context, while we know how structurally fundamental it is to understand that we are descended from the father *and* from the mother, and to be able to shout that fact to the world (or at least to one's group of peers).

A risk that many children of the separated run is endogamy, that is, the exclusion of the child from one of the two extended families—a denigrating action which turns them away from one extended family involved in the confrontation with the other, attributing good to only one branch of the kinship, while the other is cut off, removed halfway, not mentioned. In these cases, it deals with attacks on the bonds that are still very fragile, with the fatal effect worse than an explicit slander against the father. I make reference here to the cases in which the extended families of the other person begin to be viewed as dangerous, to be eliminated, in the attempt to recreate an endogamic family where everything is homogenous, where everything is good.

The extended family of the other person is seen as a threat that should be eliminated to realize an Imaginary Child, in the attempt to recreate a self-sufficient nucleus that has no need either for the models or for the money of the other (this project is at times noticeable even in the fantasy of some professionals, as we had a way of verifying in one of our studies and as some children in the group have said). In such a situation, our task as a third party is that of being able to restore to the parental bond an Oedipal perspective—to reinstate the child in the triangular relationship between the father and mother.

To participate in a *Voice Group* where the children can name their dad and mom without the danger of a framework permits them to reacquire their own space, to define the confines of their being a child without having to sleep in the bed of the parent or be informed/consulted of everything that pertains to the emotional life of the adult.

The excessive involvment of children in all the decisions of the parent with custody is very risky and, at times, these children exist in an inversion of roles, in the form of dependency of the parent to the child, to the parentification of the children with evident danger of pathology. The confrontation with other subjects involved in the same situation transmits courage and strength.

The instrument of the *Voice Group* is placed in this perspective, in the sense that it offers the children a time to recount freely that which is happening at the dad's, mom's and grandparents' houses, and to name the contrasts without fear and without having to side with one side or the other.

One of the most imminent problems for the children of the separated is that of the construction/maintenance of "roots" of the family history. The separated children live in anguish, and anger. Many times they lack a foundation under their feet because they cannot tell the mom that they were fine at the dad's house, and vice versa if they are with the mom, they cannot say how much they miss their dad. That is why in the *Voice Group* it is possible for the children to say that they are having trouble, not feel that they are alone, and within the exchange of the group, attempt to make sense of some of life's adversities.

SOME OPERATING INSTRUMENTS

We can say in summary that confronted by the three above-indicated, fundamental needs, the facilitator makes use of three types of activities.

1. With respect to the *need to be heard*, the children are told that they can tell what happens at home without being listened to by the adults and without anything being repeated outside of the group, but to other children who live the same experience. This is announced at the beginning of the encounter while sitting on their cushion and during the snack. They speak freely and even in their greetings they share very important things about their lives.

2. With respect to the *need for information* there is a specific activity we do with all the children with the goal of informing them that separation is a process, whether in the temporal or judicial sense of the term. This is done after letting them know that they will not remain in today's phase forever

where the quarreling is overwhelming (for example, someone said of mom, "its impossible to visit her in her new house because she has a new companion and the grandparents do not permit it").

For the children it also serves them to know—from the experience of others—that the phase of tremendous shouting on the telephone is not forever, or that it may occur that dad or mom meet a new companion . . . All the children who come to a voice group find themselves in a particular phase of the process of family separation. We know well from reading the national and international research, but the child, however, does not have a historical perspective of his or her process of separation. The small ones who believe that what is happening now will be like that forever are very worried.

One resource used is images in which—a puppy, for example—is portrayed in a state of mind similar to that of the child (confused, angry, loved, etc). Every child is invited to choose that image which most represents them in that particular moment. As is seen in the figure reproduced here, Emanuele (8 years old) uses a sad puppy to communicate to the group his emotions and adds a message for his parents: *"Why do you keep fighting? What reason do you have?"*

You try to inform the child that the relationship, and the emotive and physical situation, will evolve, even if it is not in the most optimal way. The accounts of the other children let every participant prepare him or herself for what will happen, or remember what has already passed, and equip them as best as possible! Ignorance of what could happen renders the children of the separated particularly anxious. Putting the critical event into a historical context offers the best possibility for life.

Resolving the need for information is not what improves the situation, because it is not the case that if they recognize the problem they no longer have it. Being with their contemporaries, in a calm context that allows them to be able to anticipate future scenarios instead of becoming frightened, encourages them to talk to the group and, later, at home.

3. To the *need of being reassured,* the parents respond directly between encounters and during the last encounter. After reading the Letter of the Group anonymously addressed to all the present parents, every adult writes on an anonymous paper their message in response. Some children's books and some stories written together explicitly demonstrate this need to be reassured. But only those directly interested—courageously called forward—can provide the words anticipated by the children, as we can see in these excerpts:

Children's Letter

Dear Dad and Mom,

It is better when dad and mom are separated because they don't argue anymore and I can sleep the whole night.

The children stay only with the mom and for the dad nothing remains.

I only see dad on Saturday and I cannot do anything to make my parents stay together.

We feel like we are to blame when parents separate . . .

Parent's Response

Mom and Dad, together, will always be close to you because our love for you is great.

Stay calm, and if we sometimes argue, do not be afraid; it can happen, but it is not about you. It is the adults that, sometimes, are a little stupid.

We will always follow you with great love.

Moms suffer with their children and hope for a better world for them.

We are very encouraged by the words that some parents have related in the successive meeting after the course: "My son is changed; there should be many groups like this for so many children; you have given our son an historical position (with a past, a present and a future . . .)."

As a father in a recent interview affirmed to a daily newspaper on the argument,

For my children who were in the group it has helped them become more serene and to speak about their situation with other children and adults . . .
it has helped us live through the separation, however possible, in a less problematic way,. . . in this phase of change we have felt united with the children.

CONCLUSION

The specific objective of the encounters can be formulated as such: helping to find a way of learning to face the difficult situation connected with the condition of children of separated parents. Therefore, we can define this as a *clinical, non-therapeutic intervention,* in the sense that a suitably prepared professional assists the child while he transitions in this complex process that is the separation of the parents. If an adult is at his side (clinical means to be at the bedside of a patient), he becomes equipped, he finds a way to face his situation; we can speak of the participation in the *Voice Groups* as an experience to learn modalities for the facing of difficult situations.

Research conducted with children of separated parents who are participants in a *Voice Group* taken in comparison to children who are from intact families or children of divorce who have not had this opportunity, has shown that the first are most in position to face the situation because their self-esteem has increased, whether it be in the dimension of scholastic competence, of social competence, of physical competence, of body image and of the conduct and evaluation of oneself.

In summary, we can thus assume the explicit objectives to which the experience of a *Voice Group* with children of the separated aims:

1. to prevent a possible marginalization of this population;

2. to offer an occasion to share this experience with those who find themselves living the same situation;

3. to clarify their perception and clarify misunderstandings with respect to the separation of the parents;

4. to offer them a sufficiently neutral and welcoming context where they can express the complex sentiments with respect to the critical event separating the parental couple;

5. to find concrete methods to face difficult situations connected with the condition of children of the separated;

6. to favor better communication between children and divided parents.

The experience and the research confirm that the *Voice Group* can be opportunely utilized as a means and place of constructing identity and subjectivity. It permits the mentalization of the bond structures born in the encounter with others and puts into action a work of psychic elaboration of this encounter. It is, therefore, a place of learning and source of interaction.

The *Voice Group* goes against the social marginalization and the sense of solitude and of diversity, through the sharing between peers and those who are similar. It becomes, for the children, easier to confront themselves and have an exchange with contemporaries who find themselves in the same family situation. This helps the children to soften the negative sentiments associated with the event, correct erroneous perceptions, transmit information and face the practical problems connected to divorce. The peer group reinforces the identifying system for every subject, thanks to the recognition that comes from within the group to which he or she belongs (in this case, the parental breakdown represents the common denominator).

The corrective experience of the group therefore opens the child to various perspectives, it permits him to position himself differently with respect to the family and the environment and to better face difficulties. In this sense, the *Voice Group* results in involving the whole family. It is expected that in intervening with a corrective experience, like that of the *Voice Group,* in a moment of crisis for the child, it produces well-being in the family web: The adaptation of the child makes a direct impression on the adults who surround him. This reflection is supported by the fact that the parents and children who participate in *Voice Groups* show a better comprehension of the inherent difficulties of separating, and are equipped with better instruments to face them and adapt. Furthermore, an improvement in the dialogue between the children with the parents, their extended family, and their peers has been observed, accompanied by a greater social and scholastic integration, and a perception of a more positive future.

I would like to conclude by reporting a brief story about separation, set in 2007 from a group of children of separated parents, gathered in a *Voice Group* in the province of Milan.

Separation
Marco, Niccolò, Gaia, Elisa, Beatrice, and Eva feel sad seeing their parents separate.
They are shocked when their parents argue [. . .]
A child's heart is broken when they hear their parents argue; but parents' hearts also break when they separate.
Sometimes, children feel angry because they must stay only with either their father or their mother.

At the beginning of the separation, children are confused and think it is their fault.

Sometimes, children are doubtful, because they do not know what the future will bring.

When children feel sad, they remember when their mother and father used to love each other.

Fathers and mothers love their children, but children also love their parents.

Children choose both parents, because there is no difference in love.

Parents were happy when they got married and decided to have a son or a daughter, but now they are not.

Children feel guilty, because their parents have not explained the reason for their separation.

We are jealous of our parents' new companions.

Parents are also jealous, and frightened of being replaced.

BIOGRAPHICAL REFERENCES

Canziani R., *I figli dei divorzi difficili,* Sellerio, Palermo, 2000.

Dolto F., *Quando i genitori si separano,* Mondadori, Milano, 1991.

Marzotto C., *Il lavoro di gruppo con bambini appartenenti a famiglie divise,* in "Politiche sociali e servizi," II, 2000, pp.387—403.

Marzotto C., *Appartenere alle due stirpi: i gruppi di parola per figli di coppie separate* in "Sudi interdisciplinari sulla famiglia," XXII, 2007 .

Marzotto C. e Dallanegra P. (a cura di), *Continuità genitoriale e servizi per il diritto di visita. Esperienze straniere e sperimentazione in Italia,* Vita e Pensiero, Milano, 1998.

Marzotto C., Telleschi R., *Comporre il conflitto genitoriale. La mediazione: metodo e strumenti,* Unicopli, Milano 2000.

Cigoli, V., Mombelli , M. Galimberti C., *Il legame disperante,* Franco Angeli, Milano, 2000.

Cigoli V., *Psicologia della separazione e del divorzio,* Il Mulino, Bologna, 1999.

Scabini E., Cigoli V., *Il famigliare. Relazioni, simboli e transizioni,* Raffaello Cortina Editore, Milano, 2000.

Guenivet Simon M., *La place et la parole de l'enfant dans les transitions familiales,* Tesi di dottorato, Università UPMF Grenoble, 2007.

Emery R., *La verità sui figli e il divorzio,* F. Angeli, Milano (Prefazione di V. Cigoli), 2008.

PART TWO

THE AFTERMATH OF ABORTION

I The Hidden Sufferings of Abortion

Being the "Good Samaritan": Between Works of Healing and the Responsibility to Educate

Maria Luisa Di Pietro

Why speak of the pastoral care of women who have lived the experience of abortion or miscarriage? Why mention the figure of the Good Samaritan who, trying to "suffer with" another who is stranger to him, stoops to cleanse his wounds and alleviate that suffering?

The theme of procured abortion has always been at the center of ethical debate (the moral status of abortion and the need to prevent miscarriage), bioethics (the status of the human embryo), epidemiology (the spread of the phenomenon), sociological (the perception of the issue of abortion and the dynamics that underlie it).

Now, there is another proposed key to understanding: how can we become "neighbor" to those in need, in particular, to the woman who has experienced the tragedy of abortion, since abortion is always—we read in No. 58 of the encyclical *Evangelium Vitae* (EV)—"an unspeakable crime ?" "[. . .] procured abortion is the deliberate and direct killing, through whatever means taken, of a human being in the initial phase of his existence, between conception and birth," and so often also causes an inadvertent but grave heartache, not only in women, but also in those around her who may have shared—in various ways—the responsibility of that decision.

It is also important to recognize the number of symptoms that may come up within the woman even some time after the abortion: emotional disturbances (anxiety, etc.), communication problems, eating disorders, relational

---

Maria Luisa Di Pietro is Associate Professor of Bioethics, School of Medicine and Surgery, Università Cattolica del Sacro Cuore, Rome (Italy), and Professor of Bioethics, Pontifical John Paul II Institute.

problems, sleep difficulties, etc. The trauma of the loss of a child can change one's attitudes, emotional behavior and affective life with the partner. Together, this represents a real syndrome: the "post-abortion syndrome."

While it is true that the life of the embryo is primarily entrusted to the care of the mother—who is often alone and desperate when she has recourse to abortion—the responsibility of this act is also profound for the others involved. In particular, the father of the child who may pressure the woman to abort, or support this decision by abandoning her; the family, the doctors, who—fearing even legal repercussions—guide the woman towards this decision all are involved (EV, 59). And even further, it involves the responsibility of those who have allowed and continue to allow the spread of a culture that trivializes sexuality, that gives no real esteem to motherhood and does not take the tragic impact of abortion on women seriously, or the wounds which are so difficult to heal.

There are still more innocent victims of abortion: the brothers and sisters of the aborted child. They are considered to have "abortion survivor syndrome," as seen in the story on the following pages—the experience of children who come to know the history of abortion in their family and have experienced a great sense of insecurity and fear, a loss of confidence, hatred against their parents, or even guilt for what happened.

It is upon all of them that the healing action of Jesus, the Good Samaritan comes to intervene: Pope Benedict XVI writes in his Speech for the Congress of the John Paul II Institute: "Oil on the Wounds," April 5, 2008—

> As the Fathers teach, it is He who is the true Good Samaritan, who has made Himself close to us, who pours oil and wine on our wounds and takes us into the inn, the Church, where he has us treated, entrusting us to her ministers and personally paying in advance for our recovery. Yes, the Gospel of love and life is also always the Gospel of mercy, which is addressed to the actual person and sinner that we are, to help us up after any fall and to recover from any injury.

A witness and teaching to concretely become "neighbor":

> Despite (love for one's neighbor) being extended to all mankind, it is not reduced to a generic, abstract and undemanding expression of love—reads Encyclical *Deus Caritas Est,* 15—but calls for my own practical commitment here and now.

The Good Samaritan recognizes the needs of others, is preoccupied with them, and takes care of them. It is that compassion, which allows him to come out of himself, to "be with" those who suffer.

Pastoral action, then, needs to have this as its purpose—first and foremost—to support and accompany the woman in this suffering condition, helping her to confront reality and to seek forgiveness with the power of faith, prayer and the sacraments. The Encyclical Letter *Evangelium Vitae* 99 reads:

> I would like to address a special word to women who have had an abortion. The Church is aware of the many factors which may have influenced your decision, and she does not doubt that in many cases it was a painful and even shattering decision. The wound in your heart may not yet have healed. Certainly what happened was and remains terribly wrong. But do not give in to discouragement and do not lose hope. Try rather to understand what happened and face it honestly. If you have not already done so, give yourselves over with humility and trust to repentance. The Father of mercies is ready to give you his forgiveness and his peace in the Sacrament of Reconciliation. To the same Father and his mercy you can with sure hope entrust your child.

A document of the National Conference of Italian Catholic Bishops for pastoral health care in 1989 defined pastoral work as "the presence and action of the Church to bear the light and grace of the Lord to those who suffer and to those who are their caretakers. It is given not only to the sick, but also to the healthy, inspiring a culture which is more sensitive to the suffering, and marginalized, and to the values of life and health."

"It is given not only to the sick, but also to the healthy," that is, to those who are not yet in a condition of suffering. In the case of abortion, this appeal should result in prevention on two dimensions. First, there is "direct" prevention through absolute efforts in support of women and in identifying the causes that may pressure women to choose abortion, in particular, looking for ways to be present to her and to not allow her to feel alone. Because being left alone—materially and morally—is one of the most serious violations against the dignity of women (and her child) and is tangible evidence of the failure of the solidarity that is meant to be the foundation of civil coexistence. Secondly there is "remote" prevention, through education on the value of new life called into existence, and on responsible motherhood and fatherhood, but above all, through education of the significance and value of sexuality and freedom.

It is not possible to build a true culture of life if you do not educate young people to understand and live sexuality, love and existence itself, in their full meanings:

> It is an illusion to think that we can build a true culture of human life if we do not help the young to accept and experience sexuality and love and the whole of life according to their true meaning and in their close interconnection. Sexuality, which enriches the whole person, manifests its inmost meaning in leading the person to the gift of self in love. The trivialization of sexuality is among the principal factors that have led to contempt for new life. Only a true love is able to protect life (EV, 97).

The Dark Side of Maternity

Eugenia Roccella

Abortion has existed for centuries. As Silvia Vegetti Finzi wrote, "abortion, practiced in a more or less clandestine form, has always been part of the technologies through which man tries to control life and death." The law can render it visible, but cannot establish it, or even cancel it: it is a phenomenon that exceeds the law, as a matter of fact; it lies outside its territory. To understand what I am saying requires a brief reconstruction of the difficult relationship between women and citizenship.

Western modernity is born reaffirming the historical separation between the public and the private, identified as the starting point of the sexual difference. On one side there is the home, the space in which the body is attended, the place of reproduction, of affections, of all that we define today as an ethic of healing; on the other hand, there is the public square, the space of the public word, of the exercise of rights and power. The existence of the public man, defined first by a disincarnated rationality, presupposes a private sphere where he can express his most intimate needs, the dependences of the heart and the body, and this division coincides with the sexual apartheid: the woman here and the man there. From the beginning, the concept of citizenship has excluded women, and this explains the difficult lot of the suffragists and the long time women spent attaining the longed-for right to vote.

The subject of citizenship is the individual. Etymologically, "individual" means "that which does not divide," and it indicates the element of irreducible subjectivity of the human. But the woman, with childbirth, is liter-

---

Eugenia Roccella is a journalist for *Avvenire*. Since May 2008, she has been Sub-Secretary of State to the Ministero del Lavoro, della Salute e delle Politiche Sociali (Italy).

ally divided; during the period of gestation there are two in one, life which contains another invisible life, by which its existence and development are safeguarded. This co-presence of subjects and of bodies is profoundly foreign to modern political thinking, in a certain sense "unthinkable" to their categories. In the public space there has never been a place for the maternal: and this has been one of the fundamental motives for the longtime alliance between women and the Catholic Church. The link between women and the Church has often been analyzed as a form of feminine backwardness, of incivility, of resistance to modernity. It is instead necessary to remember that the Church has welcomed and validated the feminine, attributing significance and importance to the ethics of healing, offering centrality to maternity, to the traditional feminine wisdom, the spiritual and moral values for which women saw themselves as their custodians and doorkeepers. It is enough just to think of the Marian devotion in Catholicism.

The juridical system and the access to citizenship are, therefore, based on the masculine body, which does not generate, does not divide; that is "individual." Women, on the other hand, divide. Their bodies are capable of containing and nourishing another, of splitting itself, of being two in one until the end, as well as after the birth: two beings linked by a chord that will be cut, physically and symbolically. Women are not "individuals." There is, therefore, an initial deficiency, in our society and in our culture that has never been filled. It is the incapacity to conceive of and include maternity, which remains a sort of anomaly of citizenship, of exceptions to the rule, where the rule is a body that does not divide. After World War II, thanks to a widening of the law, women of the Western world also entered the flux of mass individualism, though maintaining all the fitting ambiguity of the deficiency we have indicated. Emancipation (not to be confused with feminism) has ignored the contradiction, and has espoused without reservation the homogenization of the male model. In this way, maternity continues to be something not thought of, a "more" that is very private, which has little to do with the public dimension.

But maternity is much more. In the first place it is the biological and symbolic matrix of the human relation. And it is because we are all "born of woman" (the citation not being a case of Biblical expression), because we carry within us this precious experience, that we know what it is to love forever. To be born in the feminine womb signifies knowing that from the beginning we are entrusted to another, even still, to the body of another. The profound difference that separates human reproduction from that of other mammals is that it deals with an experience which interweaves in an indestructible way biology and relation. To be very clear: a cat is not the mother forever, a woman is. That initial symbiosis remains, for us humans, a chain that is not broken, a truly indissoluble link. Even today, in a world in which all relationships are fleeting, transitory, the relationship between mother and child appears as the only one which spontaneously resists, for which it is unimaginable to cut apart. When a woman is pregnant, she thus knows that she is committed for life: it does not only have to do with a concrete commitment, that is, of the time that she must dedicate to the care of her child, even if reduced to that which is today defined as "personal realization" (as if we cannot realize ourselves in dedication). It is a commitment which engages and disturbs the most profound and inexpressible sentiments and desires.

This does not happen for paternity, which is constructed in part from maternity. From only a few years back, with the DNA exam, is it possible to trace with certainty the identity of the biological father, but still today the asymmetry of reproduction in parenthood is evident. Fatherhood is always social. There are fathers who publicly recognize that a woman is the mother of his own children; a man can accept or refute his paternity, simply by accepting or refuting the woman. Only in being a mother does one experience in a full way the necessary link between biology and relation, and it is projected to the external, creating the model of conjugal love, of enduring parental responsibility, of the affective commitment and of the gift of oneself that endures for one's whole life.

This link, which is so strong, so absolute, is always a source for the woman of ambivalence, of contradictory sentiments that coexist. Behind maternity, which has always been surrounded by rites and taboos even in distant cultures, there is the terrible proximity of the mystery of life and death: every woman knows that in giving life she prepares for death, and that life that we give we do not govern, it is not an available good, totally in our possession.

Maternity is not only a joyful experience; it carries fear with it, at times depression and rejection, because it implies contact with the sacred and the elsewhere, with that which transcends us and which we cannot control, but only welcome. In the experience of birth there is an interior sense of limit, even in terms of sentiments: maternal omnipotence accepts little by little letting itself be disarmed and made powerless. The child, at the moment of conception, is totally dependent on the mother, totally entrusted to her physical protection; it has been said that expectant women are sentinels of the invisible. Then, when the baby comes into the world, he gradually becomes more autonomous, and the mother should help him to grow and leave her. The limit goes back to the condition of being a creature, to human impotence, to the absurdity of the pretense of self-determination and of completely deciding for oneself. On the other hand, maternity is connected to power, to be for the other the only font of survival, of well-being, of protection, of life. The ambivalence of the maternal is, therefore, structural, and cannot be eliminated.

This is, naturally, also from the point of view of the emotive: no maternity is completely joyful, because it is always imbued with anxiety, for oneself and for the one who is to be born. When we become mothers we do not know whether the baby will be born healthy, if everything will go well, and we do not know if we will be in the condition to be able to confront childbirth, and later to look after our child, to educate and raise him. The increasing medicalization of the delivery and pregnancy has increased instead of diminished, these profound and secret anxieties that often never come to surface. At one time, when maternal and infant mortality was higher, and the risks for the mother were serious, there existed a network of familial solidarity around the woman, that which has been defined as the chain of feminine knowing: competencies transmitted from mother to daughter, enlarged to the kinships and friendships between women, and the figure of the midwife and wet nurse. Today this chain has snapped, and the mother is often completely alone with her child, in urban contexts in which relationships are dispersed and difficult, and in which the organization of labor and of services is modeled to a time that is hardly favorable to women. For this reason countries that want to be favorable towards childbearing, as with France, anticipate a series of support services that are not of an assistance or specialist type, but which tend to reconstruct a fabric of support, that culture of maternity which has been lost. France, for example, has confronted the problem of lowering the percentage of infanticide, and has had good success; they have arranged the monitoring of at-risk women through centers which they are able to turn to for small daily help that does not require recourse to a pediatrician or to social assistance, and, provides structures for the acceptance of the most grave cases. On the other hand, the same country has not been able to reduce abortions, because it has not linked the abortion phenomenon to the dark side of maternity, but to a question abstractly rationalized from contraception and procreative planning. In all the countries where this has happened, where it has facilitated access to the diverse forms of contraception, and to that which has been defined as emergency contraception (morning-after pill), and where it has only pointed out precocious and diffused information and sexual education, abortion has not diminished, but often has grown. In this sense, Italy is an interesting exception: in Italy abortions have diminished in a consistent mode, although there is not the habit of chemical contraception, and despite the politics of spreading contraceptives to minors. In Italy abortions have diminished because it still "has" the family, because familial relationships are still a levee to social disintegration, although signs of the crisis are beginning to be seen.

Abortion is not a rational question, and it cannot be rationalized completely. If it could be, those who would have reason for trying to eliminate it, or in any case to reduce it through policies of spreading contraception, would have been right. Following this logically, contraception should cause the diminishing of interventions for the interruption of pregnancies, but instead between the two phenomena there is not a necessary correlation; it is enough to see the European statistics to verify this. In this sense, it is useless to criminalize the "futile" motivations for which some women interrupt their pregnancies. The few surveys that have been done on the explicit motivations for abortions have always been disappointing: when it does not have to do with socio-economic reasons, women do not come out and explain the profound and true reasons for which they resort to abortion, exactly because they are almost never motivations of a logical or objective type. Some studies have even spoken of it as a "failure of thought," precisely to underline the profoundly conflicted and non-rational nature of abortion. Nevertheless, it is never about a light gesture in the life of a woman, even when it is done with apparent lightness. The explicit motives, often inconsistent, mask reasons that are of a more complex decipherability, linked to the fear of not succeeding, to the incapacity of confronting an event greater than ourselves, in which women often feel completely alone.

Abortion is not comprehensible, and, therefore, neither avoidable nor treatable by medicine, if it is not thought of within the maternal condition, and from its extraordinary specificity. Without entering into the significance of the maternal, it is not possible to understand why a woman is able to commit an act of violence against the child she carries in her womb and against herself. Maternity, as we have said, is a complex event, that mixes desire and denial, life and death, feelings of omnipotence and of devastating inadequacies. It is an event that presents itself as transcendent and together with all that is imminent: life does not belong to us, but it manifests itself concretely in the body of a woman, putting into play the entire feminine identity. In maternity is embodied, literally, the dumbfounding phrase of Rimbaud, "I is another."

To socially heal abortion means to try to reduce it, that it would ideally reach zero. In order to succeed, there is a need for a policy of prevention that succeeds at individualizing and welcoming the personal and familial needs which at times are even difficult to put in focus. There is the need for attention spread throughout the territory, committed to subsidiarity and to modulated social services, more than to structures and standardized services of the state type. But none of this can be done if maternity is not re-evaluated in a strong manner. The English debate that has come out today in the press about the television operator who failed to tell her employer that she was expecting a baby is indicative. The expectant woman is spoken of as a worker that is disloyal because she has hidden a fault, something which is considered harmful to the company. No one says she is disloyal in confrontations of women and families; it is the society that does not regard the "child-good." The idea that offspring are a social wealth has vanished for some time now, despite all the analysis that is made on the deficiency of vitality, also of economics, of a society of elderly, which the West will become.

It is urgent, therefore, to put maternity at the center, on a cultural plan and on that of public policies, beyond simple rhetoric. As long as we do not succeed in this, it will be difficult to confront with efficiency the dark evil of abortion.

The Psychological Consequences of Abortive Mentality in the Family

Philippe De Cathelineau

I was a student in medicine in Paris at the time of the discussions that preceded the vote of the Veil law that liberalized abortion in France. At the time, probably somewhat indoctrinated by the feminist propaganda, I welcomed the text, ratified by the French parliament in 1975, which invented the term IVG, or voluntary interruption of pregnancy ["*interruption volontaire de grossesse*"]. The elected officials in this way intended to help women in distress due to the conception of an unwanted child, by proposing to allow access to de-penalized and medically supervised abortion, and erasing the criminal aspect of the procedure. It seemed like social progress.

I did not however, ever join myself to the misleading choir who claimed that the human embryo was just a "glob of flesh" and whose extraction posed no more moral question than having a tooth pulled. But I had vivid memories of a young woman who had been gravely sickened by septicemia perfringes, contracted from an illegal abortion, conducted without any notion of hygiene or antiseptic. Like many French, I thought that in the absence of being able to save the unwanted child, whose future was darkened by the fact that he was unwanted, society could at least protect the mother from the derelict schemes of illegal abortion providers and other "angel makers."

This discussion, built on pity and apparent compassion, did fly. In the name of charity, those of us who, like me, claimed to represent the Gospels, and to be in solidarity with others, felt that medical units specializing in the abortion procedure, which could be free and accessible to all women, should be put in place throughout the world in order to help the so-called "women in distress."

Philippe De Cathelineau is founder of the Association Splendeur de la Vie (France).

We had simply forgotten that negative actions cannot create the conditions for happiness. How many unfortunate victims have made this painful decision since the vote on this law? The road to hell is truly paved with good intentions.

I have seen so many broken women, couples in crisis, families torn apart, society destabilized . . . and I am not even speaking of the innocents assassinated, since they do not have a voice to speak.

But the drama has just begun. The new outpatient practice of abortion, coupled with a denial of its reality and aftermath, will inevitably increase the amount of grief, drowned in remorse and guilt, which, through lack of recognition and treatment, is able to vent itself only in anger and revolt, despair and violence.

A fact, however, could have disturbed democratic spirits, tied to the respect of freedom of opinion: Soon, all those voices that could speak out against the trivialization of abortion were muzzled with the utmost rigor. Its author, castigated by the media, could only be under the influence of "old demons." How had this new totalitarianism, after the century we had just lived through, not alarmed our consciousness sooner?

This is what caught my attention. I will always remember one evening discussion, in which Prof. Jérôme Lejeune, whom I had the good fortune to have as a professor of genetics—because he was a remarkable teacher—was attacked by a group of angry students, whose arguments had reduced themselves to spewing violence and unimaginable hate. And he, alone against everyone—never at that time would I have dared to try and defend him!—remained calm under attack, while some brandished their fists under his nose and patiently repeated his argument.

Peace and strength were on his side. They demonstrated, better than any discussion, the divine truth that inhabited him.

It's time to open our eyes, as we have learned to do and to face our mistakes with courage especially from now on; to correct them, to be aware of the damage that abortion leaves man with. How much suffering do we still tolerate under the pretext of protecting an already unholy act that finds justification only in the selfish and backwards proponents of an outdated ideology?

A strong witness like that of Susan Stanford[1] could have at least attracted the attention of the feminists. It never did. The women who claimed to be the spokeswomen of their sisters in distress worked hard to keep her quiet—

proof that their fight is purely ideological and not motivated by any female solidarity.

That being said, we will therefore try to see the dramatic psychological consequences that the abortive mentality introduces within the family.

It now appears indisputable that the abortion mentality generates a number of damaging sequences, which pervade familial love and engender grave psychological problems of which children are the first victims. I would like to cite:

1. The perverse ideology of the wanted child.

2. The use of a scapegoat.

3. The relationship between abuse and abortion.

4. The spiral of violence and its tragic triangle.

THE PERVERSE IDEOLOGY OF THE WANTED CHILD

"*The first right of the child is to be desired.*" This slogan was echoed by the United Nations and the bulk of the rest of the world to justify their abortive politics and birth regulation, insinuating that once we eliminate all the undesired children, there won't be any abused children. This has never been the case; we have observed exactly the opposite.

Why? Because in reality, hidden under the best of intentions, there is a war of ideas even more dangerous. Even if the first right of the child is to be desired, what about the child who is not?

In fact, the child who is not wanted no longer has rights, since he has lost the right that precedes all others, the right to exist! The ideology of the wanted child is thus a death sentence, whose pending execution depends only on the decision of parents or social services, usurping an extravagant power.

This ideology is in complete conflict with the Gospel message. From a Christian point of view, in effect, the first right of a child is not to be desired, but to be welcomed.

Even better, obviously, if the child is ardently desired! It is very important that this be the case! I am not advocating for irresponsible fertility, but quite the contrary!

However, the welcoming of the child should not be subordinated to the desires one may or may not have for him, nor in the momentary economic conditions in which a person may find himself or herself, especially because if we put forth the good will and effort, these challenges can all be met.

The same is true for the recognition of his humanity. This humanity, inherent to all human beings, does not depend on the conditions exterior to him, which vary with changing fashions and ethical circumstances.

It is this perversion of parental love, when the mother and father submit the welcoming of the infant to the fluctuations of their immediate desires, which will lead to, within the families where abortion is an option—and *a fortiori* in the families which practice this—an entire birth of the abortion survivor syndrome, which Prof. Philip Ney had individualized, before even being alerted to the signs of post-abortion syndrome in the parents.

For in these families, even though the abortion is not spoken of—and this is practically true in all cases; it is a pseudo-secret maintained with complicity for all generations—the child who has escaped knows in his subconscious he has been kept alive for fortuitous reasons through the capricious desire of his parents' decision, where the perennial nature of his existence and the recognition of his humanity were weighed against other considerations, altogether secondary and ridiculous in regard to what he is . . . or is believed to be.

There are certain people who doubt the veracity of this assertion. These people must lack a certain human experience and knowledge of children and the mysterious link that unites mother and child!

Numerous clinical observations indeed show that the child born after the abortion of an older sibling often perceives, very precociously and probably while still *in utero,* the drama through which his mother was plunged and the violent torments she underwent, rendering her ambivalent to her current subject.

It is a matter of course of a vague knowledge, subconscious, not verbalized; but the facts are there: the child is already imprinted with an insurmountable injury. Because from birth, since the days in the womb, the newborn may show serious behavioral issues characteristic of abortion survivor syndrome.

To understand the origin of this illness, it is necessary to understand that when the parents subordinate the child's survival to their desire, the infant loses *ipso facto* all intrinsic value, claiming life solely through the fluctuating desire of his parents, where through the laws of society, he is given the right to exist. He perceives that his right to life is no longer linked to his human condition, which has no value in itself, but is contingent on the opinion of others.

Therefore, to merit the right to life, or moreover to preserve the right to survive, he must try without ceasing to correspond to the desire his parents had for him. This will prove impossible.

Further troubled by personal difficulties of his parents, themselves subjected to the upheavals that make up post-abortion syndrome, the family situation will quickly degenerate into a succession of conflicts. His life threatens to become a nightmare.

In addition, the child perceives sharply the objectification of his person, and he suffers from being for his parents, (who claim to love him), nothing but a toy between their hands, which they can alternately and without notice, at the discretion of their whims, sometimes adulate and sometimes reject.

On the other hand, a child who is born to a family where abortion is unthinkable remains unharmed by the psychological perturbations caused by conflicts resulting from abortion. Not holding the right to life as a precarious chance that escaped refusal from his parents, he does not have to struggle to remain in good standing with them. But being conscious of his intrinsic value, he will respect himself and naturally respect others. He begins life with conditions that allow him to flourish.

THE USE OF A SCAPEGOAT

Men have always needed to look for scapegoats, to protect themselves from the agitation and guilt associated with the reminder of their errors and the morality of their choices. Pointing the finger at the scapegoat, punishing it, even putting it to death, allows individuals, families, and even society to exonerate themselves of mistakes they cannot come to terms with.

By diverting the anger towards the designated culprit, they sense at least temporarily a relief, a respite, that encourages the feelings of indignation that they created to deflect guilt away from themselves.

But resorting to the scapegoat, far from resolving problems, rejects resolutions and perpetuates the issues: burying all possibilities of reconciliation, reparation, and pardon necessitated by the situation of conflict, preventing a peaceful or lasting outcome.

The scapegoats are never difficult to find: all the little ones, underlings and paupers, those without vote and without voices fit the description. The ill and the mentally handicapped, the old and the dying, are all designated scapegoats. One could also include other bothersome groups: the Jews, ethnic peoples, priests. Every era has its own.

Unborn children are very convenient scapegoats, since no one fears their protests or rebellion.

They are reproached for disturbing the stability and intimacy of the couple, of ruining sexual pleasure and breaking up the household, but also they are found to be responsible for overpopulation and poverty, or to be future polluters who worsen the greenhouse effect and threaten the ozone, etc. In short, they will assume responsibility for conflicts and frustrations that adults, their parents and grandparents, have not resolved, and one will accuse them with a straight face of being the cause of many other world problems.

Once born, their parents will blame them for domestic disputes, burden them with their professional failures or inability to achieve their goals. And as scapegoats, they will soon experience the suffering of those around them.

We will further develop this topic, the fatal consequences of the trivialization of abortion, in the next chapter, namely the link between child abuse and abortion.

The conflict may remain dormant for quite some time, bursting forth secondarily. For the young child knows he needs his parents to survive. From then on, he can be brought to protect them and even sacrifice himself: thus, he will not hesitate to intervene in their disputes to divert their anger to him.

In doing so, he reinforces his position as a scapegoat, and in return, it multiplies the grounds of his abuse. But he will deny the abuses in order to avoid his parents being questioned by authorities and prevent himself from being removed from the home.

It then begins a vicious cycle that is for him a veritable alienation, gravely hindering his development.

However, despite his efforts, he will never measure up to his parents' expectations. He is a prisoner of a drama in which he himself becomes the actor, which he cannot nor will not leave. For he prefers to face the wrath of his parents than to risk abandonment.

Moreover, he may take out his frustration on his brothers and sisters, themselves often facing the same difficulties, then on his classmates or teachers, who then take their turn being his scapegoat, and then his source of affliction. He may then finally turn his back against society and become antisocial.

The victim becomes the executioner. We will see in a later chapter, dealing with the tragic triangle of violence, how the victim will be brought to repeat his own history, and tries to understand his own suffering while convincing himself that it is not really so serious.

The child-scapegoats can never be happy: they have forged a deplorable picture of themselves and hate themselves even more because they are often put in situations of failure.

The most painful position is held by the replacement child, conceived solely to overcome the guilty conscience after abortion. He has the combined handicap of being the child particularly desired by his parents and that of polarizing the hopes of his parents awarded to him by their remorse, crystallized thereafter on the lost child, now idealized. He will bear for them all the hopes they had for their lost child, while they painfully relive the aftershocks of unfinished or repressed mourning.

The child's inevitable failures will aggravate their disappointment and anger. The replacement child thus embarks on a violent spiral that, if not eventually taken care of, will often end in death or one of its substitutes (drugs, etc).

The use of scapegoats has always existed. But it has an unprecedented existence today, only limited by the madness of our times. There is not a tree that falls in the woods, a river that floods its banks, an avalanche, a clumsy fall on the sidewalk, or a late bus for which we cannot find a responsible party; and television journalists like to find satisfaction for the victims, if the suspect is severely punished, or anger if the courts are lenient.

Now we have even arrived at finding culprits for congenital diseases!

This insane, limitless determination says a lot about the problems in our society. I see the effects of the decline and weakening of Christianity in the conscience. Jesus Christ, in effect, is the scapegoat *par excellence,* the perfect victim, offered in reparation for the sins of the world: the sacrificial lamb taking all upon himself, without complaint.

The human embryo today, smallest of all men, is the new sacrificial lamb. *"Amen, I say to you, whatever you did for one of these least brothers of mine, you did for me"* (Mt 25, 40). Jesus warns of this similarity in advance, likening the smallest and poorest of our society to himself.

THE LINK BETWEEN ABUSE AND ABORTION

The cause-and-effect relation linking abortion to the abuse of children is indisputable.

It appears, in effect, that the persons who have undergone an abortion have a greater tendency to abuse their children and vice versa; those who are abused have a greater tendency to abort.

However, we are not concluding that those who have aborted will all be bad parents, nor that the victims of abuse will all be driven to abort their own children! It demonstrates only a tendency, already explainable in part because we have already revealed that scapegoats often become voluntary punching bags. But this passage, happily, is far from automatic.

It depends in part on the capacity of the person to overcome his injuries and of his own fragility. It is clear that those who already suffer from psychological illness or even from minor psychological troubles are more vulnerable than those unscathed by these occurrences.

It also depends on the path taken, by the help given to them from their peers, the presence or not of a helpful spouse, and on many individual and environmental factors, among which recourse to a peaceful religion is surely important.

Abortion and abuse are at the same time cause and effect. The link does not necessarily verify itself in the history of a single person, but certainly within the interior of a family.

I will explain here what is called the trans-generational phenomenon.

It manifests itself within guilt-ridden families whose conflicts drag on unresolved, or from unaddressed grief, buried in the depths of family history. The adults, worn out by the weight of previous generations, reject the issues that plague them from their children. For generations, one scapegoat leads to another, who abuse and destroy themselves anew.

If the idea of the wanted child is and continues to be lauded by governments, as it is across the board, it is because it suggests that aborting unwanted children will eliminate those who will be unwelcomed, and therefore —like the roads to hell which are truly paved with good intentions—one may safely eliminate the existence of abused children by removing their principal cause.

How could this be the case? That throughout the world the occurrence of child abuse is increasing, at a rate parallel to that of abortion. In other words, the increase of abortion leads to an increase of child abuse!

Why does this fact astonish some? The casual link between abortion and abuse is not surprising: elective abortion is indeed the cause of post-abortion syndrome in the parents, of which loss of stability and bouts of depression are frequent occurrences. A mother with abortion in her family history, of whom she herself may have been a survivor (because she was born into a family where abortion was practiced), will therefore be more inclined than others to fall into post-partum depression, specifically due to the fact that this birth may revive previous feelings of guilt and anxiety.

This pain may prevent her from bonding with her newborn; she may abandon it, refuse to touch or breastfeed the child. The neglected child will demand his due; his cries will drive the mother to lose patience . . . in a moment of weakness she may be brought to shake or even hurt the child. And the child, totally dependent, does not understand the situation, and not having any way to manage or improve it, sinks into incomprehension and fear.

This is an oversimplified example. It explains where this situation stems from (insidiously and inevitably most often from past wounds left ignored which have worsened over time), without having to accuse the parents of being essentially cruel. In reality, the unhappy are often alienated by their own suffering, which corrupts their judgment and bruises their good will.

All child abuses are by nature unique and from variable origins. It is necessary to distinguish the different forms of neglect.

Negligence, in which the child is ignored, is generally considered from a psychological point of view more damaging than abuse, in which the child is only considered bad. Children, in fact, know their own needs intuitively: nourishment, affection, etc. Negligence deprives them of these essentials; they are taken care of in cruelty, and are grateful to their parents, even as they receive scraps in substitution for real nourishment. On the other hand, by worsening its effects indirectly, this negligence renders the children more vulnerable to all other forms of cruelty.

It is equally necessary to differentiate between the three types of abuse and two forms of neglect, of which there are unequal consequences: the abuses can be verbal, physical or sexual, and the neglect can be physical or affective.

Contrary to popular belief, the most brutal abuses are not necessarily the most traumatizing on the psychological plane. Thus verbal abuse, when repeated, can be more detrimental than physical abuse. Indeed, it may be worse, because it is much more destructive to be told repeatedly that you are less than nothing, than to take a spanking even if it leaves bruises and a stinging pain.

Verbal abuses ("You are nothing but a little idiot! I should have aborted you! It's because of you I had my abortion!") may appear at first to be the more harmless approach. In reality, it fills the child with bitterness and follows him all of his life; becoming an adult, he will use these statements against himself when angry, these hurtful words heard in childhood, he even condemns himself of being this detestable and despicable character that his parents continue to accuse him of being.

Negligence, whether it is physical or affective, also causes the worst harm, because children who are neglected feel they have no value. Therefore, they are exposed to all sorts of abuse, desperately seeking signs of attention. And they permit this kind of abuse repeatedly as if the pain was worth more than no affection at all.

Sexual abuses are always grave, so grave that they most often generate a greater sense of guilt. Sexuality touches the most intimate part of a person, and its abuse consequently damages the person's self-image very deeply. Because they are rarely isolated incidents, most often associated with affective neglect, (they are, as we have just demonstrated a comprehensive result), the child seeks hopelessly to mitigate the lack of affection from which he suffers. Even in the absence of physical trauma (molestations, for example), it is thus likely to result in very heavy psychological consequences, which prevent the adult from maturing healthily and happily in his sexuality, with all the consequences one may imagine.

These reflections on the consequences of childhood abuse and their specific horrors in respect to their categorical appearance are easy to put into perspective. The harmfulness of the worst abuses depends heavily of course on their intensity and repetition. These remarks nevertheless emphasize that the worst abuses may pass completely unnoticed: some are more easily noticed, like physical abuse, which is more likely to leave visible evidence, while emotional neglect and verbal abuse—sometimes most destructive of the personality—pass totally unnoticed.

Or in the cases of physical abuse, the child will at least receive the building blocks he needs to construct his personality. Of course, they are poorly hewn, but at least they're there. The child's structure is thus comparatively stable, and repairs can often be made without a large degree of difficulty.

On the other hand, in the case of emotional neglect, a less blatant abuse for those involved, the child will always lack the emotional foundation that he was never given at the time, something of capital importance to bodily integrity. From then on, his emotional construction will be shaky, and its restoration will be quite a delicate process. How do we replace the foundations of a building, without the risk of damaging the upper floors, when it's found to be a wreck?

Maltreatment and lack of proper care destroy, little by little, the image that the child has of himself and impoverishes his developing personality. These wounds may heal of course, if they are properly diagnosed and treated. But these wounds leave permanent scars: a lost childhood can never be replaced.

THE SPIRAL OF VIOLENCE AND ITS TRAGIC TRIANGLE

A violent incident in life often leads to more violence, as if the violated person were to catch his finger in a gearbox. And we observe that he is carried away in spite of it, most often without his knowledge, in a sort of vertiginous spiral.

Many reasons contribute to this fact. The first is that victims of violence, through a sort of complacence and subtle complicity towards their aggressor, protect and contribute in some way to the abuse they suffer, themselves maintaining the destruction of their personality.

Still another reason stems from the fact that a victim of violence has a natural penchant to want to repeat the drama, as if it were necessary to relive it in order to understand it, trying to penetrate the mysteries of the tragedy he has suffered and analyze the circumstances which escaped him, but also to try to convince himself that what he lived through must not be so grave after all.

From that time on, he replays the drama in two ways: on the one hand submitting himself to the harm of his aggressor; on the other hand directing the abuse that he himself suffered towards a new victim.

The result of this unconscious double-movement not only perpetuates the violence—the victim places himself in the role of victim—but the tragedy turns on itself with the victim becoming the abuser.

Another part of the responsibility falls on the witnesses to the abuses; because of their silence, their compliance, and numerous justifications—"I didn't know! I couldn't intervene! I couldn't get involved!"—it is allowed to happen.

By closely examining the circumstances and the evolution of these dramas and their players, we realize that the aggressors, victims, and witnesses are linked to each other by a sort of triangular relationship that turns on itself, as if the roles, sooner or later, become interchangeable.

The victims, once they are parents, become in their turn the aggressors, as we have seen in the preceding chapter, and vice versa; the aging aggressors, abandoned without forgiveness, become victims. Daily observation shows this to be true.

More ambiguous is the role of the witness, who at first glance seems passive if not innocent. In fact, he actively takes part in the tragedy the moment he cannot admit to his responsibility in allowing its continuation to perpetuate without intervening. So, he will be inclined to exonerate himself by using the scapegoat, becoming the executioner himself, while his cowardice leads him down the slippery slope of dehumanization. For, whether he wants it or not, by washing his hands of the drama that unfolds before his eyes, he is an unconscious victim. He thus re-enters, unknowingly, the spiral of violence.

Therefore as a result, each one takes his turn, sometimes being the aggressor, sometimes the victim, and sometimes the witness, unless he can positively intervene to break the cycle.

What is important therefore, if one wanted to help in these situations, is to consider that they are all—of course in different degrees, but none the less in a real and definite manner—the victims. At least they all will be, one day or another.

In family dramas, parents as much as children, husbands as much as wives, grandparents as much as other relatives, are all prisoners of the tragic triangle of violence, drawn into the sort of spiral that is hard to escape. They are all entitled to our compassion, because they all need to be rescued.

However, this surely does not exclude recognition of responsibility and reparation for the acts committed! Healing these profound wounds, in fact, cannot be done except through a true path of forgiveness, reclaiming true pardon and thus real reparation, without which forgiveness could not exist.

But this requires us—if one wants to act in a positive way towards the participants of violence—to bring towards each one of them, even the primary culprit, an attitude of compassion, of love and of mercy, devoid of personal judgment. This attitude cannot be achieved without being a simultaneous advocate for truth without complicity, never calling something that which it is not. This is very important.

Consequently, one may understand how abortion cannot only be the cause of abuse, but also a consequence, from maltreatment experienced during childhood.

Does a worse kind of abuse exist? Certainly, it does for the unborn child who paid the price, because he pays for it with his life. It is an absolute abuse. But, even if she refuses to admit it—those who chose to abort know well in their own heart—it is also a great harm to the woman. In choosing death for her child, she knows that she is at the same time his executioner. And yet, because she has embarked on the spiral of violence, and because she feels the need to replay the tragedy of which she is the victim, (it is truly she who chooses it), beyond the pressure of those around her, she directs the abuse towards herself.

One notes in fact a vertiginous permutation of the roles within the tragic triangle of violence, and that each actor, to varying degrees of course, is in turn, the executioner, the witness and the victim.

The innocent child causes his mother to suffer because of his inopportune entry at a time when his mother was unready to welcome him: he is the executioner. He participates in the tragedy without having said a word: he is the witness. He is sacrificed: he is the victim.

The mother chooses death for her son: she is the executioner. She is abandoned into the hands of the abortionist: she is the witness. She is profoundly wounded by the abortion: she is the victim.

The doctor is responsible for the killing: he is the executioner. He respects the choice of the woman: he is the witness. He destroys a part of his own humanity by acting contrary to his vocation: he is the victim.

And society, does it not occupy simultaneously all three parts of the tragic triangle? It does not offer many alternatives to women in distress: it is the executioner. It leaves abortion to practice itself with general indifference: it is the witness. By ignoring its weakest members, it destroys itself: it is the victim.

CONCLUSION

I would like to make four statements, drawn from what I have already said:

The first statement is that the contraceptive mentality—a child when I want it!—is the door to the abortive mentality; moreover, the proof that contraception failures are almost always solved with abortion.

The second message is that in abortion, it is the children who pay the price; it is truly they—and I do not speak of the sacrificed child, because he does not say a word!—who pay the greatest price!

The third message is that we must always look on those who are players in this drama with compassion, for they are all victims.

The fourth message is that through our silence and apathy we too are knowingly the witnesses and the unconscious victims of abortion, engaged, whether we like it or not, in the process of dehumanization[2].

REFERENCES

1. Susan Stanford—*Une femme blessée*—Editons *Sarment.*

2. To learn more, the reader may reference my various publications, all available on Amazon.fr:

- *Les lendemains douloureux de l'avortement—Quand Rachel pleure ses enfants* (Preface of Cardinal Alfonso López Trujillo, president of the Pontifical Council for the Family), Editions CLD, 2003.

- *Aux sources de la culture de vie—Père et mère Il les créa* (Preface of Cardinal Paul Poupard, president of the Pontifical Council on Culture), Editions CLD, 2003.

- *L'Eglise et les réalités biomédicales—La bonne nouvelle de la vie,* Editions CLD, 2004.

- *La France entre lumières et ténèbres—D'un génocide à l'autre,* Editions Cheminements-Arsis, 2007.

The Psychological Aftermath of Abortion for Children and Families: A Clinical Perspective

E. JOANNE ANGELO, M.D.

Dr. Cathelineau's observation that violence begets violence brings to mind an 8-year-old boy who was a patient in my psychiatric practice. He was upset about a violent accident which had occurred the day before in which several people were killed. He was attending a Catholic school, and in an attempt to console him, I asked him, "What do you think happens to people when they die?" He said, "What do you think?" I said, "I asked you first." He said, "I asked you second!" I said, "I think they go to heaven." He said, "Yes, but not everybody! Adam and Eve didn't go to heaven. If they didn't eat that apple, bad things wouldn't happen. That explosion wouldn't have happened yesterday! When I grow up, I'm going to make a time machine and kill Adam and Eve!"

Although I agree with Dr. Cathelineau's understanding of the issues of physical abuse which may precede or follow abortion, I would like to address another negative psychological aftermath of abortion: post-abortion grief. The many faces of post-abortion grief in women, men, and children are often unrecognized or misdiagnosed.

In every abortion a child dies. The death of a child is perhaps the most difficult loss to mourn. When a premature baby dies in an intensive care nursery, the staff encourages the parents to hold the baby, to take pictures, to plan a funeral and a burial. Family and friends gather around the grieving parents to console them and pray for them.

Parents of aborted babies, on the other hand, typically are not given per-

---

E. Joanne Angelo, M.D. is Assistant Clinical Professor of Psychiatry, Tufts University School of Medicine, Boston, Mass.

mission to grieve. The mother is expected to feel relieved that her problem is over and "get on with her life." The father of the aborted child is expected to have no feelings at all. "It didn't happen in his body," we are often told.

Ordinarily, grief after an elective abortion is uniquely poignant because it is largely hidden. There most often are no provisions made to assist the parents of aborted children in their grieving—they have no child to hold, no photographs, no wake or funeral, and no grave to visit. A post-abortion woman typically finds herself alone to cope not only with the loss of the child she will never know, but also with her personal responsibility for her child's death with its ensuing guilt and shame. As time passes, and she becomes more aware of her truncated parenthood, her grief often becomes overwhelming.

Waves of unexpected emotion—sorrow, emptiness, guilt, depression, anger, hopelessness, and suicidal thoughts—may flood her consciousness on the date the child would have been born each year, on the anniversary of the abortion, Mother's Day, Father's Day, at the birth of another baby, at the time of another death in the family, seeing a child the age her child would have been or a baby in a television ad. Sights and sounds may cause flashbacks to the abortion experience such as the sound of the suction in a dentist's office, the sound of a vacuum cleaner, a pelvic examination, or driving by the abortion clinic. She may have great difficulty trusting persons like those who advised her abortion—her partner, her friends, her physician, her parents, or professional counselors. If she enters marriage without revealing her dark secret, her husband may never understand her mood swings, her difficulty with intimacy, her ambivalent relationship with subsequent children, or her attempts to deal with insomnia and recurrent nightmares with alcohol, prescribed medication, or illicit drugs.[1]

Men too grieve the loss of their children. As Vincent Rue has said, "For men and women alike, the feeling of emptiness may last a lifetime, for parents are parents forever, even of a dead child."[2] Men who have tried to prevent their partner's abortion and found they have no legal right to protect their unborn child feel emasculated and stripped of their protective and nurturing role as fathers. Men who insisted on the abortion, paid for it, or did nothing to dissuade their partner from engaging an abortionist to kill their child, may become overwhelmed by guilt, shame and self-loathing. Both groups of men often become angry, anxious, distrustful of women, abuse alcohol and drugs, and despair of ever being the husbands and fathers they had hoped to be.

Subsequent children born to parents who have suffered the tragedy of abortion or children who were born prior to the abortion are also burdened with the consequences of this life-changing event in their parents' lives. For example, a 5-year-old boy who was told, "Mommy has a baby in her tummy. The baby may not be all right. Mommy and Daddy are going to see the doctor. If the baby is not all right the doctor is going to send the baby back to God." This boy may forever worry that if he is not "all right" he cannot be assured of his parents' love and protection. The perceived lack of unconditional love may lead to the need for the child to lie and to hide any problems or mistakes from those who would be best able to help him, for fear of loss of their love and esteem which is essential for his survival.

Some case illustrations may serve as examples of the negative effects of abortion on children and families. The following are true stories from clinical practice or accounts written for the express purpose of being shared with others.

> "Jeannie," a 6-year-old girl, was referred to a child psychiatrist because she refused to go to school. Every morning her mother would take her kicking and screaming from the car into the school building. A terrible scene followed when her teacher and her guidance counselor tried to separate "Jeannie" from her mother, who gave her mixed messages by holding her tightly and at the same time telling her that everything would be ok when she left. This behavior which was once diagnosed as "School Phobia" is now called Separation Anxiety. It is clear that the mother and the child have mutual problems in separating from one another. Once the separation was accomplished each day, "Jeannie" enjoyed her school experience and related well to the teacher and the other children. Her mother, on the other hand, worried constantly about her all day, and often called the school to ask how she was doing. In my work with the family, I searched for the root of the anxious attachment between mother and child, and the mother's overprotectiveness and constant worry about her daughter. Only after I had gained the mother's trust did she reveal that she had had an abortion prior to "Jeannie's" birth. "Jeannie" was her replacement baby—so precious to her that she needed to be protected at all costs. When her mother's post-abortion grief and guilt were addressed, and she was helped to mourn her lost child and ask the child's forgiveness and God's forgiveness as Pope John Paul II taught in *Evangelium Vitae* 99, she was able to allow her daughter the freedom to take the appropriate developmental step of attending a full day school program.

In the next case a young adult patient reflects on the burden of being "wanted" when a sibling had been aborted.

> Doctor, I am desperate. I am depressed much of the time and often I think of killing myself. I cannot enjoy life. I know that I have not used my abilities and opportunities well. I have always been that way, but now that I have lost my joy, things are really bad. I keep wondering if people really like me and I am terrified they might reject me. I do not trust many people, particularly not my parents. Sometimes I have queer sensations of some little spirits bothering me. Frankly, I do not feel that I deserve to be alive. What is the matter with me? Am I going crazy?. . .
>
> I have had these problems much of my life. I just found out my mother had an abortion. I have suspected it for a long time. I can remember as a child my father and mother whispering about her having become pregnant and what should they do? I was surprised when I did not get a little brother or sister, but I was too afraid to ask what happened. The topic of abortion came up in a discussion I overheard the other day. My mother informed her friend that she had an abortion but insisted it did not bother her. But I do not see why her abortion should trouble me; I strongly support a woman's right to choose.
>
> Well, I guess I am just lucky. I realize they could have aborted me. I was conceived shortly after my mother and father married, but I know they wanted me. Because they wanted me I am here today.
>
> It is a good feeling. It is wonderful to be wanted. But sometimes, even now, I wonder what would have happened if I was not wanted? I wonder what would have happened if people stopped liking me? I put an awful lot of effort into being popular. I guess it is because I need to be wanted.
>
> I feel this enormous burden that I have to be the best in everything that my parents could expect of a child, almost as if I had to compensate for something. Through most of my teenage years, I tried very hard to please them. Eventually, I gave up and became bitterly rebellious. It was not because they were critical of me. It was this sense of being unworthy of all their love and attention. Now I see that it is possibly connected with knowing that my brother or sister died although he or she had done nothing wrong.
>
> There are times when I feel as if I am living with a suspended death sentence. I feel I was supposed to die, not my brother or sister, and now some event will suddenly kill me. At times I felt so awful that I wanted to die. Taking drugs did not help. I wanted to get high to escape reality. But it seemed that none of these experiences made me surpass what I was going

through. I wonder if my parents discussed whether they would or would not abort me. It is awful to feel that they sat in judgment on an innocent child's life, especially since the child could not speak and defend himself. Someday I am going to ask them if they considered aborting me. There are some things I just have to know.[3]

As painful as the truth is, it needs to be brought to light in order to prevent the festering secrets from poisoning family relationships.

In the next story, a woman recalls how she developed an aversion to her favorite doll as a young child when her mother had an abortion, even though she was not told about the abortion at the time.

> When I was four years old I suddenly decided that I did not want to play with dolls anymore. I wanted a real baby. One day I took my doll . . . and strangely enough I buried it at the end of the garden. It was only years later that I realized that my mother had had an abortion when I was 4 years old. Only now I see that to protect the image I had of my mother as being innocent I tried to make myself responsible for my mother's abortion. I have been carrying her guilt all my life and have suffered terribly from it.[4]

The next two stories illustrate how abortion can sabotage family relationships in ways that may not be obvious to medical doctors and therapists who are attempting to treat their patients' symptoms.

If the following woman were referred to a psychiatrist for the treatment of recurrent postpartum depression, it would be important to understand how the birth of each child subsequent to her abortion intensified her pain and sorrow. She writes from Australia, choosing to remain anonymous.

> It was eight years ago and I still think about it every day—feelings of grief, and loss, anger and self-hatred. After the birth of each of my children, the grief was enormous. To see their beautiful little bodies and personalities growing fills me with the pain of the loss of the first child and the fear of losing them . . . my mind is obsessed . . . I notice other children around the age mine would have been. I have confused my wedding anniversary with the termination anniversary. I have confused my firstborn's birth year with that year. My life is divided into two segments—before and after the termination. Sex reminds me of pregnancy and grief and I feel like crying and I have to stifle the emotion. I feel we don't deserve to enjoy ourselves

as a couple, such as going out together without the children . . . I feel depressed, useless, isolated.[5]

"John" was a 30-year-old accountant who entered psychotherapy because of longstanding depressive symptoms—malaise, insomnia, poor appetite, inability to concentrate at work, conflicts with coworkers over insignificant matters, and feeling distant and uninvolved with his wife and two young children. After several therapy visits, which seemed to be yielding no insights into the cause of his depressed mood, "John" had a dream. He was at the home of an old girlfriend. She brought him into the bedroom and introduced him to a 12-year-old boy saying, "This is your son." Only after the dream did he think to tell his therapist about the relationship he had had all those years ago, the pregnancy and the abortion which he had agreed to and paid for. John needed to deal with his loss and his guilt and shame about the abortion before he could invest emotionally in his present family and his work.

At times the grief after abortion can be overwhelming, especially if the grief is compounded by multiple losses.

"Bob," a factory worker who was waiting to tell his story at a training session for priests and post-abortion counselors, leaned over to me to ask if I had any antacids, mumbling something about not having had time for breakfast. I later learned that he had developed an ulcer after his traumatic experiences with his wife's abortions. When she became pregnant with their first child she had an abortion without even telling him she was planning to do it. "Bob" was overcome with anger and sadness. Sometime later she became pregnant again and announced that she would abort the child. He pleaded with her not to and tried everything he could think of to dissuade her. He learned that as her husband and the father of their child, he had no legal right to defend the life of the baby. She went ahead with the abortion. He was distraught and became clinically depressed. Somehow the marriage survived and another child was conceived. This time his wife allowed the pregnancy to come to term and she delivered a healthy baby boy. "Bob" was overjoyed. He could hardly let the child out of his sight. He changed his work shift so as to be able to be with his son while his wife was at work. The baby became the primary focus of his life. He was overprotective, smothering him with affection, hardly allowing him to crawl or to stand or to explore his environment. "Bob's" relationship with his wife was characterized by anger and disdain. She divorced him, and she was awarded sole custody of their son. "Bob" told the assembled group, choking back tears, "I didn't have three babies torn from my womb. I had three babies torn from my heart!"

This family was totally torn apart by abortion, leaving both parents permanently wounded. Although we have only heard the father's side of the story, their son is at high risk for many developmental problems and in all likelihood, diagnosable psychiatric illnesses.

As a high percentage of abortions end in divorce, children in these families carry the double burden of these two tragedies.

The next story is about a family that never came to be.

"Peter" was a gas station attendant whose teenage girlfriend had become pregnant. "Peter" had just lost his father whom he loved. He was delighted that they would be having a baby. He planned to marry her and to name the baby after his father. "Peter" was distraught when her parents intervened, forced her to have an abortion and forbade them to see one another. The multiple losses were more than he could bear. He put a gun to his head, shot himself and died.

"Peter's" suicide will not be recorded in any post-abortion sequellae research. I only know about it from his girlfriend's best friend. Two lives were lost and an adolescent girl scarred for life. Although her parents thought they were acting in her best interest, their "wisdom" proved disastrous. They too are wounded by abortion.

The next case illustrates the complex familial relationships which are often the motivation for abortion.

"Jill" was 18, the youngest in a large family and a senior in high school when she became pregnant. She was very close to her mother who was older, obese, and suffered from heart disease. "Jill" went out of her way never to displease her mother and worried that if her mother got upset she might die of a heart attack. Her mother's advice to her about dating was always the same: "Be good, and whatever you do, don't come home pregnant!"

When "Jill" found herself pregnant, her boyfriend arranged for her to have an abortion without telling her family. There were surgical complications—bleeding, infection, and fever. Jill was still living at home when she became very ill. She told her mother she had a bad case of the flu. The procedure had to be repeated. "Jill" lived in fear that in addition to killing her baby her abortion might also cause her mother's death because of her weak heart.

Overwhelmed by shame and guilt, she attempted suicide by getting drunk and driving her car the wrong way down a busy highway. She crashed into a wall, but she survived. When the police came to the scene of the accident she told them, "I just want to be with my baby!" She was admitted to a psychiatric hospital where her psychiatrist helped her tell her parents the truth about her life. "Jill" was relieved that everyone survived the conversation, which ended with tearful embraces.

Another significant aspect of her recovery was a long conversation with a Catholic priest who had received special training to deal with post-abortion issues through Project Rachel. "Jill" received the Sacrament of Reconciliation and was then able to attend Mass and receive the Eucharist with a clear conscience instead of going through the motions to please her mother and the others in her parish where she was an active and very visible youth group member.

The role of the priest is extremely important in helping those who have suffered the tragedy of abortion. Many women think they have committed an unforgivable sin and will be excommunicated for life and doomed to hell. One woman who was contemplating suicide decided to make one last attempt to find a priest with whom she could talk anonymously. She told a Project Rachel gathering of diocesan priests: "That day it was going to be either the darkened box or the bridge!" Fortunately, she found a priest in a confessional in a downtown chapel and was able to receive the Sacrament of Penance. Her witness has helped hundreds of priests and penitents understand the love and mercy of God. Two other women who have spoken publicly have said that they only felt understood regarding the gravity of their abortion experience by Catholics. They both yearned to become Catholic so that they could go to Confession, and eventually both of them did.

John Paul II's outreach to women who have had abortions in *Evangelium Vitae* is a beautiful personification of God's understanding, mercy, and love. Many women who have experienced the tragedy of abortion have come to a deeper understanding of God's mercy and love than most of us will ever have.[6]

The next case illustrates that post-abortion grief, guilt, and shame are not generated by Catholic upbringing or even limited to western culture.

"Akiko," a Japanese student at an American university, was referred to me for the treatment of what was presumed to be a severe case of Premenstrual Syndrome. One or two days every month her dormitory staff reported that she would stay in her room and not come out for meals or classes. When they tried to visit her they found her crying inconsolably—a most unusual display of emotions among Asian students in their experience.

"Akiko" had had an abortion the day before she left Japan to come to the United States to study early childhood education. Her first university class focused on prenatal development. Watching a film that showed intrauterine life, she suddenly became aware of the actual developmental stage of the child she carried within her which she had aborted a few weeks prior. From then on, on the anniversary of her abortion each month, she was overcome by sadness and guilt which she could not share with anyone.

In the course of my work with this patient, I learned how parents of aborted children in Japan deal with their grief. (I subsequently read about ritual mourning for abortions in Japan in the *Wall Street Journal*[7] and in *The New York Times International*.[8]) She explained that parents in Japan often set up small statues to represent their aborted children in Buddhist temples, inscribe their names on them, dress them in baby clothes, bring them gifts of candy and toys to relieve their suffering, and engage the monks to offer prayers for them regularly. Because these "water babies" are considered too young to have souls, they are thought to be stranded on the banks of the river which separates the land of the living from the land of the dead, and need to be guided across. Since many aborted babies are now found floating in the river in pieces, a goddess with webbed fingers can be invoked to take them out of the water and place them in the land of the dead where they can rest peacefully.

A Buddhist temple in Taipei offers to take charge of hundreds of infant ghosts of aborted and miscarried babies and ensures that they will not return to haunt their parents. These spirit babies are said to harass the living in various ways: disturbing their sleep with special cries, ruining business deals, souring love affairs, and prompting suicides. For a fee, the Mercy Temple will name the unborn child, light incense for its soul twice a day, and hold special religious services twice a year. When the spirit babies are cared for in this way it is believed that they will no longer be hateful and can subsequently be reincarnated.[9]

Abortion or attempted abortion need not permanently destroy family relationships as the next story illustrates. The following is from a new play to be produced in New York sometime in 2008. A single actress, portraying a woman in her fifties, comes on stage and tells this story.

Once upon a time there was a mother with three children who believed her family was complete. She was in her mid-forties and she had not been pregnant for 10 years, so when she missed her menstrual period, she believed it was the onset of menopause, and thought no more about it. But then she began to notice other symptoms associated with pregnancy—a sudden repugnance for the smell of coffee, morning sickness. She then knew she was pregnant and she was absolutely appalled. She told me that the only thing she knew for certain in her life was that she did not want this child. Her husband was in his mid-sixties, her elderly mother was living with them; there wasn't much money.

Abortion was not available but the lady in question did everything to bring on a miscarriage. She went horse-back riding, had gin baths, and took laxatives. But nothing would remove the pregnancy, short of the unavailable surgical intervention. She cried buckets, tears of rage, frustration and misery. But nature had its way and the pregnancy progressed healthily.

Before she gave birth, the woman went to Confession and told the priest that she had done everything she could to get rid of it, and that she couldn't repent this, because she didn't welcome it. The priest told her, "Don't trouble yourself about this, my dear. When you are old, you will be glad you had this child." The narrator looks up and continues: "And when my mother told me this story, she was old, and she added, 'I am.' That woman was my mother and that child was me."

The narrator continues, "I tell this story because I think it says something important about human behavior. People change their minds. Life is unexpected; there are surprises in store for all of us. Apparently, a third of mothers have ambivalent feelings about being pregnant even with their planned and wanted children! And I believe that it is loading women with much more guilt and depression by telling them that every child has got to be either "wanted" or "planned," because it doesn't allow for the ambivalence and fluidity which is often part of human relations. Human beings are surprising, and you never know what your relationship with your child is going to be, even if it is planned."[10]

This play called "Voices," consists of several true stories about how abortion affected the lives of women, men, and families. It will be available for production in theaters and on college campuses in the near future.

CONCLUSION

The psychological aftermath of abortion for women, men, children, and families can be devastating, leaving scars which last a lifetime for the persons involved and for all of society. The tears of grieving parents, siblings, relatives, and friends, which are shed in solitude and self condemnation, are bitter and destructive to all involved. When these victims of abortion are invited to tell their stories to a compassionate listener, and introduced to the love and mercy of God, their burden can be lifted and sorrow healed. Then their river of tears will not have been in vain.

It will be like the river flows out of the temple sanctuary in Ezekiel 47:

> This water flows east . . .and to the sea; and flowing into the sea it makes its waters wholesome. Whenever the river flows, all living creatures teeming in it will live. Fish will be very plentiful, for wherever the water goes it brings health, and life teems wherever the river flows. Along the river, on either bank, will grow every kind of fruit tree with leaves that never wither and fruit that never fails; they will bear new fruit every month, because this water comes from the sanctuary. And their fruit will be good to eat and the leaves medicinal.[11]

Then the millions of people who have suffered the tragedy of abortion will become the wounded healers of our society, exemplifying what Pope John Paul II taught:

> You will come to understand that nothing has been definitively lost and you will also be able to ask forgiveness from your child, who is now living in the Lord. With the friendly and expert help and advice of other people, and as a result of your own painful experience, you can be among the most eloquent defenders of everyone's right to life. Through your commitment to life, whether by accepting the birth of other children or by welcoming and caring for those most in need of someone to be close to them, you will become promoters of a new way of looking at human life.[12]

As we reach out to heal post-abortion grief, this suffering can indeed help to transform our society into the civilization of love John Paul II predicted when he said, "Suffering is present in the world in order to release love, in order to give birth to works of love toward neighbor, in order to transform the whole of human civilization into a 'civilization of love.' "13

ENDNOTES

1. Angelo, E. Joanne, M.D. "Does Post-Abortion Grief Exist?: Yes. Post Abortion Grief" in *Taking Sides: Clashing Views on Controversial Issues on Abnormal Psychology*. Halgin, R. Ed. Dushkin/McGraw-Hill. 2000. pp. 88–91.

2. Rue, Vincent. *Forgotten Fathers*. Lewinston, NY: Life Cycle Books 1997 (pamphlet).

3. Ney, Philip G. M.D. Peeters, *Abortion Survivors,* Second Edition. Pioneer Publishing, Victoria, Canada 1996. pp. 4–9.

4. Ney, Ibid., pp. 34–35.

5. Reist, Melinda Tankard, *Giving Sorrow Words*. Sydney: Duffy & Snellgrove, 2000. p. 43.

6. Pope John Paul II. *Evangelium Vitae,* 99.

7. "Unusual Ceremonies Reveal Doubt in Japan over the Use of Abortion." *Wall Street Journal.* June 6, 1983. p. A1.

8. "In Japan, a Ritual of Mourning for Abortions." *New York Times International.* January 25, 1996. p. A1.

9. "The Spirit Babies: Fighting ghosts of aborted infants." *The Standard.* July 6, 1990. p. 18.

10. Vitz, Evelyn Birge. Vitz, Ann Royals. "Voices," 2008. An unpublished play, personal communication.

11. Ezekiel 47: 8–9, 12. First Reading, mass for Tuesday of the Fourth Week of Lent.

12. Pope John Paul II. Ibid. 99.

13. Pope John Paul II, *Salvifici Doloris.* 30.

Abortion of the Sick Child

Agnetta Sutton

"Man becomes the image of God not so much in the moment of solitude as in the moment of communion." These words by Pope John Paul II are at the heart of my argument about abortion on grounds of fetal abnormality. Abortion on grounds of fetal abnormality is based on a eugenic ideology. This ideology is founded on a utilitarian quality-of-life evaluation of human life, an evaluation that is often linked to an exclusive understanding of personhood.

By contrast to the eugenic and utilitarian evaluation of human life and an understanding of personhood that excludes some members of the human family, the Holy Father has presented us with a relational and Trinitarian understanding of the human being in the image of God. As he explained in the *Theology of the Body* lectures,[1] the truest reflection of the One and Triune God is *not* found in the individual as such, but in human beings together in union and communion. He was telling us that, created in the image of God, we are essentially relational beings.

> Man became the "image and likeness" of God not only through his own humanity, but also through the communion of persons which man and woman form right from the beginning. The function of the image is to reflect the one who is the model, to reproduce its own prototype. Man becomes the image of God not so much in the moment of solitude as in the moment of communion. Right from the beginning he is not only an image in which the solitude of a person who rules the world is reflected,

---

Agnetta Sutton is Senior Lecturer, Department of Theology, University of Chichester (United Kingdom).

but also, and essentially, an image of an inscrutable divine communion of persons (*ToB,* 14 November 1979, p. 46).

While the focus in the quoted passage is on the man-woman relationship, it is telling us more generally that humans are created for one another and belong together. Elsewhere in the *Theology of the Body* we are told about the eschatological significance of virginity and celibacy for the sake of the Kingdom of Heaven. Here we are told that these vocations point in a special way to our spiritual fulfillment in union and communion with the saints and with God in the resurrection. We are told that our very identity and fulfillment as personal beings is rooted in our relationships with other humans—and God. This relational understanding of what it means to be a person has important implications for the question of the value of life with disability.

Very different from this understanding of the human person as essentially a relational being is Peter Singer's concept of a person and evaluation of human life. For the Princeton philosopher the criterion of personhood is the possession of certain mental abilities, among them self-consciousness and a degree of rationality. In his book, *Rethinking Life and Death*[2], he argues that, neither human fetuses nor infants nor severely mentally disabled people are persons, whereas a healthy and mature ape is a person if it shows signs of rationality and some awareness of the past and the future. Singer does not think that membership of the species *Homo sapiens* gives the individual a special status and dignity. His is a rationalist Lockean understanding of what it means to be a human person. This understanding excludes those who cannot think of themselves as themselves or look back to the past and forward to the future. And it devaluates those who lack certain intellectual abilities.

Hence, to Singer's mind, the value of human life varies; and "life without consciousness is of no worth at all" (Singer, *LD* 1995, p. 190). So to his mind, the lives of those humans with little understanding or awareness are of little value. Not possessing what he considers personal and ethically relevant characteristics, their lives deserve scant respect. Singer argues, then, that those humans who do not yet have, never will have, or have lost the intellectual powers typical of sane and healthy human adults have a lesser right to life than a mature and mentally healthy gorilla. This may shock. Yet Singer's view of what it means to be a person and of the value of human life is widely shared in our society. It has set its stamp on diagnostic practices aimed at avoiding births of sick and disabled children.

Not only is this view morally unacceptable, but as I shall show, it is not even rational. But first I want to say a few words about the characteristic elements of eugenic practices and their application to abortion on grounds of abnormality.

EUGENICS

Eugenics is usually associated with coercive state programs. I mean programs such as the Nazi programme to eliminate disabled people and any legally founded state program involving the sterilisation of mentally and physically disabled people. Programs of the last-mentioned type were found in the United States, Canada and many parts of Europe in the first part of the 20th century. Indeed, in Scandinavian countries such programs remained in force until the end of the 1960s (Broberg & Roll-Hansen, 1996).[3]

However, today, any suggestion to the effect that present medical policies are eugenic tends to be met with indignation. Nonetheless, a eugenic mentality and eugenic practices are still with us. Such practices are no longer taking the form of enforced sterilizations or non-voluntary euthanasia. Today they take the form of non-coercive eugenics. This is by way of offering prenatal tests with a view to abortion on grounds of abnormality. Pregnant women are not forced to undergo such tests. But in many countries they are under certain pressures to have them. Pregnant women are encouraged to have tests to be reassured, when the main reason for the tests is to avoid births of disabled children. It is pointed out that termination on grounds of fetal abnormality allows couples to embark on new pregnancies that may be unaffected.

Indeed, the practice of prenatal testing deserves to be called eugenic for two reasons. First, it is encouraged by ideological pressures to prevent births of disabled children. Secondly, it is sponsored by public health services and regulated by national legislation.

Another reflection of the eugenic ideology permeating our societies is the observation that in many families there is a feeling of guilt when a genetic condition is passed on to a child. Of course, such feelings are partly to be explained by the very availability of tests to detect disability, since this means that the child need not have been born. The very availability of prenatal tests with a view to abortion on grounds of fetal abnormality promotes the idea that it is part of responsible parenthood to avoid the birth of a disabled child.

Yet it is not surprising if parents who have aborted a child on grounds of disability grieve. Normally they would have been looking forward to the birth of the child. Learning that it was unhealthy would have been a major disappointment. Thus they mourn the healthy child they were hoping for. Not only that. They mourn their child. It was their child who died. Their baby! Many of these parents may also doubt they did the right thing. These people need our special sympathy. For in a society that encourages eugenic abortion, abortion on grounds of fetal abnormality is primarily viewed as a rational choice rather than as a loss of a child.

THE GROWING EMBRYO AND FETUS

To be sure, there are many who, like Singer, believe that abortion on grounds of fetal abnormality is a responsible act and even an act of mercy, but certainly not an act of killing a person, certainly not an act of murder. Very different is the position of the Congregation for the Doctrine of the Faith, which insists that we must not kill the human fetus, since "the human being must be respected—as a person—from the very first instant of his existence" (*DV*, Part I, para. 1). According to the Congregation, we have good reason to regard the human embryo as a person from the start.

True. As argued in *Donum Vitae,* of 1987, "the conclusions of science regarding the human embryo provide a valuable indication for discerning by the use of reason a personal presence at the moment of its first appearance of human life; how could a human individual not be a human person?" (*DV*, Part I, para. 1).[4]

The reference to science suggests that the statement refers to the genetic potential of the human embryo, a potential which is there from the outset. The embryo may not yet look much like a baby, but it is alive and of human origin. It is a human organism, that is, a human being. The normal human embryo is an immature human being with a genetic potential to develop into a human being with the intellectual and emotional and physical characteristics typical of mature adult persons. It is a person in the making. Contrary to what has been suggested by some bioethicists and scientists, this argument is not spoiled by the observation that some embryos twin. If they twin, they were two persons in the making.[5]

However, if our prime focus is on the original potential to develop into a highly rational and capable person, the argument from potentiality does not seem applicable to all embryos and fetuses. For some of them may grow into mentally or otherwise disabled adults. In this case, what is their status?

THE UNHEALTHY EMBRYO, FETUS AND INFANT

As noted by John Paul II, seen as created in the *Imago Dei*, it is as beings in union and communion with other persons that we are persons. It is as such that we are persons in the image of the Triune God. It is as relational beings, then, that we resemble God.

Now, our relations to other persons are of the biological and more so the spiritual, emotional and intellectual kinds. While Pope John Paul II's emphasis was on spiritual and emotional relationships, he rightly recognized that these were intimately linked to our biological nature, as is made clear by the very title of his work the *Theology of the Body*. The body, on his understanding, is the vehicle by means of which we communicate and relate to others around us.

The Congregation for the Doctrine of the Faith did well to pay tribute to our biological origins, since they are the foundation of familial relations. It is, indeed, because the human species is biological that we have reason to recognize every human being, however immature or disabled, as a person. As a biological member of the human family, the human embryo, fetus and child is one of us whatever his mental or physical disabilities.

Knitted together by God in the womb, as the Psalmist said, the embryo is already loved as a person by God. For, even if he is not yet in intellectual union and communion with one of us, he is flesh of our flesh. Biologically related to his parents, the human creature in the womb is loved by God as a member of the human family, on the understanding of the Psalmist. As somebody loved as a person by God, the child in the womb is clearly a relational being and one in the image of God. That is, whether born or unborn, whether able or disabled, the child in the womb is a person.

What kind of person he will be is another matter. That depends not only on his genetic origins but also on the events of life, his upbringing, his schooling and the society and times in which he lives as well as on something over and above all that which we call the free will.

When the emphasis is put on the familial or biological dimension of personhood, every human being must be counted as a person. For from the start he has both physical and social relationships with other persons. Being conceived by human parents immediately places the child, the fetus and the embryo, within the sphere of the human family. Abilities and disabilities are irrelevant. It makes no difference whether, because of genetic illness or accident and injury, the child will not manifest all those mental or physical abilities we normally associate with personhood. The human person is identified as such, because he is a member of the human family.

THE VALUE OF A LIFE OF SUFFERING

Having come to this conclusion it is time to return to Singer's claim that some human lives are of little or no value. Is it true that some human lives are not worth living? Would the disabled child rather have been killed in the womb than have been born with a disability? Surely, it is not for me or you to say that another person's life is not worth living.

To say that it is best for a disabled fetus to be aborted is to say that the value of a human life resides primarily in health and human abilities. This is a materialistic and utilitarian point of view. It reflects an impoverished understanding of the value of human life. It takes no account of spiritual values. It overlooks that people enjoy life for many different reasons. You do not need to be a philosopher to have a fulfilled life. And you need not be an athlete in order to be fit for life. The materialist and utilitarian understanding of the value of human life fails to recognize that we may learn from the disabled person. He might teach us courage. In his dependence, he may teach us to care for others. Reaching out for love and friendship, for union and communion, both the mentally and the physically disabled may help us to become more caring and better people. They may help us to see more clearly the *Imago Dei* in others.

Born to a life in a wheelchair, one of my students once said in a seminar that he would not want to be different. Affirming that sitting in a wheelchair was part of his identity and role in life he taught us something, just as the blind man mentioned in the Gospel of St John, taught us to have faith. As you remember, when the disciples asked Jesus if the man or his parents had sinned for the man to be born blind, Jesus answered that neither he nor his parents had sinned, but that the man "was born blind so that the works of God might be displayed in him" (*Jn* 9:1–3).

REFERENCES

1. John Paul II, *The Theology of the Body: Human Love in the Divine Plan* [ToB], Pauline Books and Media, 1997.

2. Peter Singer, *Rethinking Life and Death: The Collapse of Our Traditional Ethics,* Oxford University Press, 1995.

3. Broberg, G., and N. Roll-Hansen, Eugenics and the Welfare State Sterilisation Policy in Denmark, Sweden, Norway and Finland, East Lansing: Michigan State University Press, 1996.

4. This statement was later repeated by John Paul II in his Encyclical Letter, *Evangelium Vitae,* of 1995 (John Paul II, 1995, para. 60).

5. It would appear that monozygotic twins are not 100 percent genetically identical.

II Towards a Pastoral Outreach of Mercy

To Act According to the Merciful Example of God

JEAN LAFFITTE

> *But a Samaritan, as he traveled, came where the man was; and when he saw him, he took pity on him. He went to him and bandaged his wounds, pouring on oil and wine.* (*Lk* 10, 33–34)

The statement, "Oil on the wounds," draws explicitly from the passage of the evangelist Luke, which recounts the manner in which Jesus responds to a doctor of the Law. He asked him, "Who is my neighbor?" This title illustrates very clearly the prospective that this Congress wanted to take into account, and which is very often overlooked when it comes to abortion.

Generally, the debate is seen almost exclusively against the supporters of abortion—who base their reasons on the "right" which a woman would have to interrupt an unwanted pregnancy—and its opponents—those who claim the right to life of the unborn child, denying that women's freedom can extend to the point of choosing whether the child in the womb should live or die.

One must have the courage to admit that, among the latter, the idea is often widespread that sees the woman who had an abortion, as an unforgivable sinner, a person not entitled to the compassion and mercy of God or man. In other words, the issue of abortion has always been considered, in most cases, strictly from the standpoint of the moral responsibility of those who perform the act or those who cooperate in it. The magisterium's posi-

---

Jean Laffitte is vice-president of the Pontifical Academy for Life, Vatican City, and Professor of Spiritual Theology, Pontifical John Paul II Institute.

tion on this topic is well known. The Church considers abortion an "abominable crime"[1] and a "grave moral disorder."[2] However, the magisterium also calls us to distinguish the sin from the sinner, to reject sin, but not the sinner. Pope John XXIII said,

> "It is always perfectly justifiable to distinguish between error as such and the person who falls into error—even in the case of men who err regarding the truth or are led astray as a result of their inadequate knowledge, in matters either of religion or of the highest ethical standards. A man who has fallen into error does not cease to be a man. He never forfeits his personal dignity; and that is something that must always be taken into account. Besides, there exists in man's very nature an undying capacity to break through the barriers of error and seek the road to truth. God, in His great providence, is ever present with His aid. Today, maybe, a man lacks faith and turns aside into error; tomorrow, perhaps, illumined by God's light, he may indeed embrace the truth."[3]

The Church feels the need and duty to intervene and to do so according to the merciful example of God. Who are the people who choose to abort? In what human and social context are they living? What are the effects of abortion on these people and their lives? These are the main questions that this part of the conference has sought to answer. The speakers are representatives of associations connected in various capacities to the Church world. They deal in various ways with the assistance and human and spiritual rehabilitation of women who have directly experienced the tragedy of abortion, and who can themselves be considered victims of this crime.

Too often the discussion of abortion fails to consider the effects that this tragedy leaves on the same people who have chosen it, primarily women. If, in fact, the political and health organizations, the national and supranational institutions, carry out campaigns to promote and spread the act of abortion, with the goal of "normalizing" it from a cultural point of view, calling the destruction of embryos and fetuses a measure of reproductive health, they, on the other hand, leave women completely uninformed about the consequences, especially psychologically, that impact those who have had an abortion. The suffering caused by abortion and that indelibly marks the soul of the mother, represents the dark side, the unspoken side of these practices. This "conspiracy of silence" has allowed, in recent decades, the undisputed development of the phenomenon of post-abortion syndrome, a real malady that has affected and continues to affect thousands of mothers (but in many cases also fathers), due to ignorance of these consequences.

"The abortion event," Serena Taccari rightly says, "has much to do with the identity of the person." This means that the decision to abort is not a decision that is made completely autonomously, where the free will of the woman fully embraces the object of the choice. On the contrary, this decision is the child of an environment, which is often socially determined, that sometimes leads to that kind of choice in contrast with the real desire of the woman. But this means also, and above all, that the abortion event etches itself profoundly into the lived identity of the person, changing her very way of being and acting, of relating to others and to herself. In this sense, following an abortion, the person may "abort her own life," considering herself a murderer without the possibility of redemption and forgiveness.

The crisis of depression, the feelings of guilt, anguish and abandonment by society are none other than the symptoms of a self-produced malaise, of a motherhood lost due to one's own choice. Abortion, as Sister Mary Agnes Donovan rightly affirms, "terminates a pregnancy, but not motherhood which is instead, an eternal reality." Abortion also changes the life of the person choosing it. Comprehending the gravity of all that has transpired opens the door to an abyss. It is exactly at this moment that the right words, an outstretched hand, can bring the experience of God. The person is gently and lovingly led to come to terms with their own past, with their own sin, with the meaning of their own life. The process of healing the memory begins here. Often, stemming specifically from the awareness of what has been accomplished, a new person is born, as well as the possibility and the desire of redemption and, as testimony to the contributions of this session, the desire to *accompany* those who find themselves in the same position.

Pope Benedict XVI, in his Encyclical *Spe Salvi*, has himself emphasized the importance of suffering in order to understand hope, and to experience that sharing through which divine love is transmitted:

"Indeed, to accept the 'other' who suffers, means that I take up his suffering in such a way that it becomes mine also. Because it has now become a shared suffering, though, in which another person is present, this suffering is penetrated by the light of love."[4]

The charism which defines the four groups represented (Project Rachel, Sisters of Life, AGAPA and Il Dono) is one of mercy, of a love which does not condemn. Their specific concern is to welcome and to console: *he saw him, and was moved with compassion. He went to him and bandaged his wounds.* These are the simple gestures of one who is aware of a situation, who takes note of a suffering person, and simply because he is suffering, without demanding to know the cause of the suffering, he bends down to share the suffering and to offer comfort.

Through this love the doors of redemption are flung open: "When someone has the experience of a great love in his life, this is a moment of 'redemption' which gives a new meaning to his life."[5]

The victims of abortion's consequences offer us a fundamental testimony, that of the courage of repentance, and the search for reconciliation. From this perspective, abortion appears to be an unexpected and seemingly absurd way to a personal experience with God. The agony of discovering oneself as guilty of such a serious crime transforms itself into a way of salvation, as Benedict XVI explained in light of the experience of Vietnamese martyr Paul Le-Bao-Thin:

> Christ descended into "Hell" and is therefore close to those cast into it, transforming their darkness into light. Suffering and torment is still terrible and well-nigh unbearable. Yet the star of hope has risen—the anchor of the heart reaches the very throne of God. Instead of evil being unleashed within man, the light shines victorious: suffering—without ceasing to be suffering—becomes, despite everything, a hymn of praise.[6]

Pastoral service is essential in the care of these persons. A wounded person, in fact, sees in the priest and confessor a foothold, someone who can, in the name of Christ, help them to understand their mistake, to "open themselves to know the truth" and who can offer them the opportunity to rediscover the light. From here the need is made evident, as brought to light through the work of Dominique Vandier, to form and educate even the priest in forgiveness and mercy according to the image of the compassionate God.

The experience of abortion must not give birth only to despair, but also to that hope inherent in the Gospel message, the inheritance of all Christians: *Spe salvi facti sumus* (*Rm* 8:24).

REFERENCES

1. Pastoral constitution on the Church in the Modern World—*Gaudium et Spes,* 51.
2. John Paul II, *Evangelium Vitae* (1995), n. 62.
3. John XXIII, *Pacem in Terris* (1963), n. 158.
4. Benedict XVI, *Spe Salvi* (2007), n. 38.
5. *Ibid,* n. 26.
6. *Ibid,* n. 37.

Project Rachel: A Sacramental Response to the Grief of Abortion

Vicki Thorn

Abortion wounds the soul of those involved in it. Abortion not only takes the life of the unborn child, but also leaves a trail of pain and desperation, of broken lives and broken spirits, of damaged families and relationships unequaled by any other injustice in contemporary society. While abortion is promoted as a safe choice, a way to control the family with a simple medical procedure, in fact abortion radically alters the life of the woman. Abortion denies the father his fatherhood. Abortion denies the grandparents a grandchild and the siblings their brother or sister. No one is unchanged by an abortion. We need to be prepared to minister to all who are touched.

The Church which has so boldly and unequivocally defended the sanctity of all life from conception to natural death, has an equal obligation to minister to the multitude of walking wounded left behind in this slaughter of the innocents. In keeping with the call of Scripture, the Church must continue to preach the healing power of our God, his mercy and tender compassion for those whose lives are broken and filled with sin. Jesus always ministered to those who came seeking forgiveness and healing with gentleness and tenderness. The sin of abortion has become so pervasive and overwhelming today that it is imperative that the Church not only continue its prophetic stance in protecting unborn human life, but also call to healing the millions who have been drawn into the evil of abortion, willingly or under duress, knowledgeable or ignorant of the reality, extending to them God's forgiveness and healing. The brokenness caused by abortion keeps millions

---

Vicki Thorn is Founder, President, and Executive Director of Project Rachel, National Office of Post-Abortion Reconciliation and Healing, Inc., Milwaukee, Wis.

of people from fully entering into their faith journey, from fully experiencing the God-life within. Those involved in abortion believe they have committed the unforgiveable sin and are afraid to approach the Church if they had once been churched. The Church has always been a hospital for sinners and not a hotel for saints and yet in our humanness, we forget that at times. Because of the enormity of the abortion problem it is imperative that the Church throughout the world address this issue. (The World Health Organization estimates for 2006 indicate approximately 46 million abortions worldwide per year, keeping in mind that every abortion procured involves both the mother and the father.) Women who experience healing through God's mercy and love do not have more abortions. Men who are restored after abortion, work diligently to end abortion as do the women. Indeed, these people become the cornerstones of the Culture of Life.

The inherent reality of abortion, the rejection of the invitation to create a new life in cooperation with the Creator of all Life, results in the profound existential wound. The wound of abortion is both spiritual and human and must be resolved in both realms to be healed. Project Rachel addresses both the spiritual and human wounds.

Project Rachel embodies the mercy and compassion Pope John Paul II spoke of at World Youth Day in Denver, Colo., in 1993. He said "this personal tragedy (abortion) must be met with concrete interpersonal acts of love and solidarity."

Pope John Paul II, went further when he wrote in Section 99 of *Evangelium Vitae*,

> I would now like to say a special word to women who had an abortion. The Church is aware of the many factors which may have influenced your decision and she does not doubt that in many cases it was a painful and even shattering decision. The wound in your heart may not have healed. Certainly what happened was and remains terribly wrong. But do not give in to discouragement and do not lose hope. Try rather to understand what happened and face it honestly. If you have not already done so, give yourselves over with humility and trust to repentance. The Father of mercies is ready to give you his forgiveness and his peace in the Sacrament of Reconciliation. You will come to understand that nothing is definitively lost and you will also be able to ask forgiveness from your child, who is now living in the Lord. With the friendly and expert help and advice of other people, and as a result of your own painful experience, you can be among

the most eloquent defenders of everyone's right to life. Through your commitment to life, whether by accepting the birth of other children or by welcoming and caring for those most in need of someone to be close to them, you will become promoters of a new way of looking at human life.

Pope Benedict XVI reaffirms this teaching. In his 2007 *Ad Limina* address to the Bishops of Kenya, he said:

When you preach the Gospel of Life, remind your people that the right to life of every innocent human being, born or unborn, is absolute and applies equally to all people with no exception whatsoever. This equality "is the basis of all authentic social relationships which, to be truly such, can only be founded on truth and justice" (*Evangelium Vitae*, 57). The Catholic community must offer support to those women who may find it difficult to accept a child, above all when they are isolated from their family and friends. Likewise, the community should be open to welcome back all who repent of having participated in the grave sin of abortion, and should guide them with pastoral charity to accept the grace of forgiveness, the need for penance, and the joy of entering once more into the new life of Christ.

At the audience with the Holy Father, Benedict XVI on April 5, 2008, as part of the Congress "Oil on the Wounds," he further challenged:

The Church's ethical opinion with regard to divorce and procured abortion is unambivalent and known to all: these are grave sins which, to a different extent and taking into account the evaluation of subjective responsibility, harm the dignity of the human person, involve a profound injustice in human and social relations and offend God himself, Guarantor of the conjugal covenant and the Author of life. Yet the Church, after the example of her Divine Teacher, always has the people themselves before her, especially the weakest and most innocent who are victims of injustice and sin, and also those other men and women who, having perpetrated these acts, stained by sin and wounded within, are seeking peace and the chance to begin anew.

The Church's first duty is to approach these people with love and consideration, with caring and motherly attention, to proclaim the merciful closeness of God in Jesus Christ. Indeed, as the Fathers teach, it is he who is the true Good Samaritan, who has made himself close to us, who pours oil and wine on our wounds and takes us into the inn, the Church, where he has us treated, entrusting us to her ministers and personally paying in advance for our recovery. Yes, the Gospel of love and life is also always the Gospel of mercy, which is addressed to the actual person and sinner that we are, to help us up after any fall and to recover from any injury. My beloved Predecessor, the Servant of God John Paul II, the third anniversary of whose death we celebrated recently, said in inaugurating the new Shrine of Divine Mercy in Krakow: "Apart from the mercy of God there is no other source of hope for mankind" (17 August 2002). On the basis of this mercy the Church cultivates an indomitable trust in human beings and in their capacity for recovery. She knows that with the help of grace human freedom is capable of the definitive and faithful gift of self which makes possible the marriage of a man and woman as an indissoluble bond; she knows that even in the most difficult circumstances human freedom is capable of extraordinary acts of sacrifice and solidarity to welcome the life of a new human being. Thus, one can see that the "No" which the Church pronounces in her moral directives on which public opinion sometimes unilaterally focuses, is in fact a great "Yes" to the dignity of the human person, to human life and to the person's capacity to love. It is an expression of the constant trust with which, despite their frailty, people are able to respond to the loftiest vocation for which they are created: the vocation to love.

On that same occasion, John Paul II continued: "This fire of mercy needs to be passed on to the world. In the mercy of God the world will find peace (ibid., p. 8). The great task of disciples of the Lord Jesus who find themselves the travelling companions of so many brothers, men and women of good will, is hinged on this. Their program, the program of the Good Samaritan, is a 'heart which sees.' This heart sees where love is needed and acts accordingly" (*Deus Caritas Est*, n. 31).

These strong and compassionate words of the Holy Father are a mandate to provide care for those wounded by abortion, while recognizing the grave moral issues associated with abortion.

Project Rachel is the official pastoral response of the Catholic Church in the United States that supports the Church's unequivocal prophetic stance that abortion is wrong and never good for children, women or men who participate. This ministry is the embodiment of the vision of Pope John Paul II when he said: *"With the friendly and expert help and advice of other people."* The name Project Rachel comes from the Old Testament, (*Jeremiah* 31: 15–17). The message is one of hope for the future.

"Thus says the Lord: In Ramah is heard the sound of moaning, of bitter weeping! Rachel mourns her children she refuses to be consoled because her children are no more. Thus says the Lord: Cease your cries of mourning, wipe the tears from your eyes. The sorrow you have shown shall have its reward, says the Lord, they shall return from the enemy's land. There is hope for your future, says the Lord."

Project Rachel was founded in 1984 in the Archdiocese of Milwaukee, Wisconsin, and it is now in almost every diocese in the Unites States. It is in New Zealand, Guam and the Bahamas. The ministry continues to develop in Canada, Mexico, Australia, Hong Kong, China, Ukraine, and Romania. It arouses interest in English-speaking Africa, the Philippines, Singapore, India, many countries in Latin America as well as in Western Europe.

I began Project Rachel in response to the call the bishops of the United States issued in 1975 as *The Pastoral Plan for Pro-Life Activities,* published by the U.S. Conference of Catholic Bishops. The bishops laid out a strategy for diocesan respect of life apostolates to confront the advent of legalized abortion. This document encouraged involvement in education on the life issues, involvement in the legislative process and called for a pastoral response to aid women in a crisis pregnancy as well as to minister to those who have lost children to abortion.

My awareness of the need for such a ministry came from a friend who had an abortion forced on her by her mother. She already had placed a baby for adoption prior to that event. Over the years that followed the abortion, she shared her pain with me and she always ended our conversations by saying, "I can live with the adoption. I can't live with the abortion." When I became Respect Life Director for the Archdiocese of Milwaukee, it was clear to me, as I heard the stories of other women who had had abortions, that the Church was the place where women could be helped. The woman who had had an abortion experiences the human pain of a mother who had lost a child and she believes that God could not and would not forgive her. The wound of abortion is both spiritual and human.

In developing a plan to minister to those touched by abortion, I approached priests that I knew and asked if they had encountered women who had had abortions in Confession. I also asked them if they felt confident that they had truly been able to help her to heal. Every priest had heard the confessions and each one of them shared that they were not sure they had known how to really help her. I asked the same questions of mental health professionals who worked for Catholic Charities and received similar replies. In response, I designed a training seminar to help them understand the aftermath of abortion as well as the components of human and spiritual healing. A canon lawyer explained the Code of Canon Law as well. The priests and the counselors attended the same seminar, which gave them a common base of understanding and allowed them to come to know each other, so that a network of caregivers could develop.

As a Church, we can offer the woman spiritual care through priests and the Sacrament of Reconciliation and we can offer her counseling through our mental health professionals where possible and through the compassionate care of Sisters in countries where access to professional mental health caregivers is difficult.

Project Rachel is a diocesan network of specially trained priests, mental health professionals, deacons, sisters and other caregivers who provide one on one care to those seeking reconciliation and healing. It is always operated within a diocese with the blessing, support and agreement of the local Ordinary. The ministry serves the entire diocese so that there is easy access to caregivers. There is a central contact point in the diocese where people can receive referrals to priests or caregivers. The person seeking help is given the referral and makes the contact for care when they are ready. It is important for them to make this step in healing. The person seeking help may choose to begin with a priest or with a caregiver.

The network of priests throughout the diocese makes it possible for her to contact someone physically close to her or to see someone away from her community. The shame of abortion may make it difficult to approach a pastor, assuming she is actually active in a parish. Many who seek help are currently unchurched and the network of caregivers, who are geographically scattered throughout a diocese, makes it more convenient to seek help. The one-on-one care is crucial because it honors the unique spiritual journey of each woman. It provides for confidential care and makes no demands that she enter into a group setting. There is a great deal of shame attached to abortion and women are often very afraid of exposure and judgment. We need to assure the woman that the ministry is confidential and that she can choose to remain anonymous. The Sacrament of Confession with its anonymity is a perfect place for her to begin. The knowledgeable and compassionate confessor can help her address the spiritual pain and either journey with her through the human healing part of the process or refer her to someone else in the network for additional care. Mental health professionals who work in the Church as well as Catholic counselors in private practice can be part of the network. Sisters are the ideal companions because of their spiritual wisdom, active prayer life and accessibility. In the United States, the Sisters of Life are actively involved in this ministry and in the Bahamas, the ministry is housed in a Benedictine convent where the retired sisters answer the telephone, work and pray with the women. In some parts of the world, it is impossible to gain access to mental health professionals because of cost and stigma. Convents provide the perfect safe haven where a woman can go for help. In many countries sisters are working with women already in other capacities and this ministry is an extension of care they are already providing. As the ministry becomes established, days of reflection, support groups and retreats can be helpful. The network of trained caregivers always remains a critical extension of these one-time activities. It is important to recognize that the wound of abortion is deep and that these one-time events can open up new areas of wounding that will need attention. We as Church are obligated to offer holistic care that provides the framework of spiritual and psychological care that enables her to accomplish deep and authentic healing.

In providing a network of caregivers who can journey with the woman at her own pace, we are being respectful of her and respectful of God's timing. The wounds of abortion take time to heal and often are linked to other wounds that also need God's attention and human counseling. We need to always keep this in mind. We are sometimes tempted to think that everyone heals at the same pace and that we can fit everyone into a model for healing but that is not true. St. Francis De Sales said:

> The soul which rises from out of sin to a devout life has been compared to the dawn, which does not banish darkness suddenly, but by degrees. The slow cure is always the surest, and spiritual maladies, like those of the body, while they are apt to come on horseback and express, tend to depart slowly and on foot.

He warned that slow progress may discourage some, while the sense of immediate purification causes others to leave their physician too soon and risk a relapse. Like De Sales, we must be patient ministers, neither rushing them to a sense of immediate healing nor letting them despair at slow progress.

It is critical to train as many priests as possible to understand the problem of abortion. As a confessor, he will be confronted with the penitent who has been involved in an abortion. His response to her can bring her back to the merciful embrace of God or drive her to despair. Some of these priests will feel called to be part of a formal network, accepting referrals from the diocesan ministry, but all priests as confessors are likely to encounter abortion. Usually about 10 percent of the priests in a diocese become part of the active referral network. The inexperienced or unprepared priest can do grave spiritual harm by telling her that she has committed the unforgivable sin, that she is damned and going to hell or in some cases, by seeming to dismiss the seriousness of the offense. He is the gateway back to the Church for her. *The Catechism of the Church* in section 1465 says that:

> When he celebrates the Sacrament of Penance, the priest is fulfilling the ministry of the Good Shepherd who seeks the lost sheep, of the Good Samaritan who binds up wounds, of the Father who awaits the prodigal son and welcomes him on his return, and of the just and impartial judge whose judgment is both just and merciful. The priest is the sign and the instrument of God's merciful love for the sinner.

He must understand her pain and her shame. He must understand the need for a reasonable penance. A bishop from an Eastern European country recently shared his dismay in finding out that some priests in his country impose on women who confess abortion a penance of seven years without the Eucharist. This denies her the very grace she needs to heal. This is a harsh public and punitive sort of penance and will not bring her to the Church, but will drive her away.

Over the years since the founding of the ministry, I have spoken to thousands of women in the United States and other countries. Women tell me that they are drawn to the Church and the sacraments, and at the same time, they are afraid to approach, inhibited by their shame and guilt and by a perception that the Church is unforgiving. The woman who has chosen abortion believes that she has committed the unforgivable sin, the sin that God will not forgive, the sin that flies in the face of the Creator by destroying a life God created. Women share that they have a desperate need to make sense of this experience in light of their spirituality but are terrified to approach the confessional for fear of retribution and shame. They were frightened that the Church, through the priest, would affirm that they were indeed unforgivable. The strong pro-life stance of the Church heightened their fear. As God continued to call them, some overcame their fear only to encounter a priest who chastised them or excused them. Many speak of returning to confess over and over, trying to rid themselves of the guilt they felt, sometimes to be told by an unenlightened priest that they were crazy and should find a psychiatrist or that they couldn't be forgiven. And yet they persevered, knowing that they needed to encounter God to be healed. Men, who are the forgotten partners, share that they don't know where to go with their pain. They've been told it is a woman's issue. They've been told they have no right to feel pain. They speak of how a homily that mentioned men and abortion, or a talk on a retreat or a newspaper article, opened their eyes to the fact that help is available for them.

Priests need to recognize the power of their preaching to speak the prophetic truth about abortion, but also to proclaim the message of healing, mercy and forgiveness. In preaching, the priest does not always have to directly address the issue of abortion, but he can often include abortion when speaking about God's love and mercy and the power of the Sacrament of Confession. Priests sometimes express a reticence to speak about abortion because they are afraid that they will hurt people in the congregation with harsh words. However, there are many ways to speak about abortion, and making a point of always including the information that abortion hurts everyone and that God's mercy is available for all who come seeking it makes it possible for people to hear the message. Some priests have found that reading a letter written by a woman or man about their abortion pain and the peace they found through God's mercy can be a wonderful way to begin speaking about healing after abortion.

Abortion is still a sin apart in some countries. The priest must approach the bishop for permission to forgive the sin or the woman is sent to the bishop. Confessors have shared that this may be a question of undue burden and that women seeking absolution simply do not return, convinced the bishop will refuse. In places where Project Rachel has been implemented around the world, bishops have granted general faculties to the priests so they can grant absolution to her. In training the confessors, it is important to review Canon Law as it pertains to excommunication for the sin of abortion. There are misconceptions about what the law really says and the confessor needs to be able to address these questions with the penitent. It is important to also recognize that the question of excommunication may apply to others involved in the abortion decision, such as her parents if they force the abortion.

Project Rachel is a powerful evangelization tool, making it possible for those who have left the Church to return. The outreach invites those who are culturally Catholic and not catechized to approach the Church and learn more about Catholicism while being cared for with compassion and wisdom. Project Rachel is also available to help those who come from a different faith tradition or no tradition at all to experience the love and mercy of God through those who care about her. This in turn often opens the door for her to consider coming into the Catholic Church. Men who resolve their abortion loss through the love and mercy of the Church also embrace their faith in a dynamic way. There are many converts because of the ministry of Project Rachel.

Post-abortion reconciliation always has critics. Critics within the Church have argued that post-abortion healing ministry somehow sanctions the sin. They say we do not need a special ministry for a set group of sinners. Other critics express concern about the sort of Church we will become if we accept the presence of parents who have had an abortion. Those who support abortion rights and promote legalized abortion find Project Rachel to be a dangerous sort of outreach. The Church is accused of inducing guilt. In the United States and Britain, abortion advocates, trying to counter the work of healing within a faith-based setting are now providing outreaches to help women resolve their feelings about abortion while avoiding the hard moral questions and human questions at the core of the pain. Some critics try to dismiss the aftermath of abortion by saying that it is caused by the Catholic Church and the pro-life community. However, non-Christian countries such as Japan and Taiwan have ritual grief ceremonies to help alleviate the guilt of abortion as well as to appease the spirits of the aborted children. In Japan, these ceremonies pre-date the work of Project Rachel by many years.

Science continues to unfold more knowledge to increase our understanding. Science has discovered that women carry cells from every child that she ever conceives for the rest of her life. This is called "human microchimerism." She cannot forget her children. The aftermath of abortion is not a psychological pathology or an aberration, but a normal response of a mother who has lost her child in a traumatic and unnatural fashion. These cells that she carries may then be transferred to her subsequent children, which may account for their seemingly intuitive awareness of older siblings. Science also reveals that fathers are hormonally changed in a permanent way during a pregnancy.

The wounds are both spiritual and human. The woman believes that she has committed the unforgivable sin. That is the core of the spiritual wound. She is a mother who knows she is responsible for the death of her child; a child she never got to birth, to see and to hold. That is the core of the human wound. Society, which supports and promotes abortion, does not acknowledge that abortion is a pregnancy loss. It is labeled a medical procedure. The process of healing enables her to claim the truth of the experience. She lost a child and needs to grieve for that unique human being.

The process of healing involves spiritual healing and human grief. Forgiveness and reconciliation are at the core of the healing. She moves toward forgiveness of the others involved in her abortion. She chooses to forgive these others with the help of God's grace, but she may not ever be able to reconcile with these people because of distance, lost connection or even death. Reconciliation is about restoring relationships that have been deeply damaged. She needs to experience reconciliation with God, her child and herself.

Practically speaking, the process of healing involves telling her story with all its pain and anger, forgiving those responsible for and involved in her abortion. This is an act of will on her part, done in concert with the grace of God, which empowers her to do this. In forgiving those involved, she comes to understand that forgiveness from God, from her child and for herself might be possible.

The caregiver will assist her in approaching God. She must hear often of God's love, forgiveness and mercy so she can be led to accept that forgiveness and celebrate it in the Sacrament of Reconciliation. She is often very afraid of God. She judges herself harshly. Introducing her to the stories of Jesus dealing with women in the Scriptures can facilitate her spiritual growth. These stories include the woman with the hemorrhage, the woman at the well, the woman who washes Jesus' feet with her tears and the woman caught in adultery.

The caregiver helps her to process her grief as a mother who lost a unique child. She must put closure on her relationship with the aborted child/children which includes grieving her loss, determining the sex of her child/children and choosing a name for her child. She is invited to write a letter to her child to speak the things her heart longs to say. She needs to memorialize the dead child, establishing a new spiritual relationship with the child in light of the Communion of Saints and having a Mass celebrated for the child and the healing of the family. In the healing experience, God restores her identity as mother to her.

The final step in the process is that she needs to forgive herself which is often the most difficult part of the process, especially if she has a history of abuse in her life. In the abortion, she may have gone from being the abused one to being the abuser. Finally, she is made aware that new life circumstances may remind her of the abortion; that her mother's heart has been restored to her so at times she will grieve for her lost child, and that an on-going sacramental participation is critical to her spiritual well-being. She is helped to discern what activities to pursue that will allow her to have a positive impact on her world. We assure her that we are always there if she needs us again.

Project Rachel has had many effects beyond the healing of women and men involved in abortion. Bishops and priests tell me that they find that the ministry reaffirms the priesthood. Priests see the healing power of the Sacrament of Reconciliation in a concrete way, when they personally experience women and men being set free from the bondage of sin and made new. The experience of caring for women and men provides the clergy with a way to speak about abortion in a compassionate but truthful manner. Many priests have shared with me that through this ministry they personally rediscovered the gift of their priesthood. Many have said to me: "This is what I was ordained to do—to set the captives free!" The ministry of post-abortion healing has changed the face of the abortion debate in freeing women and men to speak openly about the tragic consequences of abortion in their lives. The growing awareness of the impact of abortion on the broader culture is changing the debate. It is the truth of their experience brought to the public square that will set us all free from the scourge of abortion in our world. Project Rachel opens the merciful arms of God through the compassionate pastoral concern and care for those wounded by abortion. It has led or brought people back to the Church. It has healed individuals and enabled the restoration of families. Many women have said to me "I regret my abortion with all my heart, but otherwise, I would never have come to know God in such a powerful and personal way. When God forgives you and restores you, you are changed forever by God's love."

Project Rachel is a desperately needed ministry in a world immersed in the Culture of Death. Through the ministry of Project Rachel, the foundation of the Culture of Life is being built, through the people who know the lived truth of abortion and who are restored through God's gracious mercy and love.

A Sacramental Journey to an Inheritance of Mercy

Mother Agnes Mary Donovan

SISTERS OF LIFE—CALLED TO AN APOSTOLATE OF HOPE AND HEALING

The Sisters of Life is a contemplative-apostolic community of religious women consecrated to God by the three traditional vows of religious life, and a fourth vow to protect human life and advance a sense of the sacredness of every human life—a vow expressing the congregation's founding charism of life. The purpose of this presentation is to share with you a spiritual work of bringing hope and healing to those who suffer after abortion, begun by our religious congregation nearly 15 years ago.

From our first days as a fledgling community, women and men who suffer the pain of abortion have come to the Sisters seeking spiritual healing. At a time (20 years ago) when there was far less awareness of the suffering after abortion, John Cardinal O'Connor, our founder, exhorted the Sisters of Life to a mission of reconciliation in the words of Christ, "Go, pick up the pieces lest they be lost" (*Jn 6: 12*). His preaching revealed a sensitive understanding of the suffering:

> The trouble with every abortion is that it profoundly and inescapably works havoc on an individual, a unique person, who fits no mold, falls into no organized category. If she has ever had a scintilla of faith, or religious conviction, or moral education, she is crushed with guilt—a guilt that may be driven deep into the unconscious by whatever forces are at work—but which is then a cancer in the very soul.

Mother Agnes Mary Donovan is General Superior, Sisters of Life.

The mother who has given her children up to death, for whatever motive or however confused and pressured, needs passionately to be convinced more than anything else in the world, that she is forgiven, not by a counselor, not only by herself but by God. These mothers must come to believe that God loves them, despite, or in a profoundly mysterious sense, even because of their weakness.

It is this intense, and still often unrecognized, suffering after abortion which I bring to our attention today. I speak on behalf of the women and men we have come to know who suffer following the tragedy of abortion and who teach us, as no one else can, the truth of God's mercy and forgiveness. It is they, and the many millions of women and men like them, who await a word of invitation to the Mercy of Jesus. Those who have encountered his mercy proclaim that the healing which often eluded them for years is found only in Christ Jesus—through his Mystical Body on earth and in the power of the sacraments.

UNDERSTANDING OF THE ABORTION EXPERIENCE

Abortion is nearly a universal phenomenon. In first-world countries, elective, legal abortion is the norm; while for significant portions of the world populations living under oppressive regimes, similarly legal, but coercive abortion (as predicted by Pope Paul VI in *Humanae Vitae,* 17) is government-mandated as a means of controlling population growth. Linked to the tragic and violent death of the little one in the womb is the human suffering experienced by many involved in this irreverence to human life—mothers, fathers, grandparents, friends, siblings, doctors, and nurses. Post-traumatic suffering is the untold story of abortion.

In the secular realm of healthcare, a conspiracy of silence has existed regarding the human suffering associated with the practice of abortion. Adequate medical and psychological understandings of abortion and abortion consequences have been seriously obstructed by the degree to which abortion has fallen sway to the political agendas. The very real and frighteningly devastating phenomenon of post-abortion syndrome has been slow to gain recognition or adequate study, for countenancing the possibility of such a condition calls into question the tenets of radical feminist and utilitarian philosophies which underlie its practice. This conspiracy of silence has left millions of women and men alone and abandoned to suffer some of the most serious psychological and spiritual consequences of contemporary society's mistaken assumptions about human life and human sexuality.

Perhaps it is important to recall the personal context in which abortion is experienced. Our work with nearly ten thousand young women and men suggests that the decision for abortion is most often an action taken in the chaos of an intense, personal crisis. It is a decision made by a woman who hopes to undo a pregnancy, who desires with all her heart to return to the day when she was not (yet) pregnant. The woman for whom pregnancy creates a crisis faces a dilemma which she experiences as life-threatening. In the crisis of an untimely pregnancy, she believes (albeit irrationally) that either her life is over, or that the life of her child must end. Preying upon such fears, those who promote the practice of abortion do so by proposing falsely that abortion can resolve a pregnancy by making one "not pregnant." In fact, an abortion will terminate a pregnancy, but not a woman's maternity. A woman who has been entrusted with life is a mother forever whether she chooses to bring the child to birth and parent the child, place the child with adoptive parents, or solicit a pre-term abortion. Maternity is an eternal reality.

EFFECTS OF ABORTION: THROUGH SUFFERING TO HEALING

Who are these women? Do we recognize their faces? So that we might with them help pick up the pieces of their lives following an abortion?

One Woman's Voice

Let me introduce you to one post-abortive woman. I will call her Teresa (not her given name for anonymity's sake). Knowing me as a Sister of Life, Teresa wrote of the years of her struggle with the effects of abortion and the beautiful healing she has found. With her permission, you will hear in Teresa's own voice the inner experience of abortion and the magnificence of God, the Divine Physician, who led her to healing and a newfound joy in life. If we are to be instruments of God's healing, then it is important to learn of His way of love with the woman who suffers after abortion so that we may better imitate Him in our apostolate.

This is Teresa's letter:

I fell asleep Friday night filled with thoughts of my child.

The next day, I walked down to the Church of the Holy Innocents. I arrived for exposition of the Blessed Sacrament, so I stayed for prayers and my rosary. I kept asking Our Lord: "What about for my baby?" No reply.

I needed activity that was lighter in nature so I went over to the Rockefeller Center for skating. The place was a zoo: tourists galore, festive with families, a riot of noise and color. As I stepped onto the ice, I met the eyes of a small boy and we exchanged a hello. Sometime later, this same boy approached me, asking me where I was from and what did I do that day? We started swapping stories of favorite saints. He relished in the telling of the story of St. Lucy. Kids really do extend love during unexpected events. His mother was nearby in her office and they were meeting at the close of skating for the day.

It was funny, but we sort of became friends, even skating hand-in-hand at one point. He was a first year altar boy named John Paul from Queens. All of a sudden it hit me and I asked his age. He was 11, within one month of my child's age. We parted with the promise of prayers for each other. As I walked back to the hotel, I knew that the Holy Spirit had set up this encounter.

Now that I know the heavenly feeling of being touched by God's love and have learned that He has a unique plan for each of us, the great sin and lie of abortion has never been more real for me. God wants these children, but we do not. Abortion is like stealing a life from God. Well, it was a long night of grief.

The following day I took the subway up to St. Jean Baptiste Church for a full afternoon of prayer. What an incredible blessing it was. All that day and night I thought long and hard about Baptism. More tears. So yet another side to the crime of abortion is the denial of the gifts and promises of Baptism. I've know this in my head, but it is now in my heart forever.

Mother Agnes, the Holy Spirit named my child for me . . . he is now John Paul, named after the Pope. It is simply glorious! The John is for St. John the Baptist. I pray for the mercy of Baptism for my child. It is in God's hands. I have been told that the final step in the healing of an abortion is accepting God's forgiveness and having a personal relationship with the child for the rest of my life. This is what has happened to me. I'll always feel the sadness, but the shame is gone. John Paul is no longer "a procedure" to me. He is a young boy, a Holy Innocent, just like the boy I met at the skating rink. What a miracle of God's healing grace!

. . . I am growing in faith and trust and gratitude. *God is so good.* How He loves to surprise us with His joy!

HOPE AND HEALING AFTER ABORTION: A PROGRAM OF RETREATS

Like Teresa, there are many women and men who are waiting to hear a word of hope for healing from abortion. As Christians we need not only experience understanding and compassion, but we need to find ways to express our compassion in words and actions. Listen to one who suffered this silence:

> I was unaware that abortion could be forgiven by a priest. I was terribly misinformed by other misinformed people. . . . Regardless of this belief, I found myself at St. Patrick's Cathedral spilling the whole story to a priest whose name I cannot remember, but whose face I'll never forget. He was so full of compassion for what had happened. He didn't condemn, he loved. It was the most exuberant experience I have ever had. GOD STILL LOVED ME!!!
>
> . . . I have gone to church religiously since my sin was forgiven and I have never once heard a priest encourage women who were silently suffering with this sin to come and be forgiven. If there is a devil, his favorite form must be ignorance.

As a way of doing our part to cast out this devil, in 1996 the Sisters of Life began "Days of Prayer and Healing" for women suffering the effects of abortion. Each month these days are repeated and new women and men come seeking healing and the forgiveness and mercy of God. A woman who has suffered abortion works with us by beginning each "Day of Prayer and Healing" with her story of the healing found in God's mercy. The day includes opportunities for sharing the pain in a confidential and understanding environment; Scripture reflections led by the Sisters and the priest chaplain; and, because we believe that the healing comes from the One who has suffered for us all, the day highlights instruction on and opportunities for the Sacraments of Reconciliation and Eucharist. An understanding of the nature of the abortion experience and a capacity to express the reality of God's mercy and forgiveness on the part of the priests who work with us are vital to the success of the day.

The graces of these days are extended by monthly "prayer gatherings" of the graduates of our "Days of Prayer and Healing," which provide continued spiritual support, through Scripture reflections, Eucharistic adoration and the common recitation of the Rosary; and week-end retreats of hope and healing.

Abortion reflects the failure of love and community, since the "choice" of abortion typically involves the emotional abandonment of many—including friends and spiritual leaders, parents and the father of the newly conceived child—so the healing process needs a proportionate life-giving, life-affirming presence of community to allow a person to break the bondage of secrecy and silence and reclaim her identity as a beloved child of God. It is for this reason that the salient aspects of the healing mission of the Sisters of Life to those who suffer after abortion are based upon a philosophy of non-abandonment which is expressed 1) by the Sisters' individual accompaniment of one who suffers throughout the time of healing, 2) in a group-based program of spiritual retreats which witnesses a realistic hope of healing and supports growth in Christian virtue, 3) reliance upon the healing to be found in the grace of the sacraments of the Catholic Church. It is the goal of this program of healing to assist the one who suffers to realize full Christian discipleship through regular participation in the sacraments, life choices guided by the Ten Commandments and the law of charity and a future defined by the freedom to love.

Like Teresa, there are many women and men who are waiting to hear a word of hope for healing from abortion. They are in our families, share offices with us at work, they sit in the pews at Church and they listen with open, hopeful ears as they long for someone to pour "oil on the wounds" of their regret. May our growing understanding of this pain experienced by so many of our sisters and brothers in Christ inspire each one of us to lend an articulate, credible, kind and audible voice of encouragement to these members of our Church and our communities so that we may all (in the words of Teresa) sing of God's mercy and forgiveness, "God is so good! How He loves to surprise us with His joy!"

AGAPA: Following Christ, Welcoming and Accompanying Those Who Experience Suffering as a Result of Abortion

Dominique Vandier

INTRODUCTION: WHO IS MY NEIGHBOR?

Let us begin with the parable of the Good Samaritan to try to answer this question.

It is he to whom I draw near while everyone passes and ignores his injury.

When the scholar of the law inquires "and who is my neighbor," Jesus replies: "A man." As much to say *all men*, who I find on my way without having looked for them, who may be suffering, who may also be far from the way of believers. And it is in this man that God awaits those who pass on the road. Because God is precisely the God of Life: he goes where life is lost. (*"C'est toi mon Dieu"*—Cerf—2006—p.65)

It is he to whom I will communicate the tenderness of Christ.

This man, the Samaritan will express *compassion and tenderness* to him. The attitude of the Samaritan gives us belief in an infinitely merciful God. He does not reproach but "his tenderness has a *father-like tone*, a call to be born to ourselves, to our freedom and thus equally to our own responsibility." (according to Etienne Grieu "la tendresse de Dieu, un appel discret"—*Croire aujourd'hui*—January 10th–31st, 2008—p. 26)

In accompanying the people touched by abortion, AGAPA helps in two ways:

1. We want to receive the other, whoever he is, whatever his choices were, with the greatest respect of who he is.

Dominique Vandier is President of the Association AGAPA (France). Cf. www.agapa.fr

2. We want to testify to the tenderness of God, which is not a tenderness that beguiles, but that which gives life to the other from himself. An uplifting force of life that brings man to his feet.

WHAT IS AGAPA?

Five characteristic elements of AGAPA:

1. A Place of Christian Welcome

AGAPA was created in Paris in 1994, in the form of a 1901 Association law but in connection with the diocese. An accompanying priest is actively present in the group. The president of the association is today a permanent deacon.

Currently, there are several satellite groups in other French towns, all created in conjunction with the related dioceses. Today AGAPA welcomes, listens to, and accompanies any person not having been able to carry out a pregnancy to term, whatever the reason.

2. An Identity Founded on Christ, His Tenderness, and His Mercy in the Gospel

The Gospel is full of meetings between Jesus and those marginalized, suffering, lost, removed from their true identity, captive in the eyes of others, who are prevented or prevent themselves from living. It is his example that we want to follow: a Christ who never judges, never condemns, but gives relief, helps others to their feet, and loves with a love that has no boundaries.

3. A Deliberate Vow Not to Enter into Ideological Debate or Controversy

AGAPA desires to be open to all who wish to come because they are suffering, listening to the person from their own walk of life or position in the debate.

4. A Space for Discussion Open to Everyone

AGAPA is a place of welcome and counsel open to all persons, Christian or not, whatever their convictions, without proselytizing. A place where the voice of those seeking help is respected.

5. A Team Composed of Well-Formed and Supervised Volunteers

Those who invest their time in AGAPA are benevolent, Christian volunteers. They have a professional education or a personal background that has specifically prepared them for this ministry. In addition, they receive a specialized education from AGAPA. They adhere to a code of ethics and are subject to routine psychiatric evaluation. In addition, they are provided with spiritual direction.

ACCOMPANYING EVERY PERSON TOUCHED BY A PREGNANCY LOSS: WELCOMING AND LISTENING AT AGAPA

Abortion Is Infinitely Complex and Always Multi-Faceted

Beyond the specific circumstances that can lead to confusion at the beginning of pregnancy and are often at play during the decision, (young age, or on the contrary, an unexpected pregnancy late in life, financial difficulties, instability between the couple, current educational pursuits . . .), the incapacity to welcome life is most often a sign of other issues most often to some degree linked to the person's history or their family background. One could say that abortion is a symptom and a sign of a more profound, painful reality.

For AGAPA, each person that we encounter has a unique history and it is impossible to try and categorize them in advance. Even if all those who come to see us have been affected by abortion, no two stories are alike.

Listening Without Judgment, Without Plans, and Without Personal Motive

The counseling given at AGAPA is always respectful of the liberty of the other, their individuality, their rhythm and way of life. The listener never knows in advance the person who comes to them. They do not give pre-fabricated solutions, nor do they try to interpret, impose, or counsel.

TO ACCOMPANY AND SOOTHE THE PAINS

All paths to healing take time and can be a long journey.

AGAPA proposes a specific support process, built with the help of psychiatrists who specialize in these particular wounds. Accompaniment takes place through about twenty weekly meetings, either individually or in a small group. The path is directed, but each person draws from it in his own way.

From one week to the next, different points of reflection are proposed, and will guide the subsequent meeting.

We will share some of the stories with you, and illustrate them with occasional remarks made by those we have accompanied. Their words can be strong, but can express better than we who have not lived the situation.

A Retelling of Their Personal and Family History

This is an important step where each person will try to shed light on their past, and understand how certain wounds from their own history or from past generations could have had repercussions on their current lives.

This return to self can, in certain cases, bring forth a new understanding of the abortion decision that was made and help to better discern the bigger picture, bringing us back to a specific moment in the history of the person: the impossible home life. Loosely it can be described as: the feeling of never having been loved, or loved only under certain conditions, unaddressed grief, abandonments, issues repeating themselves through a series of generations, problems identifying with or relating to the mother, defiance of the paternal figure, low self-esteem, various abuses. . . .

> "I am the baby of the family. A model little sister. My father would have killed me if he had known. But there again, I did what I had done to avoid reproach, to remain perfect."
>
> "I was no longer a person, only a thing. Nothing could be born from so many horrors."
>
> "Today I realize that it was not the child I rejected. I was speaking to them, as if I was saying: you see, I can live and be happy without having children."

This first step permits a better understanding of everything that has played out and also gives meaning to other past events. And because these things can be cleared up, decoded—all these familial, social, and personal sufferings—they are able to move on.

Moving Towards a Better Knowledge of Oneself and a Sound Self-Esteem

Very often, those meeting at AGAPA suffer from great attacks on their self-esteem. This is why a certain number of the encounters of the proposed journey focus on helping them grow in this area. While focusing on the positive elements they have allowed themselves to build, and in rediscovering in themselves that which makes their personalities rich, they are able, piece by piece, to find more esteem for themselves and to console the part of themselves that remains wounded.

A strong sense of worthlessness often pre-exists the choice to abort, and can be part of the explanation.

> "To be a mother seemed to me an enormous task. I was not capable of it."
>
> "I never took care of myself. Always neglected. Nothing good could have come from me."

But this poor opinion could be made worse by this gesture, at a moment of the pregnancy where the distinction between the future mother and the growing infant within her is not clear.

Some felt their integrity strained, as if they were themselves under attack, or as if they would lose something of themselves that they would never find again.

> "I felt like I had become like him: pulverized. I wasn't sure I existed anymore."
>
> "I felt as if I had left a part of myself in a million pieces at the hospital."

Little by little the proposed journey will help them to recognize the difference between an act, always specific—even if it had heavy and painful consequences—and the person who is the author of that act.

It will equally help them to put themselves back in context with others, to get their own bearings straight, which allows them to deal with the situations they encounter . . . A long path that will allow each person to return to the normal subject of their own life.

> "With the passing of weeks, I am learning to listen to myself and make myself happy, not to systematically obliterate myself in front of the will of others. I am learning, quite simply, how to exist. Little by little, I renew myself."

As they make their way through reconciliation with their history and themselves, the women and men will be able to begin the labor of mourning.

Permitting the Labor of Mourning to Open Themselves to Life

At the heart of the journey, there is an important time dedicated to the mourning of the infant who was not allowed to see the light of day. Each person will be able to go through this process in their own way, without restrictions, and will find what is right for them.

Different points of reflection are proposed to help to:

- *Cement the reality of the abortion in the reality of their history.* To accept the reality of the loss, being allowed to give it a place for what it was, when often it is denied, concealed, or buried.

> "I believed for a long time that I could erase it, forget it. Now, I no longer want to forget."

- *Soothe older mournings, if need be.*

- *Make a symbolic gesture.* For certain people, giving a place to this unborn child translates to giving them a name. For the woman, naming the child is to give them a life of their own.

> "Since I have given them a name, it has changed. As if they were finally out of me. I no longer think of them very often but sometimes, I speak to them."

For others, this will translate into a more symbolic act, and may be considered restorative.

> "I decided a few months ago to sponsor a little girl from Indonesia; I think about her, I provide for her needs, I assure she will have an education; it feels like I am reconciling myself little by little with my own maternity."

Others will turn to something more ritualized. The rite symbolizes a transformation, helping to leave the past behind and opening themselves to a new stage: planting a tree, writing and filing away a letter, going to light a candle in a church, giving a set of newborn clothes to an organization for needy women, putting the ultrasound picture in the family album . . .

- *Reinvesting in one's own life.* Dealing with loss also means accepting this loss so that something else may occur. We must continue to live by finding a new balance of life. Sometimes it is trying to rediscover a taste for life. The pain slowly fades and people will begin to be at peace with the events surrounding the loss and live life without the guilt of being alive. By coming to terms with this loss, the person will have truly lived a profound transformation.

> "When I look back a little, it gives me courage to continue to move forward. I feel like I gradually detached from the baby I would never see. And at the same time, I feel as if I gave him life."

Thus little by little, at their own pace, each woman is able to enter into this phase of mourning which is rebuilding, a period of redefinition of the relation to others and to the world, redefinition of the relation to oneself, but also redefinition of the relation to the "object" of their mourning.

Advancing Towards Forgiveness and Reconciliation

How can these wounds of childhood, life, and abortion be overcome? How do we make the slow journey towards forgiveness, towards letting go of the hatred, of the anger?

The delicate question of forgiveness requires a lot of time and often continues on well beyond the time of accompaniment.

Among those who have undergone accompaniment, they find it difficult to gauge fairly the limits of their responsibility and not remain invaded by guilt, conscious or unconscious. Listened to, they are slowly able to discern how much certain wounds from their past that have never healed could weigh on their behavior, and by doing this, acquire more concern towards themselves, accepting that their liberty is never total. This concentration on their own selves will help them to pass from culpability to responsibility.

> "This entire journey has allowed me to understand better the true reasons for having had the abortion. I can now carry my share of the responsibility without being crushed by it."

Among those interviewed, the question of forgiveness (whether to give, given or asked) is often very important: forgiveness for themselves, for a partner, for the doctors, those who were conscious or unconscious participants, forgiveness for the child who should have been born, forgiveness to God . . . and often forgiveness for the older injuries as well.

It is for this reason that one or more meetings will be devoted to this issue at the time of the accompaniment proposed by AGAPA. For those who desire it, it is also possible to meet with the priest who works within AGAPA, and to receive the Sacrament of Reconciliation.

Gradually, these women will be able to accept and say they did what they could at some point in their history, but their story does not end there. They also accept that they still have a long way to go.

> "I never said that I was infallible. I now give myself the right to have taken a path that I did not want to, and the right to get up and try again."
> "Since God has forgiven me, I must also forgive myself."

It is thanks to this journey that women will be able to believe again in the possibility of progress and transformation within each one of them, to begin for themselves.

This path will sometimes allow for a profound spiritual renewal, which will begin or restore the journey towards greater life in God.

THE FRUITS THAT WE BEAR

The fruits of all our encounters where we have accompanied the person are beyond us, it is something we do not always see.

All of the stories we encountered illustrate well that there is a singular path, open to everyone, and there is never a predetermined solution.

The path that our workers accompany women on is:

• A path of truth: all that is accomplished during the accompaniment gives a place to what was, while alleviating and giving freedom.

• A path of independence: to help to untangle oneself, to leave the fears and guilt that constrains, to journey towards greater responsibility.

• A path to greater consciousness when it comes to reclaiming one's own history, to put things into order.

• A path towards a renewed life where, without erasing the past, the person is able to bring a new perspective on events, people, relationships, and in certain cases, she will be able to welcome new life within her.

• A path of discovery or return to God. Discovery of another image of God, who is close to each one of us and shows us His Love.

- A path of forgiveness asked from God, given to others. A path of spiritual conversion whose fruits outlast the time of accompaniment.

CONCLUSION

We will close with the words of Monsignor Golfier, one of the founders of AGAPA:

> "If Christ has saved all mankind, he has saved the whole man. No healing would truly exist if all aspects of man were not truly taken into account.
>
> "A human welcome, if cordial, is not enough.
>
> "A strictly psychological focus does not satisfy.
>
> "A solely religious approach not based on the true fundamentals of the person cannot help a person too fragile to return to God."

This is why the accompaniment proposed by AGAPA seeks to integrate all these aspects, because it addresses the person in all that they are, opening a path of unification from which she will hear the words of life: "Rise and Walk," a future has opened itself to you.

The Gift of Support

Serena Taccari

A few years ago, in 2005 to be exact, my husband and I felt the need to offer our personal experience and our experience as a couple in the service of life and of women, who, deceived, found themselves faced with what has socially been put in terms of choice: to abort or to not abort but to bring their baby to term. From this desire of ours, the organization The Gift came into being in January 2006. The Gift extends particular attention to those women who face an unexpected pregnancy alone or those who have brought upon themselves the psychological consequences of a past decision for an abortion.

To date, and this shows the need for social intervention in these two areas, more than two thousand people throughout all of Italy have had reference to the association, and with our help—which only in certain cases has come in the form of economic aid—already 100 children have been born, thanks to the dedicated work of many volunteers, including a large number of those who use the fruit of their own experience of abortion to testify to the devastation this choice can leave in one's soul, and what wonder it is instead to embrace a tiny life.

I was asked to give a reflection on what sense we have today when we speak of "gift," on the kind of support we offer, and to whom.

To do this we must first take a step back.

When we speak of life, it frequently enough comes in the context of "the gift of life," but just because we say this, doesn't mean we ever stop to think

---

Serena Taccari is President of the Association Il Dono Onlus (Italy). Cf. www.il-dono.org

about it. And yet it must be significant that it is never talked about as a "present," but as a gift.

Life, in fact is not a "present" given to anyone, and yet it is appropriate to attribute to it a meaning of much more profound gratuity, with a new connotation: that indeed, of the "gift."

Although this is a very common way of speaking, today there is nothing that is really free, not even the gift of life. This society is one imbued with the relativism denounced by our Pope Benedict XVI, which has reduced human relations, as Z. Baumann affirmed, to something liquid that slides off one, without involving him too much, because "In a relationship, you may feel as insecure as you would be without it, or even worse." With this deep insecurity in their foundations, people tend to create only superficial, detached relationships in which I would only approach you to the extent that you do not become too deeply involved in my life, nor would I have to invest too much of myself in you.

This can be seen perfectly in the friendship relationships among teenagers, where—and those who are involved in youth ministry are well aware of the situation—we have cynical and anti-social kids, but you see the same type of thing in affectivity within couples. Even before this, you see similar ties between parents and children: the child burdened with the expectations of the parents. He is a good child to the extent that they are satisfied, while he is a disappointment unless the expectations are fulfilled. In this light, it is easy to see why the sick child who cannot fulfill any expectation of parents is more acceptably done away with in favor of the perfect child who can realize those parental desires.

Similarly, the daughter who disappoints and becomes pregnant is accompanied in her decision to abort, because, isn't this the way her life has to go, so that, I, the parent, can be proud? Or the woman is pregnant in the moment when I, her current companion, had other plans for my life, I am committed in a bond that I am not looking for, that requires a commitment that I do not want to offer; or for the woman, the unexpected pregnancy takes me away from my own future projects and imposes a change and a sacrifice for me, that I don't want to face. It is interesting that this society that makes us so insecure in our foundations, pushes us to make plans and projects for the future as if it were concrete, as if it could give us stability, as if then, we could belong.

And so I do not take serious commitments today because "I have my whole life ahead of me," and I can even deny my own child who is present now, in favor, perhaps, of a child I will have tomorrow under better circumstances, things of which I have no certainty! It is neither certain that tomorrow I will be able to have a child, or that tomorrow things will be better. And I would do well to realize that I am not even sure that I myself will be here tomorrow. This concept of Life as a race towards a certain tomorrow (and therefore to project yourself into a fantasy) does not permit us to live today, which is what Christians are called to do: to see in today the possibility of one's life. To live today fully is a gift, perhaps it is for this that the "gift" is called the "present."

We spoke of self-sacrifice which is often not accepted, it is precisely the dimension of self-sacrifice of one's own expectations and projects, which makes the difference between a present and a gift, but if the first is almost an obligation to which a "thank you" is expected of us, (maybe a birthday celebration requires the courtesy of a present), the second requires the acceptance or rejection of oneself, and concentrates its value in the gesture of having given himself.

A Gift is unexpected, it is precious, and it is free.

Life today has a price to pay, a price that corresponds to a standard so elevated that it is unreachable. It is not free, and if I pressure myself to arrive closer to that standard (effort that may even mean to destroy the most precious things that I have, like friendship, affections, or the life of my own child), on the other hand I ask it to pay for my efforts with immediate results and if life is not so generous, then my life becomes meaningless, and with the lack of meaning, full of despair.

We've lost the meaning of this sacrifice: we have tried to change words to soften the effect, and we have called abortion "the voluntary pregnancy interruption," to make it less objectionable, we call a particularly sad person "desperate." But no, he is not: "desperate" is the person who has lost hope, who despairs in the ability to give meaning to his life, in the certainty that his history is oriented towards something good, in the possibility to love and be loved. Those who are desperate are those who do not have God, the first source of hope.

I think it is really symptomatic of the fact that all of us working in the pro-life movement talk about unplanned pregnancy, an unwanted, undesired pregnancy. And this last admission of "undesired," is already very generous linguistically, from the perspective that what is ever wished and desired is never found instantaneously in reality. Indeed—and again this has been well-explained by Baumann—"desire" involves waiting and satisfaction, while it is more the childish "want," a whimsical demand, that we often seek in our lives: I want to go in a certain way and I must fulfill my wants.

And so comes the lack of welcome and embrace of children who are planned in a certain way and at a certain point in one's life, becoming the satisfaction of a "want" in the same way that it would be to buy the right car at the right time.

It is as in the case of a child who arrives unexpectedly, it might not yet be the time in my life to satisfy that want, but then instead, the child that I do want, as I hear the ticking of the biological clock, but does not arrive at all, I force the hand of an "ungrateful destiny" because that child which was rejected the first time because it was not the moment for him to arrive, now must arrive, at any cost.

Even more, we have been socially indoctrinated with the thoughts that a child costs: costs in sacrifices, in time, even in money, and for this reason we almost present ourselves not as much parents as tax collectors! You cost me so much and you must pay it back with interest. The immeasurable debt which we put on the shoulders of our children, borne of our expectations on a life that we think formally belongs to us . . . not only our own life, which we suppose we can dispose of at our liking, but also those who we have put in the world that have cost us so much. We are not capable of loving the Other, for he is different from what we imagined, and, yet for this reason, he is unique and precious. But for the same reasons, we are not even able to love ourselves.

Incapable of freely loving others, and first of all, incapable of loving oneself, man forces himself to wear a mask of presumed perfection or of acceptable error. Because to recognize one's own sins and to renounce them, in the face of oneself and then with others, is something fearful: it is to be naked in front of another, the nakedness of Adam and Eve; it is a letting oneself be known that puts our mutual safety at risk. Yes, because it is not as important that someone from outside points his finger at the sin of others, as much as—evangelically speaking—that the same person recognizes the *beam* in his own eye.

Today everything has a value in economic terms and one must run into the future without ever looking back, without regretting the choices that were made, since seriously recognizing the wrong one has done runs the risk of "putting myself down."

The man who despairs not only lacks the sense of his life, but also lacks the hope that he can be loved beyond his commercial value, because he is as he is, and does not remember that the price for him has already been paid: with the blood of Christ.

To be able to strip away the mask in front of another, I must know that you will not hurt me, that you will not use my sin against me, that you will not judge me to be a sinner. Or else I must be tremendously desperate, as the traveler, nearly beaten to death on the roadside, of the parable of the Good Samaritan, of whom we do not know if he had a good job, if he was brave and good, with an excellent reputation, if he had a beautiful family. All that we know is that he was unconscious and needed help. It's at this precise moment that mercy appears as the greatest gift that can be offered.

Mercy is given as a gift, not as a present. Moreover, because the gift requires much more than a present: While the "present" can be the just compensation for the one who is waiting, the other surpasses by far any kind of expectation, and is completely separate from the objectified, economic, quantifiable, assumingly subjective value; so that—for those who receive this gift—it is of inestimable value.

And so the demonstration of mercy becomes a gift of human, psychological and spiritual support; it becomes the opportunity to listen and embrace in your own heart the pain of a woman or a man who has lived such a tragedy as abortion, and to make it transparent in me that it is possible to see a person apart from the sin, that it is possible to love, for love of Christ and for love of man, those who have believed the catechesis of this world, and have idolized something to the point of sacrificing a child, and then remain destroyed by this fact; that it is possible to listen to that pain and to do so without misunderstanding the seriousness of the act, but without coming to listen to the pain full of my own preconceived judgments.

The Samaritan, in fact, brings the traveler to the inn without announcing his convictions to him, nor waving around his beliefs; he does not even know what he will have to invest for the care and cure of the traveler, and makes, we could say, a "credit" with the inn, to continue to provide for the traveler ... if he wants! Because the Samaritan does not even know if the traveler will appreciate his service or if he will complain, or whether he will stay longer at the inn, if he will ask even more from him, or if he will return to his previous life, or if he will diametrically change route.

The Samaritan offers himself in the poverty or wealth of what he has and what he is: freely and completely.

He offers the gift of that compassionate mercy that is support during healing. Today, it is so impossible to understand that the sin and the sinner are not the same thing, that one you condemn and the other you embrace . . . today when, if you steal, you are a thief (and you are so for life) and if you kill, you are a murderer (and you are for life), like a branded man, for which the possibility of conversion is not considered, because we lack mercy, the free gift of love, which comes from God, surprising us. It produces amazement. And it allows you to change your life.

Abortion is not an event cut off from the context of a person's life, and it cannot be treated as The Event. Instead, it might be compared to the tip of an iceberg and for this reason, yes, you can attend to that wound and yet you must help the total person because even if that wound heals, if we suppose that we can treat only one wound, it will be a failure.

We all have experiences of relapse, (in fact when it is done once, it makes it easier to do it a second time!) but we also know that many things in life may be "aborted": if the life of an innocent child can be aborted, one's own life can be aborted.

The effects of abortion are devastating, and they are felt by the individuals, and couples who are already fragile.

The abortion event has much to do with the identity of the person because to seriously be aware of what happened, that is, to have stopped the life of one's own child, puts the mother in serious crisis with her relationship with herself. It is to look in a mirror and to no longer see the reflection of that "acceptable" person that I claim to be, but a monster, one capable of the most shocking thing of all, to harm an innocent one in the worst way: a child, your own child.

It is no doubt that this discovery destroys any possibility to accept oneself, to love oneself, as well as to think of oneself perhaps, in relation to another child (which will never be that one, so it would be unfair to have another, because I rejected one, so I do not deserve it, because I was too evil), or even to think of oneself being happy . . . because a monster like me does not deserve happiness.

For this reason I first spoke of the possibility of aborting one's own life:

the rejection of oneself after an abortion is one of the saddest and most difficult to overcome, and it testifies to the dramatically high rate of suicides or slow deaths of mind and body linked to drug or alcohol abuse, in which many women who have aborted fall into.

And while we offer our ministry, we cannot neglect to try to frame the events that have built the ideal platform to cause a person to seek an abortion, and try to offer support, not limited to binding and medicating the visible wound today, but to building-up the person in his totality.

We cannot neglect to bring the traveler to the inn.

Precisely based on this concept of healing as "non-sectoral" but one which sees man, the person, in his entirety, in these years of the Gift's activity, the association brought the discussion concerning support of pregnancy and parenthood into an integrated vision: to do much for those who face an unexpected pregnancy—because you bring her along—and then support them in the aftermath of abortion.

It could not be otherwise! You cannot define a person with one event. To cure a cough if you have pneumonia is to make the real problem into something "cosmetic." We need to cure the pneumonia!

So support for the aftermath of abortion is to be outlined with a double track of healing of the wound (the visible one of abortion) and a permanent catechesis so that the person in her entirety can heal.

The meetings which are, for now twice a year, dedicated to people from all over Italy who have been involved in an abortion, always see new participants come: people with an open wound who need to hear a word for themselves, for their lives. But those meetings are not the only medicine: they are not the point of departure (because the journey our organization, The Gift, offers, starts before the meeting) and are not the point of arrival (because the journey goes on beyond the weekend!), but are poignant moments to reflect on life, on that "Where are you?" with which God questioned Adam, a moment when we offer the opportunity for people not to hide but to let themselves be loved by God.

And for this reason, our weekend meetings joyfully welcome all those who have already participated at other times, two, three, ten, as many times as they want, because they know that there they can continue to find a key to apply to all the events of their lives. It is, in a sense, a way of coming out of the senselessness that has become their life. This, I think, is indeed the richness of the Holy Spirit and of the Word of God that becomes present and speaks to the Today of man, in each of his "todays."

The world, our society, calls us to bring a great message of hope, to give meaning to the life of man, which, perhaps more than at other times, has become a complicit protagonist of great sins and disorientation. It is not necessary to discount the consequences, to tell people that "what's done is done, move on!" or "you didn't have any other choice." But it requires that people, priests and laity proclaim the Truth to their life.

We need people who do not try to minimize or soften what has been done but who are convinced, as we are, that yes, it is true, that because of abortion an innocent person lost his life, a child could have been, and it is our duty, as a society, to fight so that the innocent one in danger may live. To say that everything is lost is to lose hope. We need people who deeply understand that an abortion does not erase the fact that a child was given, that you cannot go back in time and undo it, and that every unplanned, problematic pregnancy always means that you will forever move on with your child, either in your arms or on your conscience.

We cannot ignore the call to recognize that each pregnancy represents a life. This life, threatened by abortion, is the one that we must take care of, we, who know that behind this culture of death is an Accuser that after having pushed you into a trap, binds you and wants to close you off from the gates of Heaven . . . we, who have for our own, a weapon that makes the difference: hope.

The support that we give is a manifestation of divine mercy. It is a vehicle through which meaning may be restored to the life of man, who while still a sinner, is loved by God and for this reason, he cannot despair; he is called to recognize, through the gift of our support, the hope of salvation.

www.ingramcontent.com/pod-product-compliance
Lightning Source LLC
Chambersburg PA
CBHW071901290426
44110CB00013B/1240